Save Send Delete

Save Send Delete

Danusha V. Goska

Winchester, UK
Washington, USA

First published by Roundfire Books, 2012
Roundfire Books is an imprint of John Hunt Publishing Ltd., Laurel House, Station Approach,
Alresford, Hants, SO24 9JH, UK
office1@o-books.net
www.o-books.com

For distributor details and how to order please visit the 'Ordering' section on our website.

Text copyright: Danusha V. Goska 2011

ISBN: 978 1 84694 986 9

A CIP catalogue record for this book is available from the British Library.

Design: Stuart Davies

Printed in the UK by CPI Antony Rowe
Printed in the USA by Offset Paperback Mfrs, Inc

We operate a distinctive and ethical publishing philosophy in all
areas of our business, from our global network of authors to
production and worldwide distribution.

For Those Who Suffer Alone.

Preface

Some years back I was wrestling with the big, hard questions. In my quest, I came across the work of a man who happened to be an atheist. I contacted him. "Save Send Delete" is based on our relationship.

There are hundreds of prominent atheists out there: filmmakers, actors, authors, poets, politicians, scientists, journalists, even some rabbis. The man I corresponded with is one of these hundreds of recognizable figures. There are no clues in "Save Send Delete" to my correspondent's true identity. I did everything I could to disguise it, while retaining the essence of our exchange. For example, Lord Court-Wright is an English lord because his location in England emphasizes the distance between him and Mira, and his lordship emphasizes the difference between his status and hers – not because my correspondent was, or was not, English, or an aristocrat.

I want you to know this, though. When it comes to my own story, I struggled to reproduce every detail as accurately as possible, right down to the orange lipstick Justin's date wore to the prom, and to the exact height – twenty-five feet – of my loft ceiling. I tracked down the man who identifies himself, in the text, as "Lamjung," and elicited from him a story he'd told me decades before. The story you read in "Save Send Delete" are Lamjung's exact words. I did this because I know that some will read this book as part of their own wrestling match with the big, hard questions. I don't want to stack the deck in favor of God or synchronicity, and I also don't want to sell God, or you, dear reader, short.

In compiling my list of acknowledgments, I became greatly intimidated. Anyone who reads a writer and lets that writer know that her work is of value does a service. Anyone who actually pays money for a writer's work and, further, shares interest in it through, for example, online book reviews, deserves a medal. I wish I could list every such supporter here. I know that I will, simply through my own failings, inadvertently miss some names, and I apologize in advance. Believe me, your support of my and other writers' work is a good deed that will count in your favor when you arrive in Heaven.

I thank below people who bought or lent me computers, typewriters, or other equipment, who fixed my computer free of charge, or who put my writing before potential publishers or other promoters. These include Regina A. Bohn, Anna M. Cienciala, Francis S. Collins, Frank DeCaro, Robert Ellsberg, Don Freidkin, Peter K. Gessner, Pauline Goska, John Guzlowski, Al and Pat Koproski, James P. Leary, Paul Loeb, Charlene Lovegrove, Ruth Maher, Amanda Moody, Antony Polonsky, Teresa Rybkowska Klatka, Kirsten and Margaret Shepard, Roman Solecki, Mark Sost, Simon Stern, Laura Strachan, Malgorzata Tarchala, Witold Turopolski, and Maria Villar.

I thank, with my whole heart and more gratitude than I can express here, those who read my work and tell me what my writing has done for them. I remember you. I write for you. You lift me up. You keep me going. You are essential to this. Thank you.

I reserve special thanks for one my heroes, Stuart Balcomb, who has been selflessly and tirelessly supporting my writing since the day we met.

I thank John "Sandy" McReynolds for being smart and funny, and for being my friend longer than anyone else.

Robin Richman Schaffer is a special angel to this book. She read it and loved it and decided that come hell or high water, others would read it, too. Her determination revivified me, steeled me, inspired me, and provided a light in the darkness.

Those are the names that occur to me now. I know this list is woefully incomplete. If you miss your name, please forgive me. You will come first on the acknowledgements page for the next book. Let's start praying right now for its publication.

Danusha V. Goska

Two days after Winter Solstice
Saturday, Midnight
Dear Lord Randolph Court-Wright, Marquis of Alnwick,
Don't you feel embarrassed going through life with such a
ridiculous name? Look, I'm an American, and I'm damn proud of
it. We fought a revolution to oust gits like you, and here we are
importing your ilk to tell us that there is no God. Me? No title; I
am not "Mira of Paterson." I am a Bohunk with a keyboard and
a modem.

I just saw you on TV – public TV, no less. My tax dollars paid
for that cushy leather chair you languished in. I kept waiting for
Bill Moyers to provide us with your resume. What qualified you
to tell millions of viewers that there is no God, and that there are,
furthermore, no soul, no afterlife, no ESP, no meaning, no elves,
no magic, no Tinker Bell – how else did you put it – nothing but
"leaden matter"? (Why "leaden"? Why not "gold"?)

Your bona fides consist in this: you are tall, you are blond, you
have an aquiline nose, you've climbed Mount Everest, and you
made some discovery about the first few seconds after the Big
Bang. Also, you speak in that insufferable accent typical of an
upper class English git. I've never used the word "git," but I've
heard it in British movies, and I want to insult you in terms
native to your lingo.

"He lives with his head in the primordial nebula," Moyers
said. "His body is amongst us, but his mind resides in a few
nanoseconds around the Big Bang." Gag me.

Moyers had other talking heads on, of course; the guest-list
was sanctioned by the Bureau of Political Correctness. There
were two women, both slender and attractive. One an actress;
one a poetess, one of those beautiful, older Irish women whose
beauty I just want to steal; we Slavs do not age well. Their thick
hair goes gray and stays thick and they all look like sages, no
matter how much folderol they mutter about mists, salmon and
St. Patrick, the Potato Famine, the Little People; Celtic harp

music rose in the background and I'm sure the PBS fundraisers' telephones rang off the hook. There was a black liberation theologian in dreads and kente cloth. One Asian, whose entire identity seemed to be that he was the one Asian. One Captain of Industry. Diverse? There were no poor people. No ugly people. No diseased people. Why do you people get to tell the rest of us whether or not there is a God? How about six million dead Jews? Isn't the Holocaust the signature event that types that question IN ALL CAPS?

I became excited when Moyers identified you as a skeptic who questions everything. I actually put down my fork and stopped chewing my pasta fazool. I question everything, and I find that that makes me very lonely. If you want to talk about Islam and terror, for example, you know that the Politically Correct will resist anything that implicates Islam. On the other hand, self-identified "Patriots" won't allow any critical statements about US petro-dependency. Abortion, euthanasia, gay marriage: people bring so many agendas to these matters that real, probing questions are never asked or answered. But you were as dogmatic in your atheism as a Monty Python parody of a pope.

Lord Randolph, just between you and me, does it matter to you at all that you lie? You lie like a Soviet propaganda minister. You create a false dichotomy: either one is a thinker, or one is a believer. Either one is a flea-bitten person of faith, scuttling about some hovel, chaining human beings to superstition and fear – you glanced at the Irish poetess the moment you said this – cruel and unfair of you – or one is a whistle-clean scientist, gleaming in the new light of truth. One is Prometheus, liberating humanity. Does it matter to you at all that these words of yours are complete, unadulterated bullshit?

Lord Randolph Court-Wright, I know that you know that Isaac Newton, frequently dubbed the greatest scientist and mathematician of all time, though he wrote reams of math and science, wrote even more about his own Christian faith. I know that you know that Copernicus and Galileo were devout Catholics. You know, also, that Louis Pasteur died with his rosary in his hands. You know that Max Planck was a church warden. You know of contemporary physicists who seek only equations and then cough up poetic admissions of ineluctable confrontations with God. You know that Einstein adamantly refused to be counted in the atheist census, though he was aggressively invited, and that he emphatically insisted on his own understanding of God as driving his science: I want to know the mind of God, Einstein said; "the rest are details." Johannes Kepler, Renee Descartes, Blaise Pascal, Gregor Mendel: Remove these Christian names and you've pretty much erased the scientific canon. I know that you know all of this. I know that you know that you are lying. What kind of a mind, what kind of a soul, lies behind lies like yours?

When I was a kid, my mother schlepped me to her home village in Slovakia. A few handmade houses plunked down between a river, fields of rye, and mountains you could hike to, hunt boar in; with another hour's climb, you entered medieval ruins; from those heights the village looked as it must have when the castle was first erected.

Mom and I arrived a few years after the Soviet tanks. The liberators who would free humanity from religious chains.

There was a priest in the village. He had been tortured. They just showed up one day and took him. He was gone for some months. They sent him back. He was broken. His body looked fine. His mind was gone. He could eat and dress and walk, but that was it. He was guided around town by the hand of a little girl. There was no question but that the villagers would tend for him. Nobody talked about it. He moved like Frankenstein. My blood ran cold.

There are these people, these people who rise up every so many years or so, and they speak really well, and they get others to listen. They get others to listen because they are smooth but loud and full of themselves and convinced that others must listen. These people have an intuition of the mob's simmering resentments, and they glom on to those incoherent grumblings, and preach them back in grandiloquent prose. And their message is always the same: "There are two kinds of people in this world. Only two. There's us, and there's them over there. And them over there, those people who are different from us, they, they are the cause of all of our woes." These slick speakers don't use their fists. No, they never hurt anyone. They pave the way for all hellish mayhem.

Is that what you are all about?

But you know what I was thinking the whole time I was watching you on TV? That this guy, in high school, got way more wedgies than blow-jobs. And that's why you don't believe in God. At least you don't believe in a God that is beyond you. Because you do believe in God, really, you believe in Lord Randolph Court-Wright, Marquis of Alnwick. You believe in your physics discoveries and your mountain climbing and your posh, Jane-Austen-movie accent. You believe in all of that so hard because when you were a fourteen-year-old science geek, before your legs bolted and your voice cracked, you were a little boy nerd and nobody liked you. The tough kids in school – there had to have been some tough kids, even just relatively tough, even in an English boarding school – the tough kids in school stole your self away from you, so you make your living stealing God away from us. And then you sit back in your squeaky leather chair and steeple your hands and look down your Viking-prow nose and observe us plebian wretches squirming, because you've just given yourself the satisfaction of snatching away the one thing that makes our miserable serf-like existences bearable.

You are so wrong I want to scream. I want to wrest from Moyers' plump and clammy hands my every tax dollar used to produce that program. I wish I could have been there questioning you. I DEMAND EQUAL TIME!!!

But, to be honest – I don't think I'm writing this e-mail just because you pissed me off. What is it about you? Is this déjà vu? I need to brush up on my metaphysical terminology. From the French, "already seen," the spooky sensation that one has lived a new moment before, met an entirely new acquaintance in some misty past ... but one cannot quite remember where or when.

Is this synchronicity? I love the story from Carl Jung. He was treating a woman who was "psychologically inaccessible."

The difficulty lay in the fact that she always knew better about everything. Her excellent education had provided her with a weapon ideally suited to this purpose, namely a highly polished Cartesian rationalism with an impeccably "geometrical" idea of reality. After several fruitless attempts to sweeten her rationalism with a somewhat more human understanding, I had to confine myself to hope that something unexpected and irrational would turn up, something that would burst the intellectual retort into which she had sealed herself. Well, I was sitting opposite her one day, with my back to the window, listening to her flow of rhetoric. She had an impressive dream the night before, in which someone had given her a golden scarab – a costly piece of jewelry. While she was still telling me the dream, I heard something behind me gently tapping on the window. I turned round and saw that it was a fairly large flying insect that was knocking against the window pane from the outside in an obvious effort to get into the dark room.

The insistent insect visitor was, of course, a scarab beetle. Jung's patient had resisted the idea that there is anything in the universe except her own intellectual excellence. She was talking to Jung about a dream starring a scarab beetle, and, at that moment, a scarab beetle burst in on her therapy: synchronicity.

Is that what you made me feel? Is that why I'm writing to

you?

It's late. I should go to bed.

Just a few hours ago, I was in the kitchen, whipping up my Saturday night pasta fazool. The TV was on in the next room. It's a ten-inch, thirty-year-old, black-and-white, and it brings in snowy images via its bent antennae. I live in a loft; there's no wall between the kitchen and the TV; right now my keystrokes echo off a shadowy, twenty-five-foot high ceiling. I heard the PBS station ID, and some maudlin Is-There-a-God type mood music, and Moyers introducing his guests, and the camera panned around the circle, and I saw *you,* and ... what? Happened? One steps out of time. Memories of those moments are inaccessible. They aren't day-to-day life. Returning to day-to-day life, you can't access the memory, because no day-to-day person, including the person to whom it happens, speaks the language of those time-out-of-time moments. Metaphysical terminology fails.

My Lord, you don't believe in moments like this, and I don't have words to name them. Communication is impossible.

But I'll tell you this, Mr. Atheist, Milord The-Sun-Never-Set-on-His-Nose. I try to watch the physics shows on PBS but I can follow them only so far. I love how they try to explain things in simple, everyday language. They'll start out saying something like, "Now, imagine the universe as a bowl of cake batter, and gravity as a stick of butter." I can relate. Cake batter – one of my favorite things. Okay, I'm with you. I'm wrapping my head around this idiot-friendly metaphor, and then the TV physics guy says, "And, that is why no one can predict whether Schrodinger's Cat is alive or dead," and I'm like, "Wait a second ... Can we please go back to the cake batter and work up to Schrodinger's Cat in slightly smaller increments?" So, no, I don't know nuthin' about physics, but I know it's all just hardware, and I know that there is a God, and I know that in high school, Lord Git-Toff Marquis of Wanker-Bugger, you got more wedgies than blowjobs.

save **SEND** delete

Sunday, 7:02 a.m.
Dear Lord Randolph Court-Wright, Marquis of Alnwick,
Wow. I mean, wow.

save send DELETE

Sunday, 7:11 a.m.
Dear Lord Randolph Court-Wright, Marquis of Alnwick,
Look, I didn't think that there was a snowball's chance that
anyone would read that. I was just trying to get a bunch of stuff
off my chest. God, this sounds so stupid. If I didn't believe what
I was writing, why did I spend two hours on a Saturday night
writing it? Great, I'm thinking out loud again, writing to myself.
Not attempting to communicate with you at all. But – you –
seven thousand miles away? How far *is* London from New
Jersey, anyway? I'm going to look that up. 3,498 miles. 5,629
kilometers. Do you use kilometers, not miles, in England? You?
Who the hell are you? Why did you write back to me? Is this a
joke?

save send DELETE

Sunday, 7:20 a.m.
Dear Amanda,
Amanda, look, if you're not online, get online. Answer this e-
mail. Amanda, the weirdest thing happened. Amanda, last night
I was cooking pasta fazool and I had the TV on and this guy
came on – Randolph Court-Wright – and started spouting off
about how there is no God, and he's a Lord, and some important
scientist, and he pissed me off, and I sent him a rude e-mail, and
he wrote back, and now I'm mortified. And I cannot believe how
quick, how intimate, and how small the world has become.

save SEND delete

INBOX:
mira … darling … what would buddha do …

online late ... almost dawn here in Berkeley ... just got back from the cast party in the city of the tarnished angels ... never guess who was there ... brad pitt can be such an cretin ... must sign off ... butterfly kisses ... yours always ... amandla

Sunday, 7:59 a.m.

Dear Lord Randolph Court-Wright, Marquis of Alnwick,

Sir, it has been more than an hour since I read your e-mail. I haven't even taken my morning shower. Having typed that I feel I should delete it; do you need to know that I am so aghast at my own behavior that it is affecting how I smell? But I promised myself that to get through this I will force myself just to keep typing and not keep chickening out and keep going back and deleting.

Please let me say the following three things as inelegantly and inadequately as possible.

I did not write that e-mail with the thought that anyone, at any time, would read it. You are world famous. Perhaps I would send it to my friend Amanda. She reads a lot of my writing, when she's not mad at me. She's an actress, in California. You may have seen her in "Female Werewolves from the Moons of Jupiter." That is not her best work; she does stuff like that to pay the bills. Her heart is in the woman-centered theater of Ibsen, Strindberg. I'm rambling. Stop.

I thought that e-mail would be like a message in a bottle tossed into the moat stretching infinitely and storming forever between your universe and mine. I live in Paterson, New Jersey, a slum. You inhabit – I imagine golden wallpaper and pearl toilet fixtures and liveried servants dishing quails' eggs for breakfast. I didn't think that "to every action there is an equal and opposite reaction" applied between the physics of my world and that of yours.

I felt no sense of triumph when I learned from your e-mail that my assumption of what typified your schooldays was accurate. I hope that the bullies were punished. There is no excuse for that sort of thing. And yet, you report your memories of school, not just with the obvious poignancy, but also with a dry and subtle humor that attests to your strength. I admire you. You triumphed over your bratty tormentors.

Your note to me was one of the most gracious documents I have ever read. Were it not so inappropriate I would compliment you on your imitation of Christ.

I apologize again. You have impressed me greatly. All the best.

save SEND delete

INBOX
mira ma belle ... can't sleep ... bastard brad pitt ... you ... another broken heart ... that's going to keep happening ... i'm afraid ... until you take my advice pumpkin ... why don't you finally break down and follow "the secret" the rhonda byrne book ... or come for a workshop ... they could get you some kind of a scholarship so it would not be so pricey ...

Sunday, 10:01 a.m.
Dear Lord Randolph Court-Wright, Marquis of Alnwick,
You are incredibly kind and gracious. I do appreciate your taking the time to say all these things. And you gave me a smile. It's a good thing you have a sense of humor – must come in handy in your work.

Me? I'm basically nobody. Thank you for asking, though. Again, you are very kind, sir, very kind.

save SEND delete

Sunday, 10:15 a.m.
Amanda, so what DID Brad Pitt do this time?

save SEND delete

Sunday, 10:31 a.m.
Dear Lord Randolph Court-Wright, Marquis of Alnwick,
Wow, but we live in a rapid age. My mother was born into a village where her psychic dreams – wait, you don't believe in that, do you? – informed her that her father in America, whom she had never met, had had a bad accident in the coal mine weeks before the telegram arrived.

Yes, I will buy and read your book. I promise. Or maybe take it out from the library.

Really, there's nothing to know about me, but thank you for asking.

save SEND delete

Sunday, noon
Dear Lord Randolph Court-Wright, Marquis of Alnwick,
Well, I'll be darned. You Googled me. Yes, I did in fact write that essay. Um ... I'm just sitting here amazed. Amazed.

save SEND delete

INBOX
mira ... my little cabbage ... my forever mira ...
just reread your e-mail ... not another broken heart ... exchanging e-mails with randolph court-wright ... well well well ... who next ... einstein ... mira you never cease surprising me ... and everyone ... do tell ... shoot some of that gold my way.

Sunday, 7 p.m.
Dear Amanda,
Must write fast. Inbox full of messages.
Um, thank you but ... I can't forward his messages to you. Wouldn't be right. Would violate his privacy. But I'll tell you what he said.

save SEND delete

INBOX
wouldn't be "RIGHT" ... oh ... please ...

Sunday, 7:32 p.m.
Dear Amanda,
I can show you my messages to him if you want.
save SEND delete

INBOX
FUCK that ... OVER and out ...

Sunday, 10:03 p.m.
Dear Lord Randolph Court-Wright, Marquis of Alnwick,
Thank you so much for inviting me to address you by your first name. But I wouldn't feel comfortable.

Well, I meant pretty much what I said. Amanda is ... an actress. And she's not ... easy.

I'm so amazed that you found those essays by me on the web and read them. I'm basically a starving writer. You know the deal. "La Boheme." Cough, cough. That someone of your status would find something worthwhile in my work is stunning.

Look – you've been very kind but I'm sure that you have more important matters to attend to. You needn't feel that you have to respond. It has been lovely receiving your e-mails. Probably the only e-mails I'll ever receive from a genius of your stature. Thank you. All the best.
save SEND delete

Monday, 6:05 a.m.
He wrote to me again. He wrote to me again, Amanda. I sent him the courteous, "Thank you for writing me" e-mail one sends when one receives e-mails from a world famous physicist that one has insulted, and "Goodbye," I said, and he wrote back.

What do I do now? I'm sitting here alone Amanda, please.

save send DELETE

Tuesday, 3 p.m.

Dear Rand,

No, no, no. Nothing like that. Please don't think that. I've loved receiving your e-mails. If you must know, I've been thinking this whole time about how to respond.

"Rand" is a lovely nickname. And I am fully aware of the pitfalls of being "Randy" and I promise that I shall never call you that.

Are you more Rand McNally, or more Ayn Rand? The Road Atlas, I hope. Not the "Atlas Shrugged." We've got too much to fight about already.

save SEND delete

Friday, 7:13 a.m.

Dear Lord Randolph Court-Wright, Marquis of Alnwick,

Hello?

save SEND delete

Saturday, 9:04 a.m.

Well, sure. I was busy, too. Dodging disaster takes up most of my day.

save send DELETE

Friday, 5:11 p.m.

Dear Lord Randolph Court-Wright, Marquis of Alnwick,

You are wrong on both counts.

save send DELETE

Friday, 5:32 p.m.

Dear Lord Randolph Court-Wright, Marquis of Alnwick,

You are wrong on both counts.

SAVE send delete

save send DELETE

Friday, 6:03 p.m.
Dear Lord Randolph Court-Wright, Marquis of Alnwick,
No, in fact, neither of your guesses is correct.

I had no intention of "converting" you when I first wrote to you, I have no intention of converting you now, and I will not change this position in the future and attempt to convert you. Ever.

You're weary of the hundreds of letters you've received: from a devout snake handler housewife in Kentucky, a politically correct if pious vicar in Lewisham, a fervid, stunningly black nun in Botswana, a secret church member in China who smuggles Christians out of North Korea.

Forgive me. I do not pity you. If you don't want all those prayers prayed for you, then donate them. Send them by Federal Express or the means of a Tibetan prayer flag that wafts good wishes onto the beneficent wind – send them to an alky derelict whom no one sees, anymore, and for whom no one spares a prayer. You celebrities have more of everything than all of the rest of us, apparently, even more of prayer.

save send DELETE

Friday, 6:20 p.m.
Dear Rand,
I think I just realized something: how easy it is for me to give Satan my thoughts and feelings and keyboard.

When I put myself first, when I make my ego the top agenda item, I am angry at everyone, and I always see myself the victim. Victim that I am, I see everyone as a cold-hearted failure who is not meeting my needs. I blind myself to others' vulnerabilities and pain and I blind myself to what I might do to alleviate those.

Rand, I think it hurt you to think that I might have contacted you not to *contact* you, not to contact *you,* but rather to claim you the way a big game hunter claims quarry. Rather than wanting to hear your stories about what those naughty classmates did to you in high school, or rejoice over your latest good news, you think I just wanted to step past your individuality, and empty you out of yourself and discard that as I would the guts of a bagged trophy, and claim your hide as a prize in some game of Christian celebrity conquest.

Please don't think that, Rand. It's you I value, it's you I enjoy, it's you I've come to cherish, it's you I want to –

save send DELETE

Saturday, 6:04 a.m.
Dear Lord Randolph Court-Wright, Marquis of Alnwick,
No, I am not trying to convert you.

No, I am not a Christian just because I was born a Christian and I don't know anything about any other faith.

save SEND delete

Saturday, 9:45 a.m.
Yeah, well.

Look, lemme cut to the chase.

You sent me a flurry of e-mails that ...

God, men and women fight over this stuff all the time.

But we aren't men and women, are we?

Right now you and I are nothing but keystrokes and binomial code and black and white patterns waltzing across a liquid crystal display.

And you are a "Lord" and a celebrity and I am an undistinguishable member of the faceless mass, a smudged extra in a Kathe Kollwitz crowd scene.

You sent me a flurry of e-mails that showed interest and got me excited and when I began to engage with you in a reciprocal manner, when I let my guard down, you disappeared.

In real life women are permitted – expected, even – to nag when a man says he will phone and a man does not phone. Does that rule apply to us? No. There is scant and contested etiquette for e-mail, and there are no rules for how a celebrity behaves with a nobody.

When you suddenly dropped out of our interaction without so much as an "It's been fun; let's wrap this up," I … hate to admit this. I Googled you. Usually a stalker has to park in front of the guy's house. You being you and this computer age being this computer age, even without crossing the ocean and parking in front of your mansion, I discovered immediately what you were doing rather than e-mailing me. You'd been lunching with the queen. "Lunching with the queen" was not a metaphor for a chess gambit or an obscure sex act. You'd literally been at a luncheon with the Queen of England. What cards do I have in my hand that match that?

We live in a pseudo-Democratic age when everyone is equal and we are all on a first-name basis and any boy can grow up to be president, and any e-mail can reach any atheist, but, still some animals are more equal than others. Woe betide the mouse that forgets that.

So, no, I do not want to call you by your first name. Calling you by your first name sets up expectations in my heart that this interaction will never satisfy.

My bosses want me to call them by their first names. I do. Because they want me to. Because I'm the employee and it's my job to give my bosses what they want. Because it would raise too many suspicions if I did not. I remind myself – Do not be fooled. This is NOT a first-name relationship.

save send DELETE

Saturday, 10:00 a.m.

Dear Rand,

Thank you for reminding me to call you by your first name.

As for your questions, they are both big ones.

I hesitate to answer them.

Are you sure you want to know?

Will you misinterpret my replies and conclude that I am, after all, talking to you merely in an attempt to convert you?

save SEND delete

INBOX

plz frwrd attchd flr ...

"Amanda Clitheroe brings a fierce fire to Ibsen that will long burn in the viewer's memory"

    "Preview audiences were in tears"

    "In our post-feminist age, the jaded Ibsen aficionado might well question what could be done with 'A Doll's House' that hasn't been done, excellently, before. This new production, featuring completely nude actors manipulating hand puppets elaborately costumed in Norwegian Gilded Age bourgeois finery, brings colors and dimensions to Ibsen that would astound the playwright himself. Essential viewing."

    "Amanda Clitheroe is a revelation. Her manipulation of her hand puppet is masterful."

    Full frontal nudity. Viewer discretion is advised. Tickets on sale at the box office or through Ticketmaster.

Saturday, 9:22 p.m.

Dear Rand,

I'll take the easier of your two questions first.

I never really planned it. I can just tell you that I've been to Bethlehem, the Wailing Wall, the Dome of the Rock, Hagia Sophia. I've been to Lumbini, where Buddha was born, and Sarnath, where he preached his first sermon. At Chiwong Gompa, I witnessed a Mani Rimdu, a Tibetan Buddhist dance drama celebrating the victory of dharma over darkness. I trekked through caves where Milarepa meditated and I spun the prayer wheels of Muktinath. I've sat zazen, and more importantly, soaked in the hot tub, at the Berkeley Zen Center. I've hiked through Pagan in Burma, and visited stupas and wats in Bangkok and Rangoon. I've been worshipped on Bhai Tika. I arrived on Varanasi's ghats in the middle of the night and walked through cremations and streams of raw sewage to find lodging. The Parthenon, the Vatican, Stonehenge, the Badlands, the Ark Church in Nowa Huta, an African witch doctor, a shaman, a Native American who kept a pet wolf; The Koran, "Zen Flesh, Zen Bones," Talmudic scholarship, the "Bhagavad Gita," the "Ramayana"; the big and small atheists: Marx's "The Communist Manifesto," Freud's "Totem and Taboo," Bertrand Russell's "Why I Am Not a Christian," Antony Flew, Vashti McCollum, Madalyn Murray O'Hair – will admit I've never read, and without aid of Google, cannot spell, Nietzsche – attendance at Catholic school, at a Seder, at a Rainbow Gathering, on a Kibbutz, in a Cistercian monastery; Ganesh puja before embarking on a new enterprise; Buddhist study with a man trained by Goenka-ji; life in the workers' paradise; in-the-flesh encounters with the Dalai Lama, Pope John Paul II, Lech Walesa, Robert Thurman, Edward Said, Bernard Lewis, Elie Weisel, Salman Rushdie, M. Scott Peck: check.

Again, I didn't plan it, but one day I looked around and realized that I had had relationships with an Orthodox Jewish rabbi, the son of a Holocaust survivor, a Buddhist meditation teacher, and a couple of self-identified Muslim terrorists; I also dated a couple of Muslims who were not self-identified terrorists. There were atheists too, of course; the Boy Scouts had refused one the Eagle Scout status he had earned because he was a militant atheist. There was also a devout follower of Rosa Luxemburg who sold communist pamphlets on the subway. On Rosh Hashanah, with a Yiddish-speaking rabbi, I threw my sins into the River Wisla, and I broke the Yom Kippur fast after services at the sixteenth-century Remuh synagogue. I broke the Ramadan fast with my boyfriend – we could finally kiss – and with a slew of Muslim co-workers – we ate mountains of rice and stuffed grape leaves and goat. I broke the Teej fast with my

Hindu women neighbors. I enjoyed a Christmas feast at a Bruderhof.

I wanted to live in a village where no one had even heard of Christianity, and see how Christianity looked from that perspective. I did want to try these other faiths on. I asked myself, had I been born into another faith, would I be a Christian? And I did my best to discover the answer.

So, no. I'm not a Christian just because I was raised a Christian in a Christian environment and it never occurred to me to be anything else.

save SEND delete

Sunday 9:05 p.m.

Dear Rand,

Did I just mention in passing that I had relationships with self-identified terrorists? Yeah, I guess I did. Ah, the limitations, ah, the untamed power, of e-mail. Okay. Let me answer your question, and type with less speed and more care.

His name was Muhannad. He used to hang out at a community college where I was teaching. Students told me he'd been in prison in the Middle East for terrorism. This was all years before 9-11.

Paterson, New Jersey is a very tough venue for the teacher. One of my students bragged to me that he had dealt crack to a pregnant mother in front of her little daughter. That was how he paid tuition, and, "Your salary, Prof." Another student confessed to me, for the first time she had confessed this to anyone, that her step-father regularly dragged her to the basement and raped her. I had to get her to the police; to the hospital. There were students who had cripplingly bad body odor – body odor so bad it was the central fact of their life. Others made life-stunting choices in personal apparel, and some brought in arts and crafts projects just because no one had ever complimented their work, or even seen it. Muhannad's rumored dark past was just one potential distraction. My policy was to focus on the noun-verb agreement that I could do something about, rather than on extracurricular mini-dramas about which I could do nothing.

Muhannad was different. It was as if he moved in his own weather, stormy and dark. Around him, kids who were rushing to grab hold of the American Dream dropped any mention of what they'd just seen on TV, and started reciting the Koran. Around him, they went through that change you go through when you walk from a crowded, sunny street into a funeral parlor. Yet, your eyes shot right to him, silent and still as he was. His energy was concentrated. As if you could touch him and receive a jolt.

Muhannad wasn't aware of only a wading pool world, of what he'd eat for lunch that day or his brother's wedding that weekend. Even if you mentioned the president's name to some of my students, they would not recognize it. They chose suffocatingly low horizons.

He never referred to himself. He let others go first in lines. He bought students food in the cafeteria when they were low on cash, while he himself went without. He organized fundraising when some international disaster struck. He stated openly that he planned to kill. You wanted to dive in and rescue. The perversion of power is an affront. You wanted to redeem Muhannad not just for himself, but for your own idea of what valence charisma should have. Electricity should be used to light lamps, not to shock, not to kill.

My students used to drag me to the cafeteria to debate him. Arabs and Poles are both different from Americans in some of the same ways: we value family, hospitality, honor, poetry, and tradition. We fight doomed battles, and we love debate. As different as we are, sharing territory outside the mainstream made us the same. Their words and sentences were like dolphins bucking and contorting through acrobatics and ocean spray. With them, unlike with most Americans, I opened the tap on my intensity. They got so excited when someone scored a point: "Masha'Allah!" They didn't care if it was their side or the other side. You could feel the air ping.

I stayed well after my workday was finished. In that cafeteria, surrounded by guys I would never marry or even see in two years, I was having a rollicking great time. I should have been able to experience that level of enjoyment with a Joisy girl with fake fingernails, sipping a Long Island Iced Tea in a franchise bar with a fake Irish name and a plastic "thatch" roof. The Mr. Right I should have been looking for was "like me" not because he had a living relationship with the God of his understanding, not because he could recite poetry by heart in the classical language of his ancestors, and not because he thought that there were things in life more important than money. The Mr. Right I should have been looking for was "like me" because he was Catholic with a blue-collar background and a foothold, however shaky, in a white-collar job. That Mr. Right would relegate his exhibitions of passion, not to discussions on the fate of the world, but to hours-long sessions of watching sports on TV.

Muhannad cited the lunatics' catalogues of quotes, like Thomas Jefferson's: "The tree of liberty must be refreshed from time to time with the blood of patriots and tyrants." I'd come right back with Gandhi's kicker, "An eye for an eye makes the whole world blind." For Muhannad change had to happen *now* and it had to have *his* name on it. Violence was not his imperative – immediacy and copyright were. The world changes slowly, if at all, and we rarely get to be the star of the narrative, unless we decide to create our own special effects.

Muhannad started showing up at places where he knew I'd be, standing a little distance off, and staring. One day he showed up at my apartment. I had not told him where I lived. How did he get into the building, get past the guard? Maybe he just hung back and waited for another resident to enter and followed silently after, confident he would not be challenged, confident he could meet any challenge. It wasn't for himself that he acted, but for the cause.

I peered out the peephole and opened the door and tried to remain calm. As a traveler, I've had men pull guns on me, knives. And not be afraid. Because I could not afford it; fear interferes with your ability to grab the gun, to dodge the blade. All Muhannad had were words. I was terrified.

"Would you like some peppermint tea?" If I made one false move, that would inform him of how frightened I was. That's how frightened I was – that I thought it necessary to conceal my fear.

He took the glass of tea. He perched on the edge of the seat of my one comfortable chair. "You and I are both different from other people," he began, "and that makes us both the same."

"I've been watching you," he said. "You are not like so many people who go through life only half awake. You know about injustice. You don't believe powerful people's foolish lies. You have a sense of the divine. You can satisfy your craving to get close to God. I can help you. You can help me. We can help each other."

As Muhannad was speaking, I was watching a rash of red specks arise on my wrists.

"I know that I am special to you."

It wasn't until he said that that I realized that it was true. I was horrified. It had been obvious. Maybe not to the others, but to him. I had thought that I was the one performing the anthropological observation. He had sized me up, and was using my fascination to entangle me.

Muhannad continued uncoiling. "I would like you to become my wife."

I watched the specks multiply rapidly as if a swarm of red ants.

"Do not become alarmed. I am a good man and will treat you with respect. I will not lie to you. I have a wife back home. She is my cousin. She knows about you. She approves the plan. I can marry more than once. You will become Muslim, and this will all become clear. For now, you need not become alarmed."

It was all so soft and silky and paralyzing. He didn't have to tell me about the wife back home. Ethics: I had to admire that. Perhaps he knew I'd admire it.

"You and I both know that the world is a terrible place. What kind of justice allows children to starve, to be bombed? Your conscience will not allow this any more than mine. It would not be right for you to become a soldier. You have a woman's heart. You will be a soldier's wife. You will serve by serving me. I will serve the cause."

I took his glass. "Thanks so much for coming by. I can promise you that I will think about your offer."

I could have done what I did when I was teaching. I could have put extraneous drama on hold and focused on the human being in front of me. I abandoned the human being; I leapt out of the moment. I was ashamed that I had been so uncool as to allow my fascination for him to show. I was ashamed that I had been so uncool as to feel that fascination. I was ashamed that my fascination exposed my hypocrisy. If I had really meant the things I had been saying about pacifism and Christianity, why was I getting squiggly over Muhannad? His agenda: the separation of limbs from limbs, muscles from bones, blood from arteries, in cinematic productions that did not discriminate between baby and soldier. Why did I tune to that channel?

I shuffled him out the door, locked that door, and never responded to Muhannad in any human way again. What I feared transpired: he won. During those moments he was in my apartment, his commitment to violence was stronger than my commitment to Christ. My fear and disgust pushed me away from his humanity. I let The Terrorist replace the human being. It's not that anything I might have said or done would have made a difference to him, but it would have made a difference to me, to

the amount of lived faith in this world. Instead, just for convenience's sake, I contributed to the amount of fear and hate.

Ten years later. It was an exquisitely beautiful September
morning. I was gazing out at a green backyard in Bloomington,
Indiana, putting the finishing touches on my dissertation. Bob
Edwards, the basso profundo of National Public Radio, with an
almost exaggerated calm – his voice, like that morning's weather,
was just too good – announced that one, no, now, two planes had
hit the World Trade Center. Many, when first hearing that news,
thought it a freakish accident.

I immediately knew, and I immediately remembered
Muhannad, who, like a roller-coaster, had been both fun and gut-
wrenchingly terrifying. As far as I know, he wasn't involved. But
six of Paterson's Arabs were. Our mayor told the press, "Nobody
ever saw them at mosques, but they liked the go-go clubs."

save **SEND** delete

Sunday, 10:02 a.m.

Dear Rand,

$$$??? It's funny you would even ask! I don't have any. I hitch-
hiked through France; that's how I got to Chartres. In Varanasi, I
slept on bare wooden boards and got chilblains; it was a record
cold winter. All I spent in Burma was the profits from smuggling
whiskey and cigarettes. I traveled by night train so I wouldn't
have to spring for hotel rooms. I discovered how polite the
Burmese are because I fell asleep on a couple of them. I traveled
on the back of a Sudanese smugglers' truck. I met Salman
Rushdie purely by chance. I walked into a bookstore, and there
he was. I told him that "Midnight's Children" was so fine that
after I read it I couldn't write a word. He looked deep into my
eyes as if his own destiny depended on my fulfilling his urgent
commission: "You must keep writing!" There's no way he would
remember that. I'll never forget it.

I know you don't believe this stuff, so it's hard to communicate. The right people always showed up at the right moment and said the right thing. One day I was bushwhacking through jungle, with my recently purchased field-guide to the birds of India. I thought, "Wouldn't it be neat if I met Salim Ali?" I looked up – the person walking toward me at that very moment was Salim Ali, the ornithologist author of my newly purchased field-guide. I know that you do not – that you cannot – believe in that kind of synchronicity. I know it happened all the time.

High Holydays at the Remuh synagogue? I didn't even know it was Jewish New Year; I had never heard of this historic synagogue. I was traveling in Poland and someone made a comment that I thought might be anti-Semitic. It was one of those comments that you could take either way, and my Polish is not fluent. Had I really heard what I thought I heard? Not sure whether I should speak up, I ventured, "Excuse me. I'd like to visit this city's synagogue. Please direct me?" I thought that that would be subtle enough that it would work one way or the other. Mind – I had no intention of actually *going* to the synagogue. I wanted to break away from the group so I could snag some luscious Polish full-cream pastries, which, in those Communist days, you could purchase for three or four American cents.

All of a sudden, these Poles couldn't do enough for me. They practically carried me to the Remuh on a palanquin. An American broke out of the group and came into the synagogue courtyard with me and whispered in my ear, "Mira, I'm so glad you've come out of the closet. I'm Jewish, too, and I've been lying low..." He dragged along this nineteen-year-old, six-foot-two-inch, neon blond German. I was aghast. Would Krakow's tiny community of surviving Jews want Hans or Horst or Adolph or whatever the German's name was in their midst? The gatekeeper was a four-foot by four-foot block of very-bad-attitude, Soviet female. She told us that they had been holding off High Holyday services because they didn't have a minyan. The two men who came with me – the American closet Jew and the German blond – completed the number of males necessary for worship.

I huddled near the courtyard wall, a wall made up of broken Jewish gravestones. It was twilight; a mist blurred the gray stones' jagged, puzzle-pieces edges, and Hebrew letters I couldn't read, anyway. We would have to go in to the synagogue soon – my first time in a synagogue. Three women stood in front of me. From what I could make out from their conversation, mostly in Polish but also with English, Yiddish and Hebrew tossed in, they were meeting this night for the first time since World War Two. One had emigrated to the US, one to Israel, and one had stayed on in Krakow. I practically fell forward, I was straining so hard to hear.

"Our red is much too blue."

"This Polish crap here I wouldn't use on my dog."

"This one feels greasy. Here. Let me swipe this on your hand. See what I mean?"

"It's a nice color."

"Color shmolor. It feels like schmaltz!"

"Nu, at least it tastes good, maybe?"

The long-lost friends were debating the relative merits of Israeli, Polish, and American lipstick!

"Why are we even talking? The American is best."

And, with that, the American woman took a few tubes out of her purse – probably already used; they didn't look new – and unceremoniously distributed them to the Pole and the Israeli.

That was the most amazing disquisition on the Holocaust that I have ever heard. Jews survive. Poles survive. People survive. Evil's triumphs are temporary. Beauty endures. Love endures.

Did I ruin that story by overburdening it with a moral? One can't tell with e-mail; I didn't want you to think I was being snotty in saying that the best commentary I ever heard on the Holocaust was listening to three old ladies debating lipstick.

I'm dyslexic. I never learned to read a map. Did not carry camera nor compass, watch nor alarm clock. I traveled around the world, alone, a woman, a backpack, a canteen, sleeping bag, pen, diary. One day I said I'd had enough of being the grasshopper – the wandering mendicant in iffy underwear, and never the ant – the carefully planning hoarder. I'd had enough of faith in some invisible destiny keeping me aloft; I looked down and realized I was treading acres of invisible air. I wore my first watch, and I really did learn to read a map. Ever since that day, nothing in my life has worked out. It's as if buying my first pair of pantyhose unplugged the magic in my life.

save SEND delete

Sunday, noon
Dear Rand,
Look, if I ever decide that I really need a man in my life I can toss dirty clothes on the floor and leave dishes in the sink. I can buy a big-screen color TV, tune it to the sports channel, turn up the volume, and hide the remote control. Oh, yeah, and I can rig the bathroom mirror so that every time I pass it, it barks, "You look fat!"

save SEND delete

Sunday 3:03 p.m.
You're allowed to hate God but I'm not allowed to hate men?

save SEND delete

Sunday 7:09 p.m.
Do I have to insert an emoticon? I thought you were smart. ;-)

save SEND delete

Sunday 7:59 p.m.
Dear Amanda-rama,
I am so impressed by the fliers, and so proud of your great reviews. Do they keep the theater warm?

Listen, I hope you don't mind if I talk about my stuff for a

28

minute. I'm still e-mailing with that famous smart guy atheist. Something about this has got me going. It's as if he's got a switch over there in England and he throws it and I just – I don't know.

One minute he'll be all professorial and he'll say something about the first few seconds after the Big Bang. I need to catch more PBS science shows. My question is, given that watches had not yet been invented, how were there "seconds" after the Big Bang? How did you do in physics in school?

And then he'll, without any transition, make some totally sophomoric *crack* about sex! I mean, he asked me this big question: Was I a Christian cause I had been raised a Christian? And not a Hindu or a Muslim or a Jew? I thought, well, that is a big question that no one has ever asked me. Does he really want to hear the answer? Probably not. So I tried to avoid answering, thinking he'd just let it pass, but he *didn't*. Three e-mails, You haven't answered, are you dodging me; he's really drilling me. Can a man be manly in an e-mail? I creamed my jeans. I love the cold, smart, determined boys. I often preferred Basil Rathbone to Errol Flynn, Alan Rickman to Bruce Willis, Billy Zane to Leo DiCaprio, Buddy Love to Professor Kelp.

And so I gear myself up to answer rigorously, and I'm telling stories, that I've never told. I resorted to the Salman Rushdie anecdote! Just, basically, baring my soul, and I press SEND and what comes back, almost immediately – did he even have time to read my message? – but this kind of icky e-mail. All he says is, So, you are a loner, *how do you take care of yourself?* And I'm like, why did I just send that e-mail to this teenager?

save SEND delete

Sunday 8:17 p.m.

Dear Rand,

How is it that you can talk about the first few *seconds* after the Big Bang? Watches had not yet been invented.

save SEND delete

29

INBOX:

slow deep breaths pumpkin ... slow deep breaths ...

the performance ... the masses could never comprehend what it takes for an actor ... preparation all day ... certainly consume no dairy ... after the show roar in ears for next hour ... as if on fire ...

torvald has got to learn to stop eating foods rich in polysaccharides ... during rehearsals his pants leg acted as a stovepipe and channeled his farts toward the floor ... now they diffuse into the ambient air ... nora has suffered enough!!!

the salman rushdie anecdote ... do so adore it ... told it so many times as if it happened to me ... have to remind myself it happened to you ... could pay you residuals ...

your new smart englishman atheist egghead geek boy dirty old man

MIRA!!! you are the GO dess! say with me sister! i am the GO dess!

read riane eisler ... when men approach us it is to worship ... we do ourselves no favor by allowing them to "drill" us ... unless by mutual consent ... is he also a dentist ... it's been a long time since your teeth have had an advocate

Sunday 9:01 p.m.

Dear Rand,

Thank you so much!

save SEND delete

Sunday 9:32 p.m.

Dear Amanda-panda,

He just sent me the answer! For that alone I want to ... clean his house.

He said that the beginning of "time" is a measurement of what theorists think of as the time from effectively infinite density and zero size to the point where protons were not overlapping each other. But it gets very confused because of the immense gravity. Spacetime is very warped, so time didn't flow like we think of now. Evidence indicates that it flowed far more slowly, in a sense because everything was so squashed together. Time is a measure of the increase in disorder in the universe. Time didn't "flow" in those early states because the entropy was constricted by the lack of available possible new states to move to, compared to the universe fourteen billion years later. So time still flowed 100,000,000 years ago, even if no dinosaur had a wristwatch. But before 13.67 billion years ago, time didn't flow, because there was no universe.

The weird thing is I think I almost understood.

save SEND delete

INBOX

does your new smart englishman geek boy dirty old man rugby fan e-mail installment plan ... never sleep?

Sunday 10:03 p.m.

Amandelicious,

I see your point.

I'm a complete stranger. A nobody. I send a famous guy a snotty e-mail. He's writing back, all hours of the day and night, esp. over there in England, all hours of the Greenwich Mean Time. Asks personal questions. When I don't respond, Googles me.

Is this a prank? Is some snotty MIT grad student reading his e-mail? Is somebody, somewhere laughing over my soul-baring anecdotes? My lack of faith eats away at me.

But, I'm enjoying this so much. Would I want to know? If it is some snotty MIT grad student, is that such a bad thing? Why investigate something that feels so good? Why not just go with the flow?

SAVE send delete

Sunday 10:33 p.m.

SAVE send delete

Sunday 11:02 p.m.

SAVE send delete

Sunday 11:33 p.m.

save SEND delete

INBOX
sweet highness of silliness ... have him call you ... ring you up as brits say ... you'll recognize if it is the voice from the tv show

Saturday 7:06 p.m.
Dear Rand,
I know. It *has* been a while.

No, it's not about you.

Something happened at work. I don't smoke, but if I did, I would be, right now.

I'm sitting here on the window sill, staring at traffic and rain.

save SEND delete

Saturday 7:29 p.m.
You just took my breath away.

That was the kindest possible thing to say.

Let me brew myself some peppermint tea, and gather my thoughts.

save SEND delete

Saturday 8:04 p.m.
Dear Rand,
As warm-up, before I get to the nub, let me describe my place.

Soundtrack. At this very moment I am listening to Paolo

32

Conte. He's Italian and he smokes and, I would have to guess, stays up very late. His voice is all trench-coat, thunderstorm, the last scene of "Casablanca," the kiss from a subtitled movie, the kind with the guts to end bittersweet. I want to cook him up a big mountain of spaghetti marinara snowy with extra Parmesan cheese. When I can't see any sense in life I listen to this CD and his seen-it-all, loved-it-all, dolce-vita baritone creates for me some kind of pattern, some kind of reason.

I live in Paterson, America's first planned industrial city, the brainchild of Alexander Hamilton, our most colorful Founding Father. He was a Caribbean bastard. His mother served time. Paterson's falls are the second highest east of the Mississippi. Used to run Silk City's mills. After labor strikes, jobs went overseas. No jobs in Paterson now. Lots of trash in the streets, including two-legged. Why do I live in a slum? Long story.

Someone got the bright idea to refurbish the silk mills. Mine is almost two hundred years old. Twenty-five feet above my head, a couple of exposed beams run a foot wide and twenty feet long. I imagine the trees, the lumberjacks, the transport, the energy, the young country raring to go. Mill workers once toiled under this ceiling. Sometimes I just lie on the floor and stare upward and count my blessings.

Windows rising ten feet face south. I watch the moon progress across the sky; I watch it grow fat and thin, dissolve into ether and then spring right back up over steeples.

There's more space than in the house I grew up in, with seven other people and a slew of pets. To this day, I am amazed that I get to pee when I need to; showers are blessings, every time. Never get old, never.

There are no posters on the acres of white wall. I like plain, and this is my apartment, and I get to do what I want. Life is an inexhaustible series of entertainments for one who grew up poor. What do kids who grew up with flat screen TVs in their bedrooms have to look forward to?

There is a moat between my mill and the noisy, gang-infested street. It is full of garbage. There are also urban mallard ducks, skunks and a very fat woodchuck. The moat used to be a raceway; it channeled water from the falls to run the looms. When the sun hits the water, rippled reflections dance across my ceiling, taunting me: beauty is a whore who blesses what she pleases and appears where she will.

I have two chairs that I carried in off the street where they were abandoned, a bedside table that I carried in off the street – it was pouring that day – the table's veneer is worn from that rain. I have two floor lamps; one was carried in off the street, and one was a donation from St. Vincent de Paul. I have a bed, donated by a Christian librarian named Doris Beasley.

And then there is the TV, on which I first saw you.

Do you feel like you are here, now, Rand?

Want to describe your place?

save SEND delete

Saturday 8:43 p.m.

I can just see the coffee stains, the filing system run amok, the unread papers reproducing every time you turn your back. "Spontaneous generation," indeed! That you work in such a cramped, windowless space violates what I've learned about celebrities from People magazine. You could have a penthouse with a sweeping vista and a solid gold table!

The Raquel Welch poster! Good gosh but I remember that! I'm not one for the objectification of women, but no one fills out a fur bikini quite like Raquel Welch. If I lived in One Million Years BC and if the women all looked like her, I'd go gay. No doubt.

I often turn my eyes away from M.C. Escher. His work makes me a bit queasy. But the one you've got on your wall – "Hand with Reflecting Sphere" – is one I can handle.

What is it with you Brits and central heating? A space heater tucked into a non-functional fireplace – is that really the best that a world-class physicist can do?

Okay, to tell you what happened this week at work I'm going to have to give you some background. I'm an adjunct professor. After a year of full-time teaching, I earn half of what someone working a minimum wage job earns.

Adjuncts have no job security. This semester, last minute, I got a job teaching Postcolonial literature. I didn't even know how to spell "Postcolonial," but I was offered the job, so I took it. I spent the next month locked in my apartment reading everything I could get my hands on about Postcolonial literature.

This university gave me my own office, which is pretty good. On most campuses you have to share. It's in the corner of a high rise, full of cobwebs, dying potted plants, and a broken radio from 1963. And, of course, on the window sills, stuck in the keyboards, the dead bugs. No one is invested in adjuncts so no one cleans the spaces we inhabit, our offices, our ladies' rooms. On every campus, we see the same dead bugs. There really should be a field guide to the dead bugs of adjunct professor university offices. This office is either very, very hot (heat on), Bob Cratchit cold (heat off) or pleasantly warm and snowy (heat on; window open).

My students don't get that I am an adjunct. They don't get that I'd never been on their campus till the day I taught the first class, or that I'll never be on their campus again. I don't know how many times I've fought back tears when a student has asked me, "What are you teaching next semester? I want to be in your class!" My students don't know that the "real" professors have their little rituals to establish their superiority over me, like cutting in front of me in line at the copy machine. They don't know that I can't afford a car and walk to campus in sweatpants and change in the ladies' room; they don't know that the material I taught them so confidently that afternoon I had crammed that morning. They don't know that I don't know my own boss' name, the approved method of contesting a grade, or even how much

I'll be paid. Their ignorance of my true status is my ally.

They witness me exercising the puny powers of assigning them work and knowledge and grades. They extrapolate from that and think I am much more powerful than I am. There's a metaphor in there somewhere that an atheist would like, about people witnessing the relatively puny powers that the winds or tides or pharaohs or adjunct professors exercise over mere mortals, and extrapolating deities where there are none. I'm not going to stop the car to pick that metaphor up right now.

Monday I was sitting in my drafty garret office, feeling like Rochester's mad wife, abandoned in her cell, feverishly prepping a lesson I'd never taught before and would never teach again but that I demanded be pitch perfect. A knock. I smoothed my skirt and opened the office door. It was Tom. I smiled. Tom is a nice kid.

Tom sits in back, crushing his sandy, bouncy curls against the cinder block wall. He's six foot and built. He does construction. His hands are big, hard and rough. He comes in some days smelling rank. It's not an affectation; he didn't not wash or wear deodorant to take any kind of political or aesthetic stand. He just came from laying bricks. Tom's curvaceous, well-defined lips and slightly flaring nostrils could have been set from the mold of a Classic Greek statue. He reads Ralph Waldo Emerson and Paolo Freire and blurts stuff out in class. He'll take one line from a text, a cheesy text, and weave it into something in Gramsci, and suddenly you can see that, inside his head, he's liberating the masses. Tom gets so much more out of the identity-politics drivel in Postcolonial Literature than the authors ever dreamed of putting into their work.

My eyes reluctantly broke free of the magnetic pull of the computer screen. I think I was on a brief breather and rereading an old e-mail of yours, Rand.

"I don't want to interrupt you," Tom said.

"No, no, not at all. Come in, Tom. Nice to see you. What's up?"

"I wanted to talk about Castro's 'Words to the Intellectuals.'"

"A topic close to my heart. Have a seat."

Tom talked. I gave him my full attention. Filled in details when he ran out of steam. Suggested scholarly articles he might read.

When I talk to students, my brain is like the dashboard of a car. The speedometer warns me if I'm going too fast. The odometer reminds me how far I've gone. The gas gauge lets me know how much farther I can go before a refill. Someone with my temperament is well advised to keep a weather eye on the temperature gauge. I was monitoring all these functions when Tom's eyes were turning pink and glimmering. I folded my hands in my gray wool lap and waited.

Tom set a record for continuing to talk about academic matters after his eyes first welled up. There were several dark stains on his t-shirt before I finally got up and went to the Ladies' room and came back with tissue paper. I didn't have tissue paper in the office; another price of being an academic gypsy.

"I'm sorry," Tom said.

"It's okay," I said.

"Some things are just getting to me, I guess."

I nodded. I noticed how green his eyes are. The contrast with red emphasized their color; the tears magnified their intensity. He was sizing me up.

"If you want to talk about it I'm happy to listen. If you just want to sit for a while, we can sit for a while."

"It's nothing," he said, blowing his nose and looking toward the window. "Your window is open," he said.

"Yeah," I said.

Tom kept looking out the window, beyond his own reflection in the glass, beyond the gray storm clouds. "I don't know if I'm going to be able to finish the semester."

"Why's that?"

"I always panic," he said. "Around this time."

"Any special reason?" I asked.

He broke into sobs.

I took his hands. That is why I know that Tom's hands are big, and hard, and rough. I kept gazing at his eyes, though he was looking down at his hands. Lots of tear stains on his t-shirt.

Tom's dad is beating him. A big, young, hard male like Tom could take a beating from an old man. It's that it's his dad, and the things he says. Even though I've not told you "Tom"'s real name, I won't repeat the things his dad says to him. Malicious messages honed to wound. To repeat this filth would violate Tom all over again.

"That's not true," I said. "What your father said is not true. Don't give it a moment of belief, because it's just not true."

I want to wrench Tom out of that house with a crowbar. The kids who have it worst are the last to leave. Twisted parents twist them around so they don't really get it that the house has a door and they have feet and are capable of ambulation and can leave and never look back. Twisted parents convince their kids that they could never make it on the outside. Convince them that they couldn't even snag a waitressing job or pay rent on a basement room. Good parents raise their kids to fly. Evil parents never release the clutches holding the child down.

"You are a wonderful kid," I said. "A pleasure to have in class. I would be proud of a son like you. If I had a daughter, I'd want her to marry you."

I listed resources: shelters, counseling. I made sure that Tom knew, at least intellectually, that there were alternatives.

Then this beautiful young man cried out, "I wish I could feel that someone could someday love me, but I know that no one ever will, because I am so ugly, and covered with scars."

He stood up, and took off his shirt, and I saw them: scars from bottles, from knives. You'd notice the scars, if you were unabashedly checking Tom out on a beach, in bright sunshine, but the scars don't lessen him; they just make him a beautiful, hard young man, who is scarred.

Tom said, "I so wish that someone would hug me." His head hung low and tears fell on the floor.

My resolve is to give my students whatever they ask for that I can. I did not hug Tom. I sat in my chair. He stood there, crying, naked to the waist.

SAVE send delete

Saturday 10:27 p.m.

SAVE send delete

Saturday 11:01 p.m.

SAVE send delete

Saturday 11:33 p.m.

save SEND delete

Saturday midnight
Dear Rand,
Omigod, that … your e-mail … you. I am crying, finally, for the first time this week. Your incredibly kind words broke the dam and brought forth the tears. You are an angel. I can sleep now. Good night. "See you" tomorrow. Am looking forward to it.

BTW, can we, sometime, soon, talk on the phone?

save SEND delete

Sunday 1:01 p.m.
Amanda! Amandarama! Amandarillo in Amarillo! IT IS HIM! Or, rather, to be grammatically correct, IT IS HE!

By the way, are you ever going to tell me what Brad Pitt said?

save SEND delete

INBOX:
who he? … or to be grammatically correct … whom him?

39

Sunday, 2:13
The famous atheist who's been e-mailing me! It IS him, not some
sadist grad student. He called! Just now! He said he couldn't talk
long but he wanted to hear MY voice, and jesus buddha
mohammed thor IT WAS WHOM!

save **SEND** delete

INBOX:
intuited as much ... must learn to trust your intuition ... now
reassured my little pumpkin or experiencing new doubts ...
not some sadist grad student ... perhaps some sadist famous
atheist ... having you on as the brits say ... in americanese
pulling your leg ... toying with you ... girls nowadays a bit
more crude in language as in everything ... fucking with you
... faith mira now what do you believe about famous nonbe-
liever ... and since when do u care about brad pitt ... are you
becoming a starfucker?

Sunday 3:04 p.m.
No, I was just trying to talk about *your* stuff – you said you had
gone to a party and Pitt was rude to you, or something, and I
didn't want all my e-mails to be about *my* stuff. So much for
your appreciation of my good intentions. Let's just talk about my
stuff.

Amandalene his e-mails blow me away. It's as if he *knows*
what words I most crave to hear and is speaking them, one after
another, in some order designed to move me to the maximum. If
he is a sadist, he's damn good at it.

But his words are just glowing bits on a computer screen.
Even if he came to America, even if he came to *Paterson* he'd
still be in Famous People Land, and the border guards would
deny me entry.

He described his office: messy, stacked papers in all kinds of
chaos. I've been typing so freely with him, not censoring

anything. The first thing that came to my mind was, "Doesn't your wife nag you, or clean up after you?" and I didn't type that.

He has never, not once, so much as mentioned his wife. Yes, he is married. Google is the stalker's best friend.

Something happened this week with a student that left me aching and impotent. I told Rand about it and the e-mail he sent me back was simply the kindest thing I've ever read. I felt as if healing balm were flowing from the screen. Is it possible to fake that kind of benignity? Am I looking a gift horse in the mouth?

The Heisenberg Uncertainty Principle: Do I alter the inter-action by observing it?

Pascal's Wager: Should I just lay back and enjoy the ride?

Have I become the scabrous atheist who can't see it because she doesn't believe it?

save SEND delete

INBOX:

quote e-mail he sent me back was simply the kindest thing i've ever read unquote now that's gratitude missie i've been sending you supportive e-mails thank you very much for noticing … really sometimes mira i do wonder about you

Sunday 7:03 p.m.

Dear Rand,

No, I don't want to be an adjunct. Yes, I would love to get a full-time job. No, that will never happen. Yes, I am just adjuncting until I figure out what to do next. Academic hiring is political, in a way that I cannot crack.

save SEND delete

Sunday 7:31 p.m.

Dear Rand,

How very perceptive of you.

Yes, I do love Paolo Conte.

And, yes, I do love my student Tom – in, as you say, a maternal way.

And, yes – in your words – ergo, the evidence suggests that I do not hate *all* men.

Your point?

save SEND delete

Sunday 7:40 p.m.

Dear Lord Randolph Court-Wright, Marquis of Alnwick,

You are so totally wrong. You do not understand women at all.

save SEND delete

Sunday 7:47 p.m.

Do you even realize what you just said?

Yes, I do go around saying that I hate men. So what? When we spinsters achieve our goal of world domination and send men to re-education camps it will be a different story, but till then, you can sleep at night.

What you said was glib and you could say it at a cocktail party and no one would call you on it. Do you even think about what that means? That you can imply that all women are prostitutes, trading their love for cash, and that no one would challenge you, "What a misogynist thing to say"?

save SEND delete

Sunday 8:04 p.m.

Dear Lord Randolph Court-Wright, Marquis of Alnwick,

You *say* politically incorrect things. I *am* a politically incorrect thing. My very existence is heresy. The inerrant dogma of Political Correctness stars two characters: guilty, privileged whites and suffering people of color. I am neither. My Slavic ancestors gave the world the word "slave." My great-grand-parents: serfs. My grandparents: peasants born under colonial regimes that maintained discipline with whips and chains and racks. My father was a coal miner. My mother cleaned houses. My biography violates – no less than Galileo's heliocentric universe – sacred scripture. I am anathema, from my first semester as a grad student, when I was told I was the "wrong minority" to receive funding, to this past semester as a professor, when my boss told me that in spite of "fantastic, wonderful" evaluations from students, she can't hire me full-time because "we must hire a minority." Which one of us, Rand, you, speaking words that irritate Christians, or me, in Politically Correct academia, has been burned at the stake?

save SEND delete

Sunday 8:07 p.m.
Dear Rand,
Is this why you never mention your wife?
   Have you been hurt?
   You're not talking about things in general are you? You're talking about someone who hurt you one time, aren't you?

save send DELETE

Sunday 8:20 p.m.
Ignore the last message I sent you. Can we talk on the phone?

save SEND delete

Sunday 8:37 p.m.
Okay, if this isn't a good time for a phone call.
   Look, maybe we should just both take a breather. Talk again tomorrow?

save SEND delete

Sunday 8:50 p.m.
Good question. It was my grandmother. She made me.
   She was a Slovak peasant. Flint hard; you can see that in her photos. Not an ounce of fat. Worked the fields. Lived in a one-

43

room house my grandfather built of stone, wood, mud, and wattle. Lost her first baby to influenza. The next was deafened by fever. She came to America with two kids who didn't know their father; he'd been over here working the coalmines, getting emphysema, sending money back. She worked hard. Died young. Before I was born. I never met her.

I'd be all alone in the library stacks, tracking down dusty publications. My grandmother would join me. She would remind me that she was smarter than I'd ever be – she could look at a newspaper in Hungarian, and read out loud in Slovak. These are two completely unrelated languages. She'd never had the chance to go to school. The Hungarians destroyed the schools Slovaks built for themselves. She told me, "I don't care if you are unhappy here. I don't care if those stuck-up bastards never let you have a job. Do you think I was happy sweating out in those fields? Stick it out. Read. Learn. Write. Something for your people." And you, Rand, do not believe in this sort of thing, so you've just written me off as nuts.

save SEND delete

Sunday 9:59 p.m.

NOOOO!!!

Are you trying to playact the clueless male, or do you really not understand women AT ALL?

And given that you completely misunderstand 50% of the human race, how can you claim to understand GOD????

save SEND delete

Sunday 10:02 p.m.

Amanda-bonanza-remanda-salamanda, oh, most magnificent one. I approach your throne room in search of knowledge.

How is it that men are the masters of the universe? How is it that they dictate who – including God – lives and dies?

save SEND delete

Saturday 9:03 p.m.

Amanda, Dear:

Do Cole Porter's lyrics provide the verbal paradigm for all peregrinations of the heart? "It was just one of those things." I'll say.

It's been three weeks since I heard from him.

My ability to write provides the index for my life. For the past ... how long? Months, years, I don't know. I do know. It's been two years. I have not written anything, no grocery lists, no e-mails to you, nothing. It was those last rejections on the manuscript after hope had seemed so reasonable. I mean, I had signed a contract. That was the straw. Haven't written anything since.

There was something about Rand, that I cannot put my finger on, that opened my heart, and made it flood. That made me not just able to write, but that made me need to write. I would be on the train to work and full sentences would ping around inside my head. I told him about Muhannad, for heaven's sake! I've never told you, or even myself. Never wrote about him in my diary; never devoted the thought to piecing together how a self-identified terrorist came to propose marriage to me.

Some women primarily *dress* – they are all about their clothes. Some primarily mother – they are all about being *mom*. Me, if I'm not writing, I'm not breathing, and I haven't been writing for a very long time. And he, this famous, faraway atheist, made me want to breathe. To write. To continue the story. Since the story is life, he made me want to live.

save SEND delete

INBOX:

doll's house closed to standing o's ... had reservations about appearing nude ... never again ... nudity accomplished so much ... and of course we were not completely nude ... those puppets on our hands ... their victorian costumes stifling ...

what poor nora had to endure in that corset ... could hardly breathe ...
squeezems and i now travel to redwoods for retreat to pen a retelling of hamlet as a black woman avenging the death of her mammy against her uncle claudius a rich white male ... i will play hamlet ... nothing could be more subversive than a white woman playing a black woman playing a dead white male ... your atheist ... he asked you questions ... that is why you wrote to him ... to answer

Saturday 9:27 p.m.
If it is that easy, if we could so heal and comfort and vivify each other just by asking questions and listening to the replies, why don't more of us do it?

save send DELETE

Saturday 9:45 p.m.
Dear Amanda,
Break a leg with Hamlet. And my regards to Squeezems. Always so hard to wrap my head around your being married.

save SEND delete

Saturday 8:14 a.m.
Dear Lord Randolph Court-Wright, Marquis of Alnwick,
Well, look at what the cat dragged in.

save send DELETE

Saturday noon
You –
So, am I supposed just to follow your lead and act as if these weeks of silence never happened? That I did not notice? It did happen. I did notice. I put work into "getting over you" –

save send DELETE

Saturday 1:02 p.m.

My Lady, Amanda,

He wrote again.

And that quality in his e-mails that I can't name or overcome. It's there.

How can a man make you feel this way just through an e-mail? So much for pheromones.

Eventually he'll stop writing.

save SEND delete

INBOX:

don't be silly … know that will be hard for you … write to him

Saturday 1:10 p.m.

Why?

save SEND delete

INBOX:

you enjoy it

Saturday 1:14 p.m.

It's dangerous

save SEND delete

INBOX:

doesn't have to be … rich … famous … charming … obviously has something for you … for once in yr life do what other women do … be smart be careful look out for number one … never give too much away … while getting what's yours

Saturday 5:03 p.m.

Dear Rand,

Hi, how nice to hear from you.

You are correct. You did ask me a very big question that I

never answered.

Let me consider my reply carefully. Let me go for a long walk and think about it. I'll get back to you.

TTFN

SAVE send delete

Saturday 5:04 p.m.

SAVE send delete

Saturday 6:03 p.m.

SAVE send delete

Saturday 7:08 p.m.

SAVE send delete

Sunday 5:57 a.m.

save SEND delete

Sunday, 7:24 a.m.

Dear Rand,

Back in from my walk. I kept trying to invoke Augustine, to quiz him on his insistence that the Donatists be compelled to accept orthodoxy. I tried to conjure Saint Luke to demand an exegesis of chapter 14, verse 23. Instead of unlocking deep truths I could propound here, that you and I might be called before queen and pope to accept our awards after publication of this e-mail, I kept fixating on a boy I shared one class with in high school.

Justin van Peenen was tall and had hair so uniformly thick and blond he could pose on a box of L'Oreal luxury dye. Dolls would kill for a nose as pert as his, for lips as bee-stung. The skin on his pencil-thin fingers was translucent. I can't imagine a kid from our end of the track fashioned from his straight lines. Justin's profile included no racy swerves around biceps or nipples, barely iced in thin t-shirt cotton, no risky detours into crotch bulges, barely sheathed in snug blue jeans. Justin wore suit jackets to class.

Justin became a Christian after reading a Chick Publication. These are pocket-sized comic books that depict a man assuming he's living a pretty good life, suddenly dying, encountering an angel who points out to him that he rejected Jesus, and then burning in Hell. If Catholic, he is treated to horrific visions of his children and grandma burning in Hell. Jack Chick "loves Catholics enough to tell them the truth."

Justin's Christianity was like a track meet, with high scorers earning commemorative plaques and applause. Evangelicals maintain case studies of their champion proselytizers. Justin reported to me, with stars shooting from his big baby blues, that one champion Evangelical had converted every student and teacher at his high school.

I thought of approaching complete strangers in the high school cafeteria, clapping them on the back, asking them if they needed help with their homework, and, by the way, if they had heard about the cool dude from Nazareth. I realized that within no time at all, I would be labeled a slutty loon. A female, alone, approaching a stranger will never, anywhere, be understood in the way that a male would be.

If someone with excellent teeth and piles of dollar bills approached me and said, "Do what I do, and your wallet will also bulge, you will lose ten pounds, and teachers will like you," I might have given it a try. All things being equal, a handsome kid in nice clothes will make more converts for the Lord.

Me? – I was a poor kid in bad clothes. Covering my skin were bruises, whose size – large – and color – rich as summer storm clouds – and frequency – constant – announced my identity and biography as unequivocally as any brand. All of my many older brothers had been in jail. One of my brothers got killed while I was in high school, and I was sad the whole next day in class. I had to live in my boyfriend's car, for a while there, when my mom was threatening to kill me. I worked full time as a nurse's aid. I can just imagine my cafeteria pitch: "Believe in Christ. Your life can be like mine. Really, that's a *good* thing."

Catholicism assured me that I had a place as good as any rich kid's in the kingdom of Heaven. Powerful nuns never allowed anyone to doubt that a woman can wield authority, without reference to how pretty or rich she was. Our big saints were people like Francis, the poorest of the poor. And, as bad as our lives were, we knew nobody suffered more than our big saints. Inside a Catholic Church, I never doubted my worth. There was no reason.

Justin's Evangelical, athletic-competition approach to Christianity reduced me to garbage as thoroughly as did popular culture. As for the comfort I felt inside of a Catholic Church, Justin's Protestantism demolished that, too. The Pope was the anti-Christ, and the church was the whore of Babylon. That I was a Babylonian whore with one foot in Jack Chick's graphic Hell did not stop Justin from flirting with me. He made sure to do so when no one was looking, and to hold himself back, just barely, from ever touching me.

In our high school "Catholic" meant "working class, parents arrived at Ellis Island, last name ends in a vowel." "Protestant" meant "at least one parent's ancestors arrived in North America on a sailing ship not less than one hundred and fifty years ago." Even if that had been a slave ship, if your ancestors were above or below deck, you were of a different class than the blue-collar ethnics, our Catholic smells, bells, and spells. The Evangelicals were taller than average, slimmer, blonder. They wore earth tones and natural fabrics. They received higher grades. They drove nicer cars. They shared little habits – the girls sucked on buttons to lose weight – and in-jokes that everyone knew to laugh at. "Remember Betty and her muffins?" was always followed by: Ah ha ha ha ha ha ha.

In Justin's church one Sunday – I succumbed to his invitations – an awkward visitor, I stood close to the back, and gazed forward and saw more blond hair than I had in any other venue. Children were confined in a glass-walled, box-like vestibule, so that they would not disturb.

My quiet arrival in the church had not gone unnoticed. Kimmie Ryerson invited me to her house for dinner. Kimmie was the kind of alpha girl who had new arrivals over quickly after they first began showing up, to vet them, and to allure the right ones into full membership. I was always hungry, and I couldn't wait to eat to dinner at the house of this rich Protestant.

When I arrived at Kimmie's sunshot Victorian home, and oohed and ahhed at her stained glass windows looking out over a spacious garden, she informed me that she had just finished the Evangelical bestseller, "Rich Christians in an Age of Hunger." This book convinced her to simplify. She served me one small bowl of vegetarian soup – she had thrown the bowl herself, in ceramic class – and one slice of whole wheat bread, no butter. Even just typing this up, I feel the chilly hunger I felt that night.

Next Sunday, I returned to the whore of Babylon – Catholic mass. I was among white, black, brown and gold skins. There were designer clothes and Salvation Army cast-offs. There were people in heavy cologne, macho guys with close shaves and don't-mess-with-me stances, people who sobbed while praying. Scattered babies warbled and cried. Outside of the subway, Catholic mass is the *only* place I have had that experience of diversity. Certainly not in the touted as "diverse" halls of academe. Catholicism really is small-c catholic. Each Protestant denomination is largely wedded to its sixteenth-century hometown.

This next part won't surprise you – I had a crush on Justin. He was like Greenland. I wanted to explore. We were in creative writing class together. He was sensitive and creative and worked with words. It has taken me decades to realize that "sensitive and creative and working with words" is not synonymous with "good." After all, Joseph Goebbels was a novelist before becoming Hitler's right-hand man. The world had been forcing itself on me with brutality since conception – I was supposed to have died in the womb, and my life had been going steadily downhill ever since. My flesh has grit imbedded in it – tattooed striations across my arms and legs. Given how filthy I always was, my scars sealed over small stones. I grew up in that foreign of a world – it never occurred to me to wash my many injuries, even as they suppurated. I have carried little bits of my hometown all over the earth. Justin was so pure. Like a vanilla ice cream cone, I wanted to lick him, to experience that flavor.

Justin went to the prom with Louise. I went with Imre, a Hungarian-American drug dealer and spiritual seeker who did bare knuckle push-ups on gravel. He used to extemporize poems on my back. It was no matter that with my next shower his poems would travel, letter by letter, down the drain. It was a spiritual discipline, Imre said. He strove not to cling to material reality. After the prom, Justin rhapsodized about the orange lipstick Louise wore, and how that lipstick complimented the color of her gown. Imre tearfully, stutteringly confessed that he was probably in love with me – he'd never met a girl quite like me – he'd become addicted to my inquisitive mind. I suffered a spiritual crisis. How could the most religious man I knew look at his woman and see only the physical? Not just the physical – the aesthetically incorrect – who looks good in orange lipstick? Not Louise. Imre, a Pagan criminal, loved me for my mind. Justin never talked about Louise's mind. He did talk about mine, while emphasizing that I was not good enough for him. I gave up fantasies of converting everyone at my high school. After that orange lipstick comment, I wanted to convert Justin.

I just Googled him. Justin has made good on his high school vow to become a man of the cloth. He serves an all-white township where incomes run tens of thousands of dollars above the national average. It's not easy to put together an all-white township in New Jersey. As in the past, Justin can afford to be untouched by life.

His faith never waivered. Justin's faith was like his new clothes, his great height, his pure blondness, his construction from straight lines: all were above reproach. Did one need to be as virginal as a marshmallow to be perfect in Jesus Christ? How did it transpire that a crucified Jew, friend of whores and lepers, became the personal property of WASP American suburbanites?

My faith *did* waver. My faith has always wavered. When I inhale, I am a devout Catholic. When I exhale, I "curse God and die," to quote my kinswoman, the wife of Job. Absent Justin, I have never had much desire to convert anyone. And this is how I wanted to convert him: I wanted to feel my body grind into his. I wanted to reconcile, maybe not Heaven and Hell, but at least Hell and what is understood by many to be Heaven. I didn't want to work this out intellectually through even the cleverest, most watertight of essays. I wanted to feel this reconciliation in my flesh as my flesh rubbed against, became one with, Justin's flesh. I wanted the God of the comfortable and the secure and the God of the wretched to become acquainted, and unite. I wanted bits of me to abrade Justin's pure white flesh and be healed over under Justin's translucent skin. Decades later, when Justin was preaching a sermon to his marshmallow congregation, I wanted tattoos of me, dark striations in Justin's flat, glimmering white chest, thighs, hands, cheeks, to wink up at him, as he testified to his fortunate flock. I wanted my tattooed bits of grit, stuck in Justin's flesh, to complicate every one of his periods, the structure of his every sentence, the noun-verb agreement, especially the exclamation points. I wanted to be the future stutter in his sermons. I wanted to be assured that Justin's God, the God of winners, could love me, and I wanted Justin to know that my God, the God of Gehenna, always watches him.

save SEND delete

Sunday 8:01 a.m.

Is it because you are famous and we have never met, and never will, so, very much as I did in the first message I sent you, I feel free of any constraint, and just write whatever pops into my head?

But it's not just the lack of constraints that draws my words forth. It's *you.* It tugs on me: my conviction that you are out there somewhere, waiting for my words, hungry; that you will pore over my reply, that you care, that you respond. You tear words out of me. No one in my life knows about Justin. *I* didn't know about Justin. I was aware that I'd once known a guy in high school named Justin van Peenen, but I had no idea how deep those feelings went. I didn't even realize it at the time.

In writing that to you, I learned something about religion, if only I could put it into words. The only way I could get close was to tell the gossipy, painful tale of Justin. To speak of God, apparently, one must speak of high school.

save send DELETE

Sunday noon

Dear Rand,

I would LOVE to watch you punch out Justin! Your e-mail was delicious!

"Pecksniffian:" That word is PERFECT!!! If only I could gin up a way-back machine and turn to my right in Creative Writing class and declare, "Justin, you are so Pecksniffian."

If you ever need me to punch out anyone – although I could never hope to be as funny as you – do not hesitate to ask.

You Are The Best.

save SEND delete

Sunday 12:19 p.m.

No. It's not just because I don't want to be like Justin, and because I don't want to make others feel as small as he made me feel.

I believe in something called "Universal Salvation." Origen, one of the church fathers, believed it. So did Julian of Norwich, thus her most famous quote, made up of the simplest words in the simplest pattern, but profoundly moving, "All will be well, and all will be well, and all manner of things will be well."

In John, Jesus says, "I will draw everyone to myself." In 1 Corinthians, Paul says that, after death is conquered, God will be "all in all," and "just as in Adam all die, so too in Christ shall all be brought to life." Time, as the nuns hammered home to us, is of this mortal dispensation, and doesn't mean, to God, what it means to us in our world of clocks and calendars. God uses time to bring his children home to him, in their own good time, which is nothing like his. So says 2 Peter 3:8-9: "With the Lord one day is like a thousand years and a thousand years like one day. The Lord does not delay his promise, as some regard delay, but he is patient with you, not wishing that any should perish but that all should come to repentance."

And there's a second reason I don't proselytize. There's a quote attributed to St. Francis: "Preach the gospel always; if necessary, use words." We are supposed to teach by example, to live in a Christian way. Merely in typing that, I am made painfully aware of all the ways that I don't live my life in a Christian way. If nothing else, I offer living proof that even crummy people can be Christian.

The third reason I don't proselytize: I haven't mastered any of the big guns. I've tried to do something so simple as to figure out who St. Thomas Aquinas was. He is one of Catholicism's most important thinkers. Realizing that I believe in God without being familiar with Aquinas' arguments is like realizing that I love to cook, but I don't know anything about Julia Child.

I resolve to remedy the situation. I read the most basic encyclopedia entry on St. Thomas Aquinas. I complete the entry and realize that I understood nothing. I reread the encyclopedia entry. I quiz myself. I retain two facts. One: St. Thomas Aquinas was enormously fat. My mind wanders: how much rancid meat, wormy apples, and insipid gruel would one have to consume to become enormously fat in the Middle Ages? It's not like they had m&ms or ice cream in the thirteenth century. They didn't even have *forks.*

The second fact: St. Thomas Aquinas never completed his Summa Theologica, the single most important theological work ever written. In December, 1273, during mass on the feast of St. Nicholas, Thomas had a vision. He later confessed, "I cannot go on ... All that I have written seems to me like so much straw compared to what I have seen and what has been revealed to me." Three months and one day later, while journeying to meet the pope, Thomas died.

I understand the hard work Thomas poured into his Summa Theologica. I don't understand the work itself, but I get his devotion. I've worked hard; I come from hard working Bohunks. I also get it that one vision made it all seem like straw.

A thousand years ago, Tokusan was a devout Buddhist seeker who used to pilgrimage around China with his exhaustive notes and commentaries on the Diamond Sutra, a Buddhist scripture, lashed to his bowed and aching back. Tokusan met a master named Ryutan, who taught him late into the night. After hours of study, Ryutan urged Tokusan to go to bed. As Tokusan headed out into the darkness, Ryutan handed Tokusan a lighted candle, which Ryutan then blew out. With that one gesture, Tokusan achieved enlightenment. The next day, he burned his notes and commentaries on the Diamond Sutra.

What I'm trying to say is I do not understand Aquinas' Summa Theologica, and I do not understand Tokusan's notes and commentaries. I have not been blessed with a "step-by-step" kind of mind. All I resonate to is that moment when they are suddenly flush with what it is they were trying to get to through each studied step. This is why I am inadequate to talk about God. I have an "Aha" kind of mind, a "That's a forest!" kind of mind, not a step-by-step, identify-each-individual-tree-and-then-conclude-it's-a-forest kind of mind.

Even if I were gifted with the kind of mind that could follow the painstaking, philosophical steps Thomas took to justify belief in God, I would not believe in God because of Thomas' steps. I don't believe in bees because a big name philosopher took methodical steps that convinced him of the existence of bees. I don't believe in bees because I pored over illustrated break-downs of bees' anatomy and physiology, and aerodynamic analyses of bees' flight patterns and chemical assays of bee venom. I believe in bees because I've seen bees, been sung to by bees, been stung by bees, and tasted peaches and pears and honey. I'm of the lower orders. I believe in God for the same reason I believe in anything: its impact on my flesh.

save SEND delete

Sunday, 3:02 p.m.

Oh, but you read me so very well Mister Man.

Of course I do. Of course I feel unworthy to speak of Christ to others. That's so obvious I didn't even bother to type it out.

save SEND delete

Sunday, 3:14 p.m.

Now, see, on the one hand I could say to you, "How insignificant you assess me that you are convinced that I never sin. Because you define sin as something that only the Big Boys do: war, pillage, stock market manipulation.

Or, I could remind you that God does not see with man's eyes, and neither does Satan. That may be the one feature that God and Satan have in common: Just as to God, I am every bit as important as a Wall Street Tycoon or Master of War, I am equally as important to Satan. In the same way that a widow's mite could pave the path to heaven, a widow's spite could pave the path to hell. Though I do not ostentatiously rape, pillage, or defraud, do

I sin? Do bears sit in the woods?

I'm a word person. I sin with words. I love to swear. Swear words in six different languages raced through my brain just while typing that last sentence: "Kwa ti mama ti mo!" "Maa cheekne manchhe!" "Kurwy waselina!" These all mean very bad things, but that's not enough for me; I invent new swear words. I try to discipline myself, and then immediately refer to my sister-in-law as a "botay bayunk." This is a very bad insult in a very obscure language and I will *not* translate it.

Jesus says that he who calls his brother "raca," an Aramaic insult whose meaning we can only guess at, is liable to hellfire. I see the sense in that. I dehumanize Trixie by referring to her as a "botay bayunk." I remind myself that her cruelty is rooted in her vulnerability. When I remind myself of that, I feel compassion for her. I feel my sword melt, if not into a ploughshare, at least into a wilted sword, too droopy to serve as weapon.

But that "Kumbaya," "let's-sit-in-a-circle-and-talk-about-our-feelings" approach doesn't do all the work that needs doing. The thrill writers get from hitting upon the right word, "le mot juste," is not just our drug of choice. Naming is one of the first steps in any path to goodness. A refusal to name plays into evil's hands. Naming was one of God's first priorities. Then assessing. Then discriminating.

> In the beginning, when God created the heavens and the
> earth,
> God said, "Let there be light," and there was light.
> God saw how good the light was.
> God called the light "day," and the darkness he called "night."

When we have to recreate our world after it has been shattered, we repeat the naming process. Tadeusz Rozewicz survived World War Two in Poland. He wrote,

I am looking for a teacher and master
let him give me back my sight, my hearing and my tongue
let him call all things and notions by their names again
let him separate the light from the darkness.

Evil can continue simply because bystanders don't have the courage to call it by its true name. How long have we debated whether or not to label what is happening in Darfur as "genocide"? Witness the testimony of parents accused of killing their own children. They always balk at being labeled "abuser," at their actions being labeled "abuse." "I loved that child! I was just disciplining a disobedient child!" I've heard people say that they did not begin the long recovery from rape, abuse, or even cancer until they could summon the courage to say "rape," or "abuse" or "cancer." It takes courage to use these words because there is a penalty for using them. "Kill the messenger" isn't always metaphorical. The truth may set you free, but your neighbors may stone you for it.

Teachers – writers – my vocations – are the designated name callers. I do not want to surrender my outrage against ugliness; I want to call it by its true name. I want to take that first step toward healing. A surgeon can't heal unless he first cuts, people can't heal without truth.

Jesus must have felt the kind of outrage that I feel. In the same Gospel in which he preaches against insulting anyone by calling him "raca," Jesus calls contemporary religious leaders a "brood of vipers" and "whitewashed tombs." Jesus addresses the crowd, adjuring them to emulate what religious leaders say, but not what they do:

They preach but they do not practice. They tie up heavy burdens and lay them on people's shoulders, but they will not lift a finger to move them. All their works are performed to be seen … They love places of honor at banquets.

Then Jesus turns on the religious leaders themselves:

> Woe to you, you hypocrites. You lock the kingdom of Heaven
> before human beings. You do not enter yourselves, nor do you
> allow entrance to those trying to enter ... You traverse sea and
> land to make one convert, and when that happens you make
> him a child of Hell twice as much as yourselves.

This is no mauve, mythological vapor. This is no Osiris or Mithra
or Dionysus. This is no allegory approaching the human but not
quite. This is one flesh-and-blood, human man. You can see the
corded veins bulge against his forehead; feel the rising pulse
pound against his neck. His righteous, frustrated rage sizzles off
the page. I feel his fist clenching and unclenching. The little kid
in me wants to crawl under the formica-topped kitchen table. But
I also want to venture out between the table's chrome legs to ask,
"Are you hungry? I baked some cookies today." Anything to get
the scary man to stop.

I feel the same impotent rage Jesus feels, against hypocrites
who tell you you can't get to Heaven if you are gay or a woman
who isn't the right kind of woman. I feel his rage crest and mine
crests, too, and it feels good, and then the catharsis leaves him
spent and slack and he goes quiet again, and I do, too. He offers
a peek at the thwarted tenderness, the unrequited love, that
fueled his rage. He's ranting against *us,* humanity that continuously rejects God: We who kill the prophets and stone those sent
to us; how many times Jesus yearned to gather us children
together, as a hen gathers her young under her wings, but we
were unwilling! Even after that glimpse of tenderness, his final
words are chilling: "Behold, your house will be abandoned,
desolate." And he gets his revenge: "I tell you, you will not see
me again until you say, 'Blessed is he who comes in the name of
the Lord.'"

It appears that Jesus *could* badmouth other people. Does

that give me permission to do so? Jesus gave sight to the blind and made the lame walk. Maybe when I can do that I earn the right to denounce my sister-in-law.

But what about St. Jerome? His sarcasm almost got him killed. Of Rome's fourth-century Christian clergy, Jerome said, "It is bad enough to teach what you do not know, but even worse, not even to be aware that you do not know"; and, "The only thought of such men is their clothes – are they pleasantly perfumed, do their shoes fit smoothly?" St. Jerome pilloried men who became priests "only to be able to visit women more freely ... when you see such as these, consider them men betrothed rather than men ordained. Some, indeed, spend all their zeal and their whole lifetime in learning the names and households and characters of married ladies ... what he approves of is a savory dinner with a big, fat bird." He even zinged their vanity about their facial hair: "If there is any holiness in a beard, nobody is holier than a goat!" Of one enemy, Jerome said, "If he will only conceal his nose and keep his tongue still, he may be taken to be both handsome and learned." Jerome is a Doctor of the Church.

As a Christian I walk a tightrope. One micrometer to the left, and I am an impotent wet tissue of compassion. One micrometer to the right, and I am a porcupine of stiff, spined outrage, driving away any fleshed creature with my infinite supply of stinging barbs. Compassion, outrage, compassion, outrage, compassion, outrage: juggling them is a full-time job. I do not have it down.

save SEND delete

Sunday 5:04 p.m.

Dear Rand,

Oh, come on. Quoting the Old Testament like that without context makes as much sense as taking a whale out of the ocean, and putting it on display in a cage in the Bronx Zoo. You cherry pick: you speak only of the angry God of Exodus who brings plagues on Egypt. You don't mention that angels want to sing praise songs to God for the drowning of Egyptian charioteers in the Red Sea. God forbids this celebration: "Don't sing praise to me to celebrate the drowning of my own handiwork," he says. This is a God who loves even the Egyptians who enslaved the Jews. That story is from the Talmud, by the way, and you need the Talmud to understand how Jews understand the Old Testament. Judaism is a family, one that has ever been in a perpetual conversation. Community is built right in to Judaism. You need ten adult males – a minyan – for public prayer. Women tend to be more religious than men. Women will show up. Getting the men there is the challenge. The minyan builds into Judaism the need for men – and community. It's just one of the traditions that have kept it alive for thousands of years. Look at a page of the Talmud. Commentary circles text. Everybody gets his two cents in. God is known and lived through give and take.

You label the Genesis creation story "ridiculous," one "an intelligent person" like me must ignore. Not so. It's one of the most stunningly profound stories ever told; its depth confirms my faith. God created us. Things were good. We needed to know that. The only way for us to know God, to know our relationship with God, and to know ourselves was to step outside of our relationship with God. A fish really doesn't know it is in water. We define by contrast. We had to gain knowledge of the opposite of God in order to know God. We had to know good and evil. We chose separation from God. God allowed us our choice. God, like any lover, wants us to choose him. We can't choose him, or anything, without free will.

That's what I believe. How about what I do?

My practice is one that attends more to what I do to live up to my own ideals than to telling others what they are not doing to live up to my own ideals. I pay more attention to writing out checks to charities, being a good teacher, and controlling my temper than I do to telling women not to have abortions and gay people not to get married.

Historians have had to ask: how did early Christianity go from a marginal, impoverished, persecuted group to the majority faith in the Roman Empire in three hundred years? One answer: Christians like the Plague Martyrs. In 261, the plague broke out in Alexandria, Egypt. Christians, who were already persecuted merely for their beliefs, further risked their lives by making a public demonstration of their faith. They nursed the living and provided the dead with civilized burial – for both Christians and Pagans. Early Christians, by doing what they said they believed, rather than by telling others what to do and not to do, attracted converts.

I pray. I pray this prayer, most often, all day: "God bless you." I see a woman struggling with her purse and her car keys and a grocery cart and what looks to be a fifteen-year-old, retarded son in a supermarket parking lot: "God bless you." I see a Maya Indian here illegally from Mexico waiting for a bus in a rich suburb after a day of landscaping: "God bless you." I see a working man with slumped shoulders and a blank face: "God bless you." I see a lively girl with unkempt hair skipping ahead of her mother, who is juggling three other kids: "God bless you."

The other day I was at a conference on campus. Adjuncts teach most of the classes. We teach the largest, toughest freshman classes. The money, the privilege, and the power tenured professors enjoy, they reach by standing on adjuncts' backs.

All the adjuncts around the table were what are dubbed, in our country, "white ethnics": We were Italian-American, Bohunk-American, Greek-American. We were children of factory workers, garbage haulers, waitresses and cleaning women. We got our undergraduate degrees at state schools. None of the tenured professors were white ethnics. They were dressed in leather and silk; we were dressed in cotton and polyester. They whined about having to wait for compensation from the university for the gas mileage of driving to the conference. We adjuncts just looked at each other. We would receive no compensation.

The tenured professors preached loudly about diversity. One insisted that you don't really have to write well to be successful; after all, she and her friends all had trouble finishing up their dissertations and yet held tenure-track jobs.

We adjuncts whispered together. Catholic primary schools had hammered into us that you finish your work on time, you do not whine, and you master the language of the power group, no matter what language you spoke with your parents at home. No one made easy excuses for us; everyone made punishing demands on us. We finished our dissertations well within deadlines, and though we had all grown up in multilingual households, our committees complimented us on our command of Standard English grammar.

Most painful for us adjuncts was the tenured professors' insistence that standards do not matter. The adjuncts are in the trenches. We teach functionally illiterate college students. The tenured professors are hand-fed the cream of the crop. A glance between the adjuncts spoke a thousand words. That's always the case with the disempowered. We develop new ways to communicate. Our eyebrows became samizdat mimeograph machines.

Rand, one of the reasons I love writing to you is that I can actually speak. With my students, and even many of my fellow professors, I must speak s l o w l y and d i s t i n c t l y. I use irony with caution. I censor every word. Many cannot understand, say, "elm," "rain check," "mocha," "pancreas" or "magic trick." This is not the result of economic deprivation. My students grew up during the "irrationally exuberant" 1990s stock market boom. They drive their own SUVs to campus. One told me he spends three hundred dollars monthly on new electronic gadgets. They would not be caught dead in the wrong sneakers. More money is spent on abysmal inner city schools, per pupil, than in many a high-performing Catholic school.

These students are functionally illiterate because they are force-fed a mind-crippling toxin: Politically Correct education. "Don't know a word? Don't purchase a dictionary. That word you don't know is just part of the Man keeping you down. How do you feeeel when you read that word? It's your feeeelings that matter most. There Are No Wrong Answers. Let's all sit in a circle and make a communal collage expressing our anger at our enemy – rich, white, heterosexual, Christian, American men." Less harm could be done by strapping these kids down and injecting undiluted horse manure directly into their brains.

At the workshop, I scanned the table with the penetrating glare of Robespierre memorizing names of class enemies to be jotted down later in a little black book. In my imagination, I herded the tenured professors into tumbrels, and sent them off to be guillotined.

I realized that if my thoughts were displayed on a screen they would be more lurid than the latest teen slasher flick. And then, Rand, the funniest thing happened. I thought of you. You, professional atheist you, made me excruciatingly aware. Would you cackle triumphantly when viewing the video of my vengeful mental Revolution? Let the games begin. You are a champion atheist. I refuse to be a last-place Christian. That competitive urge was all that motivated me.

I decided to pray. I read, years ago, of something called "The Jesus Prayer." Its roots are with the Desert Fathers and Mothers, Christians who, in the third and fourth centuries, retreated from Rome's persecution and decadence to poverty and meditation in the Egyptian desert. I did not remember the exact text of the Jesus prayer; it is more popular among Orthodox than Catholics. I jerry-rigged my own: "Lord Jesus Christ crucified, have mercy on me, a sinner." I wrote it out on the yellow legal pad that was one of the hand-outs at the workshop. I acknowledged the truth of each word. I asked to be made open to whatever happened as a result of praying that prayer.

I suddenly noticed that one tenured prof had exceptionally kind, humorous, and twinkly eyes. I thought of how lucky students might be to have a teacher with the kind of soul that often shines out from such eyes. About the utterly clueless politically correct princess, I reflected that while our stated purpose was to teach, God's reason in bringing us together might differ. Perhaps God summoned her here to learn. The handsome prof's narcissism suddenly morphed into a visible handicap – thinking unkind thoughts about him seemed as ungracious, suddenly, as being impatient on a bus with a passenger in a wheelchair.

I laughed. I contributed. People opened up to me, were nice to me, said, "That's an excellent suggestion …You must be a great teacher … Please give me your e-mail. I'm going to be coming to you for advice."

It didn't occur to me to pray, "Transform my anger into compassion; let me see the humanity I share with my class enemies; help me to focus on aspects of life other than the material. Don't let my victimization be the only reality I see." I prayed solely out of a petty, ego-driven competition with you. I just prayed, "Lord Jesus Christ crucified, have mercy on me, a sinner." And things changed.

save SEND delete

Saturday 5:59 a.m.

Dear Rand,

Hi, nice to hear from you again. Yes, it's been a busy week for me, too. I hope you felt no pressure to respond before today.

Okay, let's get down to these brass tacks you've tossed under my tires. And, yes, I'll admit – I started it.

I report only my own reasons for not accepting these faiths. I'm not arguing that these faiths don't play a role in the depth and beauty in the lives of their followers. I know that they do. I hope you can hear that. Shall we take them in alphabetical order?

Atheism. I could never be an atheist like you. Long story. For another post.

Buddhism. There are many emendations of Buddhism. Buddhism combined with Hinduism in India; Confucianism and Taoism in China; with Shinto in Japan. Thomas Merton popularized Buddhism plus Catholicism. The Dalai Lama embodies Buddhism-plus-freedom-struggle. The Avalokitesvara tradition presents Tara, a beautiful, compassionate, goddess savior, as sensual Buddhism. At the opposite end of the spectrum you've got Zen Buddhism, stripped of all adornment, and its clever, witty koans, short-story riddles: "What is the sound of one hand clapping?" It's all good, and like Merton, I'm grateful to embrace Buddhism's gifts, like meditation, that don't contradict my own beliefs.

Buddhists have developed all these emendations of – these commercials for – Buddhism because unadulterated, bedrock Buddhism is a very tough sell. Buddhism demands that we transcend everything – not just our pettiness but also our strength; not just our passing appetites but also our eternal thirst to give and receive love; not just our egos but also our search for meaning. Buddhism insists that that everything that we transcend is mere illusion. It's not just that, say, terrorism is an illusion. Your baby's face is an illusion. Both are blocks on the road to enlightenment.

Buddhism offers, in place of the everything that we transcend, a bait-and-switch. Buddhism's wise stories exist to get you beyond story and beyond wisdom. Buddhism's compassionate saviors exist to get you beyond any contact with any other. "Nirvana" doesn't mean "heaven" or "understanding" or "meaning" or "love" or "redemption" or "peace" or "spiritual growth." Nirvana means "to extinguish a light." Both Buddhism and Christianity emphasize compassion. In the Beatitudes, Jesus tell us that God knows, cares about, is engaged with, and will be there at the end of all our struggles for what's right. The hunger and thirst for righteousness will be satisfied. The merciful will be shown mercy. The meek, the persecuted, the peacemakers: all will inherit the kingdom of heaven. In Buddhism, these worthy souls will reach Nirvana – the extinguishing of their light.

Nirvana sounds a lot like nothingness to many, and they recoil. After its initial expansion, Buddhism retreated; it was almost extinct in medieval India. Buddhism gussies its message up with a lot of attractive accessories – images of the sensuous savior Tara, for example. But that promise of Tara is not to be fulfilled. She's the pretty girl in front of the car in the advertisement. Buddhism's many attractions exist to draw the Buddhist in to Nirvana, where the bliss, love, and compassion promised by that image, like everything else, will deliquesce.

There's no getting around it. We humans are hot-blooded creatures, and Buddhism is, ultimately, as cold as empty space, and it demands that we be, as well, and we cannot. That we have capacities that Buddhism insists we deny is Buddhism's problem, not ours. We don't best anesthetize our horses; we best saddle and ride them.

On the mundane level, I can say that the Tibetan, Burmese, and Sherpa Buddhists I encountered in Asia were exceptionally admirable people. OTOH, a good percentage of the Americans I know who converted to Buddhism are representatives of a very distinct species of jerk. That's not a reflection on Buddhism, but on these particular converts, who were disdainful, holier-than-thou misfits in their own American hometowns and home faiths. They wanted to shop in an exclusive spiritual boutique. They wanted to leave behind the mass of commoners at the supermarket. They were too precious to invest in the world they were born into. They yearned to join a "pure" group far from the taint of their own community.

I've met Jews who've never heard of Jewish mystics like Martin Buber or Isaac Luria or Baal Shem Tov who insist that they had to become Buddhists because there is no mysticism in Judaism. Some raised as Christians were utterly deaf to

Christianity's teachings of "compassion." Their ears pricked up when they heard the satisfyingly exotic term "karuna." Complete ignorance of the map of your own hometown retards you in deciphering the map of a foreign city. Grounding in your hometown prepares you to plumb the world. If someone approached me and said, "I want to convert to Christianity because everyone in my church is a loser, and your religion doesn't have scandals, like mine does," I would feel duty bound to educate that seeker on how far he was from readiness.

These American converts' conviction that they had joined a superior group makes them even more callous, more unaware, and more arrogant. Conversion has robbed them of the chance to take a good, hard look at themselves. One need never confront an identity in motion. They are foreigners among Buddhists. They never speak in their native tongue; they are never fully understood. Reading alien texts and moving through alien rituals, they understand nothing completely. That lack of depth allows them to continue to interpret everything as they please, to think that there had never been a bad Buddhist, to think that they had found and joined the "pure" group, the emblem of their superiority. If I knew nothing else about Buddhism, this group would scare me out of ever considering becoming an American convert to Buddhism.

Once, in Nepal, I was sleeping in a trailside tea shop. I woke in the night to find a Buddhist monk trying to rape me. I realize that he was not a representative of Buddhism. He was one loser. At a hospital founded by Sir Edmund Hillary, who was my host for an unforgettable night of drinking and storytelling, I met monks who had just escaped across the Himalaya from Tibet, with nothing on their feet but canvas sneakers. I didn't think that these heroes, or the would-be rapist, whom I simply beat up, were the representatives of their faith; it takes all kinds to make a world.

There is no pure group. The true spiritual seeker will,

eventually, have to confront the dark side, and you may as well confront it in your home faith, as in any other. There may be good reasons to convert, but the search for purity is not one.

Hinduism. The Bhagavad Gita is one of the best spiritual books I've ever read. Gandhi read it daily; I recommend it to my students. Ancient Sanskrit writings on the big questions are the textual equivalents of the pyramids. They are awesome, and they make one feel small, in a way that is also exalting: people like me achieved these heights, thousands of years ago. Heck, I feel a huge amount of admiration for the Sanskrit *alphabet.* It is aptly called "Devanagari," the script of the city of the gods.

Hinduism's questions awe me. On creation, from the Nasadiya:

What stirred? Where? In whose protection? Was there water bottomlessly deep? Was there below? Was there above? Who really knows? Who will here proclaim it? Whence was it produced? Whence is this creation? Perhaps it formed itself, or perhaps it did not. The one who looks down on it, in the highest heaven, only he knows, or perhaps he does not know.

Some mind from an unreachable past is calling out questions to us. We ponder these questions today, millennia later, with as much humility, curiosity, skepticism and wonder as the ancient author. Doesn't that give you chills?

I lived Hinduism's answers. Women and girls in the village where I taught, in the only Hindu kingdom on earth, slept outside when they had their periods. They could not speak their husband's names. They washed their husband's feet first thing in the morning, and drank some of the wash water. They were all but non-persons after a husband died. You know about sati? It is the custom whereby a usually young wife walks, alive, into the funeral pyre of her often elderly husband because, after all, widows are inauspicious. Thanks to those culturally insensitive imperialist bastards, the British, sati became less common, but it has happened recently. All of my neighbors denied their youngest daughters the protein and health care that they provided sons. These youngest daughters developed kwashiorkor and slowly died – from a cold they couldn't shake off, or simple diarrhea. Amartya Sen talks about one hundred million missing women and girls in Hindu, Muslim, and Confucian Asia. I witnessed a few of those deaths.

The caste system is there at Hinduism's beginning, also in the Rig Veda, the same three-thousand-year-old collection of hymns in which the Nasadiya appears. The body of a god is divided up and humanity is created from the corpse. High caste Brahmins were created from this god's mouth; warriors from his arms; thighs produce the common people; peasants are from god's feet. The law of karma-samsara, or reincarnation, further justifies caste, and, indeed, any human suffering. People earn low status – as insects or battered wives – by making bad choices in their previous incarnations. From the Upanishads:

According to his deeds and according to his knowledge he is born again here as a worm, or an insect, or as a fish, or as a bird, or as a lion, or as a boar, or as a serpent, or as a tiger, or as a man, or as something else in different places.

From the Garuda Purana:

The murderer of a Brahman becomes consumptive, the killer of a cow becomes hump-backed and imbecile, the murderer of a virgin becomes leprous, all three born as outcastes. Who steals food becomes a rat; who steals grain becomes a locust; who steals water becomes a Chataka-bird; and who steals poison, a scorpion. Who steals vegetables and leaves becomes a peacock; perfumes, a musk-rat; honey, a gad-fly; flesh, a vulture; salt, an ant.

The devout Hindu's only hope lies in living out the destiny his own karma has made inevitable. If you are a mathematical genius, but, thanks to bad deeds in a previous incarnation, you are born a low-caste woman, your only virtuous choice is to ignore your mind and submit to your husband and your low-caste status. To do another's dharma is death – so dictates the Bhagavad Gita.

The caste system and karma-samsara, or reincarnation as justification for it, is the spinal column, the muscle and bones, of Hindu ethics. Had Hindus founded the United States, the sentence "All men are created equal" could not have appeared in the Declaration of Independence. When you see a feces-encrusted Untouchable emerge from a sewer where, he – and his father and grandfathers, his sons and grandsons – is cursed to cleaning other people's feces with his bare hands – and that is deemed justice because his own ill deeds in his past life have brought him here – you have second thoughts about that inextricable answer Hinduism provides to life's big questions.

Islam. I didn't learn about jihad from a book; I learned about it from Narin, a girlhood friend. Narin was an extraordinarily beautiful Circassian who would go on to marry a man I'd later work for. My county in New Jersey hosts a large Muslim population. One sunny day, as we walked home from class, Narin turned to me and calmly – I'll emphasize her calm – informed me that when the time for jihad came, she'd kill me if I did not submit.

I've had Muslim friends, neighbors, bosses, coworkers, lovers, roommates, landlords and students, and, like any other group of people, they have been, variously, kind, cruel, intelligent, dense, delightful, frustrating.

Islam is not Muslims. Islam is an ideology. The unchanging command that Muslim men must commit jihad and establish universal dominance is unique to Islam. No other world faith mandates the nonnegotiable, continuous and all-pervasive denigration of women and girls that has proven central to Islam.

Hinduism has some very dark passages, but Hinduism is a vast, flexible, multi-cellular organism. Local enforcers populate every village – the high-caste mayor, the tight-knit family – they'll kill you if you marry outside your caste – but break free of them, move to the city or America, and there is no Hindu pope to mandate orthodox Hinduism. There is no such thing as orthodox Hinduism.

Islam allows no criticism, and, therefore, no growth, no change. A Muslim shot Theo van Gogh, slit his throat, and impaled him, on an Amsterdam street. Van Gogh had made a film critical of Islamic misogyny. The film was ten minutes long. It aired on public television. In Holland. What would they do to someone who made a blockbuster Hollywood movie critical of Islam? Crucify him? As mandated in the Koran, 5:33?

Islam's Politically Correct apologists insist that Islam is peaceful, sophisticated, and able to withstand intellectual criticism. Then they prove that they don't really believe that by clamping down speech codes. The Iron Curtain around speech about Islam renders the world a less safe place for Muslims.

The most frequent compliment writers hear is, "You said exactly what I think, but what I could not put into words." What happens when words become taboo? On September 11, 2001, I walked across campus in Bloomington, Indiana. I saw a pickup truck with a crude, handmade sign in the rear window. The driver was threatening to beat up Muslims. I approached him. He was young, muscular, with a shaved head and heavy boots. I talked. He responded. He was convinced that his comrades, men in uniform, had been killed in terrorist attacks. He wanted revenge. He began to cry.

I didn't spank him for "Islamophobia." I didn't prescribe a course in multiculturalism. I listened and I nodded and I acknowledged his pain. I also talked – about Muslim friends, neighbors, and students, people who were kind, hospitable, and caring. All I did was move ideas around with words, rather than with fists. The man in the pickup truck didn't beat up any Muslims that day.

Last spring I lead a discussion at school. When it came to Islam, participants froze up. They had been well-trained. If they said what they really thought, they risked punishment. In America, on a university campus, I saw the kind of rigid and fearful facial expressions I saw in the old Soviet Empire.

One of the participants was a lovely student, a future teacher, and herself a woman of color. English was not her first language. As she left the meeting, she handed me a note. My jaw dropped as I read. This gentle woman, who breathed not a single taboo word, wrote that she despised Muslims. She was certain; she'd never change her mind. Perhaps if I had gotten her to speak, we could have moved her ideas around. But she would not speak. She knew the barriers, and the penalties, as well. This build-up of resentments against Muslims is not doing anyone any good.

Judaism. As a Christian, I think of myself as a Jew, in that I am an inheritor of the God of Abraham, Isaac, and Jacob. I also think that Jesus is the Messiah. In any case, the Jews are God's chosen people. His covenant with them will never expire. "Theirs is the sonship and the glory and the covenants and the law and the worship and the promises; theirs are the fathers and from them is the Christ according to the flesh." So spoke the Apostle Paul, so spoke the Vatican in Nostra Aetate.

Paganism. Funny how the word "Pagan" has such a pleasant vibe in our New Age. The kind of person who says "I'm spiritual but not religious" – whatever that means – often adopts a few Pagan totems: goddess key chains, Wiccan solstice pot-lucks, Stonehenge posters, whimsically penciling "Druid" onto a census form. Rarely do you hear eclectic adopters of soft-core Paganism mention the 80,000 humans Aztecs boasted of sacrificing over a four-day period, the ripping out of still beating human hearts, the post-sacrifice banquet of roasted thighs and arms, the wearing of human skin flayed from living victims, the Aztec family homes decorated with human heads. They don't mention Tezcatlipoca, "The Enemy," the deity who created war to provide food to cannibal gods. When an Aztec speared a pregnant woman through her belly, aiming for the child within, he wasn't a renegade war criminal. He was a devout Aztec.

Neo-Pagans don't often mention Cronos, to whom Carthaginian parents in North Africa sacrificed their babies. Without a baby of their own, they purchased the baby of a poor woman. Ovens were cleverly designed to resemble a beast god; the god's outstretched arms automated the passage of your baby to the flames. Plutarch reported that if the impoverished mother "let fall a single tear" as her purchased baby was being cooked, she forfeited the money. Flutists and drummers drowned out audible cries. Ancient Jews noticed this soundtrack, and named the sites "Tophet," from the Hebrew for "drum."

Modern-day Druids emphasize the ancient Celtic religion's respect for oak trees. I share that respect; one really can't say enough good things about oak trees: their majesty, their shade, their acorns. Fans insist that talk of human sacrifice – like Julius Caesar's account of a "Wicker Man" a wicker cage within which Druids burned live humans – is a conspiracy cooked up by the Druids' enemies. While some would think it naïve to underestimate the power of the vast anti-Druid conspiracy, archaeologists, and commercial peat-cutters, find so many ritualistically murdered corpses buried in ancient Celtic settlement sites to give one pause.

I love a good didgeridoo solo as much as anyone, and I can never forget that when Europeans first arrived in Australia, there were 150 Aboriginal men for every 100 women. Someone was killing a lot of girls in Australia for a very long time. A modern tribeswoman in nearby New Guinea was named "Break It and Throw It Away" because that is what her father instructed when she, a girl, was born. Her mother defied him, so she lived to tell her chapter of the genocide against females that she, barely, survived.

No, I am not a Pagan. Were I, since I am the youngest female child of a peasant couple, I would be the one selected for elimination. Rodney Stark emphasizes that one of Christianity's biggest impacts was that it allowed female infants to continue breathing. Were it not for Jesus Christ, Lord Court-Wright, world famous atheist, I would not be here now to type these words to you. It's not for nothing that Heinrich Himmler was a fan of Paganism, and that Nazis marched under the swastika, a Pagan symbol.

save SEND delete

Sunday noon
That's not what I said.

save SEND delete

Sunday 12:16 p.m.
No, I did not say that, either.

save SEND delete

Sunday 2:02 p.m.
Dear Lord Court-Wright,
Look, let's try something novel here, shall we? Why don't you try actually reading my post? And, then, oh, say, responding to something I actually said, rather than bravely taking a series of huffy, principled stances against things I NEVER SAID.
Or have I wandered into the Haymarket and do you deal only in Straw Men?

save SEND delete

Sunday 2:11 p.m.
Amanda,
Why do we even bother with them?

INBOX

hmmm ... let me guess ... "we" earthlings "they" extraterres-
trials ... "we" drivers "they" traffic signals ... wait ... no ...
think i have it ... "we" women "they" men ... could that be
what you were thinking?

save **SEND** delete

Sunday 2:19 p.m.

Mandala,

There's no fooling you. We women they men. We nurturing they
competitive. We gatherers they hunters. We try to say something,
IN RESPONSE TO A QUESTION THEY ASK, and they stomp all
over it and beat their chests. I wonder if he has hair on his chest?
I hope not. I do hate wasting a good hairy chest.

save **SEND** delete

INBOX

and there you have your answer dear ... shall i rub some more
rogaine on your boobies

Sunday 2:27 p.m.

Amandarama, it wouldn't be the same.

save **SEND** delete

INBOX

would not be the same

Sunday 2:58 p.m.

You want me to be specific? I'll be specific.

I never said that Christians, nominal or genuine, from
Conquistadors to Nazis, don't do bad things.

I'm not "ethnocentrically arrogant" and "ethically numbed by
the opium of the people," as you so generously put it. There's
something very disturbing to me in your inability to *see* *me*.

What I'm saying at baseline is that I want contact with you. As long as you are focused on your stereotype of me, rather than on *me,* you and I can't touch.

Do you just want to voice the exact same canned gripes and insults, word for word, snort for snort, obscene joke for obscene joke, that you delivered on the PBS show?

Is it possible for you to jettison your warmly indulged prejudices: that I am a Christian because I am stupider than you, less honest than you, less perceptive than you, less brave than you, more bigoted and imperialistic than you? Can you allow yourself to think: I am a Christian though I am just as intelligent as you, just as honest, just as perceptive, just as courageous, just as respectful of other cultures, just as aware of all the horrible things Christians have done? Why can't you see that my reaching different conclusions than you doesn't make me an armored crusader or an imperialist bigot or a door-to-door proselytizer, and that I am someone you'd have to work as hard to get to know as you work to get to know anyone?

Do you work to get to know anyone? Are celebrities relieved of that duty? Or are atheists so relieved?

People suck, Rand. That's my first noble truth. No one is righteous, not a one: Romans, 3:10. People are magnificent. God created us in his own image: Genesis 1:27.

I don't go around preaching about "tolerance" and "diversity" but I've trusted my fate to persons of many faiths. I didn't base those decisions on what creed those people espoused, but on what I saw in their eyes. A woman, alone, unveiled, I hitchhiked through rural, Muslim Turkey. Farmers tried to get me to take one of their watermelons on the road so I'd have something to eat. I don't think that they were quite aware of the concept of "hitchhiking" and how carrying twenty pounds of ripe, juicy melon would interfere with that method of travel.

Politically Correct cultural relativism does not equal tolerance. I was renting a room in the Berkeley Hills. My landlady was a Politically Correct hippie heiress. She gave me a very hard time for being Catholic, and for criticizing Islam. I had an Arab boyfriend. She told me to be careful when I had him over, *because she did not want to get lice*!

If you can hear me at all, can you just, for one moment, think of a story I'm sure you've heard – the Good Samaritan. Three men come across an injured stranger. One of the passersby is a priest, one is a Levite, and one is a Samaritan. Samaritans were a despised, outsider group. Jesus tells us that the priest and the Levite pass the injured stranger right by, but the Samaritan risks all to help. Read the Old Testament story of Ruth. Ruth was a Moabite, an outcast group. She's a better daughter to Jewish Naomi than her own biological kin.

God hammers it into Christians and Jews – we hold no patent on virtue. Persons not of our confession often do God's will much better than we.

Christians and Jews acknowledge the failures of our faith. You? With the obsessive exactitude of a Soviet censor, you wield your Exacto knife to slice out of your argument any sentence, any sentence fragment, any syllable that does not play into your Christophobic agenda.

Jews and Christians have not invaded, have not killed, have not fought wars absent the same mitigating factors that cause any population to go to war. The price of grain goes through the roof or falls through the floor; microbes mutate and plague breaks out; a warlord has a pissing match with another warlord; an underdog ethnic group good at nursing grievances suddenly gains power; a ship sinks and no one knows why, a baby boom of young men wants to test themselves – *all* humans go to war for these reasons.

It's a false equivalence to say, "Muslims have jihad but Christians fought World War One." Muslims fight wars, just as the rest of us do, over the price of grain, over disputed borders, over bad royal marriages, over soccer, but Muslims *also* make war because Allah demands it. Islam adds to an already overburdened humanity an extra trigger for war.

Hernan Cortes, Francisco Pizarro, Andrew Jackson – all of those who laid waste Native American empires – they did what *any* population would have done, and was doing, including Native Americans. Native American empires were defeated with Native American armies. Pizarro brought down the Incas with 168 European soldiers, and thousands of Native American ones. Those Indian troops were fighting back against the Incas. The Incas enslaved their neighbors; the Aztecs ate them. What the Europeans did was ugly, but it was no exotic import, no innovation.

Do you really think that if Muslims or New Age Hippies or celebrity-atheists-who-appear-on-PBS had discovered the New World it would have gone any nicer? No population with guns, armor and small pox would have come upon a people rich in gold and real estate, but poor in weaponry and biological resistance, and politely negotiated for gold mines and beachfront property.

I'm not saying this just because the Conquistadors were nominally Christian. During World War Two, prominent Buddhists worked overtime to promote Japan's fascist and genocidal regime. Cambodia had been Buddhist for fifteen centuries before the Killing Fields gobbled up a fifth of the country's population in an auto-genocide. Buddhist monks in Sri Lanka support civil war against the island's Hindus. But uses of Buddhism to support violence contradict the critical mass of Buddhist scripture, Buddhist interpretation, and Buddhist practice, all of which are radically anti-violence. There is no canonical Buddhist concept of holy war, but Buddhists, like anybody else, can screw up and exercise their religious sway in support of wars caused by other factors. Cambodia was caught in the crossfire between Americans in Vietnam and the Maoist Khmer Rouge. Any population, following any religion or none, might have gone mad under similar circumstances. If you want to see an exemplar of Buddhism in those days, you don't look at the Khmer Rouge, who were following atheist Maoism, you look at Thich Nhat Hanh, the Buddhist monk and peace activist.

Unlike Buddhism, Islam *does* include a call for holy war. That doesn't mean that every time a Muslim kills that jihad is the cause. When Indonesians, twice in the last fifty years, raped, tortured, and slaughtered the ethnic Chinese living in Indonesia, it wasn't Islam that made them do it; it was, rather, the tension-producing "Middleman Minority" economic system. Chinese control a disproportionate share of the wealth. Osama bin Laden tells us he is killing infidels in the name of jihad. There's no reason not to take him at his word, but it's folly to assume that all religion is the cause of all violence. That's like saying that having two legs is the cause of violence, because most killers have two legs. You've got to account for one-legged killers; you've got to account for two-leggeds who never kill.

European killers of Native Americans were not following Biblical dictates. Who was? Bartolome de Las Casas, a Catholic priest who gave his life to the Native Americans. De Las Casas prompted the pope to issue Sublimus Dei, which condemned racism as Satanic, and stated uncategorically that there is no difference between one human being and another in the eyes of God. Sublimus Dei condemned slavery and the theft of Indian property.

De las Casas' insistence, at the risk of his life, that Native Americans were, essentially, no different from Europeans was an expression of nothing but Judeo-Christian faith. Nobody else was saying that all human beings are equal. In Hinduism, karma-samsara makes some of us high caste, and some of us untouchable. The Incas, too, had a caste system; the rulers believed themselves descended from the sun and carefully guarded their purity. Scientific Racism and Social Darwinism explain human differences as expressions of the inferiority of some races – blacks, Jews, Slavs – and the superiority of others – Nordics like yourself. In 2007, atheist James Watson, a Nobel-Prize-winning scientist, stated that scientific tests prove that blacks are intellectually inferior to whites.

I'm not reporting, here, that Sublimus Dei made all humans' experience of life equal. Conquistadors were on top. Indian slaves toiled in mines. I'm saying that Sublimus Dei and the Judeo-Christian insistence on human equality and human dignity give humans an essential tool that they absolutely need to achieve greater equality, a tool utterly unavailable to subjects of empires built on the idea that the folks at the top are fashioned by a different, superior God – or set of genes – than the folks at the bottom.

The first revolutionaries are always writers. They compose new words that refashion reality. You can't struggle without a vision. Nobody has fought a liberation struggle based on the idea that my group descended from the sun, and therefore, we deserve slaves, treasure, and territory. Nobody has fought a liberation struggle while waving, as foundational document, a scientific test proving the intellectual superiority of some races and the inferiority of others. Nobody in the Americas has ever founded a school or a hospital for the poor using atheism as a founding document.

I'm not saying that Peter Claver was able to make life anything but hell for millions of New World slaves. I'm saying that that ideology that says that Claver – a university-educated citizen of Barcelona, who could do whatever he wanted with his life, should spend that life in the fetid hulls of slave ships, awash in human waste, with doomed, terrified Africans who did not share a word of language with him, feeding them, washing them, befriending them – is an ideology with which I agree. I'm saying that that ideology that inspired Wilberforce, John Brown, Harriet Tubman and Fannie Lou Hamer to create a unique movement that insisted on human equality, is the ideology with which I agree. I'm saying that I disagree with the ideology that says that slaves are objects to be raped and murdered at will, as Classical Paganism and modern Nazi Scientific Racism did.

In 1 Kings, a voice tells a prophet to stand outside; God is coming by. There was a wind, there was an earthquake, there was a fire. God was in none of these. Then there was a still, small voice. That's where God was. In the still, small voice.

Jim Zwerg was a white, Wisconsin college student who joined the Civil Rights movement. Back in 1961, in Freedom Rides, whites and blacks rode buses together throughout the American South, to challenge Jim Crow's insistence on segregating the races on public transportation.

Jim Zwerg knew that, simply by being a white man riding with blacks, he was risking his life. His parents knew that as well. His mom was afraid that if Jim got killed, the heartbreak would kill his father. She hung up the phone on Jim when Jim told her what he was about to do.

Throughout May, 1961, violence against the Freedom Riders escalated: a bus was firebombed; riders were hospitalized; the KKK surrounded a bus and beat riders. Alabama's governor refused them protection. "They ought to stay home ... you just can't guarantee the safety of a fool." Before one of their most tense days, Jim stayed up all night meditating on Psalm 27, "The Lord is my light and my salvation; whom do I fear? The Lord is my life's refuge; of whom am I afraid?" This line was written as if expressly for Jim: "Even if my father and mother forsake me, the Lord will take me in."

The next day, in Alabama, a mob armed with sticks and bricks surrounded the bus. "It was like they were possessed," one of the Freedom Riders said. Jim Zwerg decided to get off the bus first, knowing full well that as a white man he would be singled out for brutality. The mob held him down while they kicked him in the spine, smashed his suitcase into his mouth to knock out his teeth, and stepped on his face. Jim was hospitalized and unconscious. The mob came to the hospital. A nurse gave Jim extra anesthesia so that he wouldn't feel anything, in case the mob lynched him.

Jim was asked later how he had the courage. "I bowed my head and asked God to give me the strength and love that I would need, that I put my life in his hands, and to forgive them. And I had the most wonderful religious experience. I felt a presence as close to me as breath itself, that gave me peace knowing that whatever came, it was okay."

Stefania Podgorska was a seventeen-year-old village girl in Nazi-occupied Poland. She didn't even know her own birthday. She was already hiding one Jew when he suggested to her that she find a bigger place to hide more. Her mother and brother had been taken to Germany for slave labor. She was taking care of a six-year-old sister. With no idea what to do, she went for a walk. A voice said to her, "Go farther, and you will see two women with brooms. Ask them where you can find an apartment. Go." She went. Stefania met the women with brooms. They found her a place. Thirteen Jews survived the war thanks to Stefania Podgorska.

You are doing the math. Six million Jews murdered, verses thirteen saved. One white man willing to risk death, verses millions who upheld Jim Crow. You're a material guy. Let me ask you this material question. If just one person managed to run an automobile on air, wouldn't you sit up and pay attention? Or would you say, "Sorry. There are billions of autos running on petroleum. No point in paying attention to just one car."

Your math doesn't work. The Talmud's math works: one who saves a single human life saves the entire world. The rabbis taught that in the same way that coins are minted from one die, all humanity, from the creation of Adam, is stamped with the divine. All the horror, all the injustice, all the bloodshed, does not erase Jim Zwerg or Stefania Podgorska. The light shines in the darkness, and the darkness has not overcome it.

Rand, you wave your arms on PBS and you shout murder and mayhem. You attempt to drown the still small voice. You grant your followers permission to regard their fellow humans as beneath them, and life as a nothing but a slaughterhouse. You grant your followers permission to be cynical, and to assume that, since no one has ever lived up to the challenge to be perfect, that no one needs to challenge himself to be decent. You deny your followers the strength available in Psalm 27, in Fannie Lou Hamer's "This Little Light of Mine," in prayer.

save SEND delete

Sunday 4:00 p.m.

No. No. No. No. No. No. No. NO. No.

save SEND delete

Sunday 4:29 p.m.

You want a system? Here's my system.

1.) What does the critical mass – not exceptional passages, but representational ones – of canonical scripture and interpretation say? What does the critical mass of practice based on that scripture look like?

An example. Christian scripture talks about feeding and housing "the least of my brothers." During World War Two, Maximilian Kolbe fed and housed 2,000 Jews escaping Nazism. The Nazis sent Kolbe to Auschwitz. Our scripture says it is great love to lay down your life for another. Kolbe gave his life for a fellow prisoner at Auschwitz. To me, that is all really clear. I don't see anything unscientific.

2.) Difficult passages occur in every document. Is there a mechanism for interpretation?

Christians and Jews are in constant dialogue with our scripture. That's been the case from the earliest days. Abraham argued with God about nuking Sodom. Mary pestered Jesus into performing his first miracle. Church-going Catholics are working to pave the way for women priests. We're doing this through our scripture.

3.) People screw up. How does the ideology handle screw-ups?

The Judeo-Christian tradition demands confession and repentance. We screw up; we confess; we make amends; we vow not to do it again. That all sounds kind of quaint, until you realize that Muslim Turkey has yet to admit that its genocide of Christian Armenians ever happened, that Japan has yet to apologize to Korean comfort women, and that twentieth-century Communists and atheists, working very much to advance the ideology of a god-free world, left the most gigantic pile of corpses in human history. Communists and atheists have yet to so much as say "Oops," never mind apologize, reassess their own atheist dogmas, or pay one cent in reparations.

4.) What are the facts on the ground?

Muslim countries have a skewed sex ratio. Muslims destroy their females at rates disproportionate to the rest of the world. Muslim women's literacy rates are an embarrassment. People vote with their feet. Women are not breaking down borders, fighting to get out of Christian countries and into Muslim ones.

You can tell me all you want that the Judeo-Christian tradition oppresses women. Let's look at the facts on the ground. A disproportionate number of female United States senators are Jews. The one woman on the Supreme Court is a Jew. A Jewish woman, Rosalind Franklin, should have been co-recipient of the Nobel Prize for discovering the structure of DNA – she was ripped off by atheist male peers. Rabbis like Rachel Adler reconcile Judaism's difficult passages with feminism.

Next to Judaism, Catholicism is the best family of powerful, intelligent, admirable women: Sor Juana, Hildegard von Bingen, Teresa of Avila, Therese the Little Flower, Brigid, Lucy, Mother Teresa, Blandina, Junia, Monica, Katherine Drexel, Clare, Mary, Elizabeth, Veronica, the Polish nuns who sheltered Jewish children during World War II. Sunlight shot through these women's faces in the stained glass windows under which I sat in some of my earliest memories. Their comments came up in family conversations. They taught me that a woman can spin the globe with every bit as much authority as a man. Nobody else gave me that message: not magazines, not newspapers, not TV, not movies, not atheist scientists like Watson, who wanted "Rosy" Franklin to wear more lipstick, to be "put in her place." Only the Catholic Church applied the same gravity to women as to men.

In her mosaic portrait in the Basilica of San Vitale, Empress Theodora drips rubies, emeralds, sapphires and pearls. But she was born poor, the daughter of a bear wrangler and a stage mother. Before she was 16, she gained fame performing a pervy burlesque of Leda raped by Zeus in the form of a swan. She traveled the Mediterranean, converted to Monophysite Christianity, married the emperor, and became a protector of women. I claim her as my ancestress. I can also turn to Therese de Lisieux, a nobody, who went nowhere and did nothing, and, before she died at 24, wrote one of the world's spiritual classics. I am in the same boisterous family as Dorothy Day, radical pacifist, and Joan of Arc, mighty warrior.

save SEND delete

Sunday 8:02 p.m.
Dear Rand,
No, that's not what I said.

save send DELETE

Sunday 8:07 p.m.
Dear Rand

save send DELETE

Sunday 10:04 p.m.

Dear Rand,

Look, maybe it's best if we just part ways right now. I'll never forget ... any of this. All the best to you.

save **SEND** delete

Sunday 10:59 p.m.

Dear Rand,

Okay, you say you'll phone in about ten minutes? I'll disconnect the computer so that the call can

save send **DELETE**

Sunday 11:01 p.m.

Dear Rand,

No, I don't think that a phone call will accomplish anything. I do wish you all the best.

save **SEND** delete

Sunday 11:31 p.m.

I could do the same thing to you, you know? I could look at you and see Stalin, an atheist even more famous than you, who murdered monks and nuns. I could see Pol Pot who ordered the torture and murder of tens of thousands of Buddhist monks. I could see the Chinese in Tibet, who have been torturing monks and nuns for half a century now. On a more intimate scale, I could see Leopold and Loeb who, claiming inspiration from Friedrich "God is dead" Nietzsche, decided, just for the fun of it, to murder their friend.

I *don't* see these famous atheists in you. When I write to you, I see the goofy, weird, endearing little jokes you insert into your e-mails to me, your poignant mentions of your late mother, your accounts of your hiking trips and your excitement over seeing a new species of bird. I see *you,* or I'm trying to. Good bye.

save **SEND** delete

Sunday 11:35 p.m.

Amanda,

Be a man, Mira, suck it up, Mira. Tears are pointless, Mira. Why are you even bothering, Mira?

I've got no answer.

save SEND delete

Sunday midnight

Rand,

Try this. Read my most recent posts, and tell me what I said.

I'm schoolmarming you. But you asked me what you could do to make me comfortable talking to you again, and that's what immediately came to mind. It's called "mirroring."

save SEND delete

Monday 1:20 a.m.

Rand! Good grief, I see that you've written back already. I can't read that right now.

I was drifting off to sleep and I remembered. In my first e-mail to you I called you a "git" and a "wanker." And here I am chastising you for stereotyping me.

But that was so long ago, Rand, and we are different people now, and we're doing something different here, aren't we? And it hurts when you refuse to see me.

SAVE send delete

Monday 1:34 a.m.

save SEND delete

INBOX

cry … cleanses the sinus chakra … releases stress karma … remember … there will always be chocolate …

Monday 3:03 p.m.

Dear Rand,

Hi, just back from campus, and have had a chance to read the e-mail you sent me last night.

Thank you for being willing to do that.

You've summed up my main points. That is exactly what I said.

save **SEND** delete

Monday 3:32 p.m.

A man Duh

Thanks for reminding me of the eternal existence of chocolate. Sometimes I do lose faith.

save **SEND** delete

Tuesday 8:04 p.m.

Dear Rand,

Yes, I am listening to Paolo Conte. You're very perceptive. It could be worse. I could be listening to tango.

save **SEND** delete

Tuesday 8:27 p.m.

Our first fight.

save **SEND** delete

Tuesday 8:32 p.m.

Wait, didn't we start out with a fight?

save **SEND** delete

Tuesday 8:40 p.m.

You're very funny. Even when you're being a radioactive, mutant, asshole.

SAVE send delete

Tuesday 8:42 p.m.
You're very funny.

save **SEND** delete

Tuesday 9:09 p.m.
Dear Amanda,

save send **DELETE**

Wednesday 7:36 p.m.
Dear Amanda,

save send **DELETE**

Wednesday 7:48 p.m.
Amandelicious

save send **DELETE**

Tuesday 8:00 p.m.
Dear Rand,
Last night, I was thinking of you and – forgive me for this – I "stalked" you via youtube. How do you go cold turkey on a man when you can get a video fix from the internet? It was a debate between you and an Anglican priest, somebody like "Neville" or "Nigel" or "Colin" or "Rowan."

I clicked the cursor and, presto-change-o, there you were – monumentally tall, splendid navy suit, sterling silver tie, hair the hue of winter sun, glacial eyes, that plumy accent to which the entire world succumbs. The cleric shook your hand, and called you "Randy."

"Uh, oh," I thought.

He was trying to be nice, but he never asked you what you prefer to be called. He just assumed that familiarity from his high station to your relatively dwarfish one would constitute a gift. Though it was, superficially, an attempt to be humble, it really was as grand a gesture as this from a bygone era – proffering his fist and waiting for you to kiss his ring.

You didn't correct Neville or Nigel or Colin or Rowan; you fixed him with a look. He was already as good as dead.

I contemplated metaphors to communicate what your opponent faced – invading Vikings, Normandy Beach – these seemed over the top; I scribbled them out on my yellow legal pad. I glanced back up at the youtube screen. I dropped my head and scribbled, again, "Invading Vikings, Normandy Beach," and added, "Praying Mantis." Out of respect to you I spelled it p-r-e-y-i-n-g. I stopped the video. I stared at the still frame. I shivered.

If I had been hitchhiking a country road through sleet at sunset, if you had pulled onto the shoulder, and I opened the car door and saw that face, I would not have entered. Death by sleet would have been preferable to any fate the man behind that face had in store.

You would destroy this priest, and you would not enjoy it. You would allow nothing, not even self-congratulation, not even sadism, to function as so much as a pebble on your tank's highway to victory.

A man can pull off a face like that only when he is completely confident that he does not need to ingratiate himself to *anyone*, that he can acquire his own meat.

I kept the video on pause and paged down through the accolades your groupies had posted. "He made that God believer his girlfriend!" "Finally someone tells the truth about godshit!" "I've got a man crush on Court-Wright!"

I clicked the "go" arrow again and watched a few more minutes, sure that I'd already seen the money shot. I had not.

The hamsters turning the exercise wheel that runs computers on our campus must have run out of breath, because the computer stopped. In a serendipitously frozen frame I saw something on your face I never would have predicted.

Just before the clip suddenly stopped, your priest opponent had asked you a velvet-glove question. "Are you happy?" From a spongy High Church Anglican cleric, with a fuzzy salt-and-pepper beard, a corduroy jacket, and, I'd have to guess, groovy, vegan sandals, the question unmanned you.

I wanted to reach into the screen and hold you. You looked about twelve. It was as if, even for a nanosecond, a unit of time that only celestial hamsters can measure, once you let down that killer pose, you have no pose at all, and you are as sweet and flexible as any boy trying on life for the first time in a town without street signs.

I've seen that look on my students' faces. Not the thugs, but the ones who come to my office with impossible questions and equally impossible hand-written manifestos, the ones who find authors like Thoreau on their own and hoard those words to share them with me, "Prof, have you heard of this guy? He built himself a cabin and went to live in the woods!"

Maybe the thugs make that face but they do it much more briefly. If that frame had not frozen, I never would have seen that look on your face.

Then the hamsters, having done their duty, set the exercise wheel to spin again, and it was as if time were an eraser, moving backward, erasing itself. All I saw was that man with whom I, hitchhiker I, would never get into a car. The priest was left in pieces on the floor like an Ikea chair after an encounter with a diet-club drop-out.

save SEND delete

Thursday 6:01 a.m.

Amanda,

I saw a video of him on youtube. I saw something – and I thought that if I mentioned it, he'd kill me, because what man wants to be reminded that he is human, especially by a woman?

He wrote back, a few hours later. The words he used, it wasn't just the essence of what he said. It was the specific words. He used the word "afford" – "I hope that you will afford me the

93

opportunity to get to know – to get to see – you as accurately as you have seen me."

He wants to *see* me.

I'm lost, Amanda. He unmans me.

save SEND delete

Friday 6:59 p.m.

Dear Rand,

Sausage, pepperoni, mushroom. Otherwise, pepper, red or green, onion, olives, salami. Never, not on my planet, anchovies. I wouldn't fight a crusade over pizza with anchovies. Live and let live, just not in my backyard. I *would* fight a crusade over pineapple and ham, but anyone so perverse as to put pineapple and ham on pizza obviously has other issues for which he needs to be drawn, quartered, and burned at the stake.

So, do you have pizza over there in England?

save SEND delete

Friday 7:23 p.m.

Oh, I don't know. Fish and chips? Bangers and mash? Curry? Boiled beef? Boiled potatoes? Boiled socks? Boiled Irish babies?

save SEND delete

Friday 7:46 p.m.

Hey! I've read Jonathan Swift. I know what you English are capable of, ESPECIALLY when it comes to the Irish! Those poor bastards have suffered so much, if they suffered any more, they'd be Polish!

save SEND delete

Friday 8:58 p.m.

What!!!??? You can't be serious. Is this public knowledge? It has to be –

I just checked the New York Times website. There it is in black and white. "Court-Wright was a postulant in a Carthusian monastery ..." That's Catholic supermax. That's cold porridge eaten out of a wooden bowl. Your beverage of choice? Room temperature water. Carthusians are allowed to speak, what, once a week? You *totally* out-Catholic me. It would have surprised me less if you had told me that you're a cyborg.

Hey, have I mentioned that it was me on the Grassy Knoll? That's right; *I* shot JFK.

save SEND delete

Friday 9:59 p.m.

ARE YOU KIDDING ME?

It's so weird corresponding with you. We know each other only through e-mail, and behind a keyboard, anyone can be a blond six footer with a buff bod. That's exactly what I am. At this very moment, I'm wearing a fur bikini.

BUT THAT'S WHY YOU STOPPED BELIEVING IN GOD?

Because you were embarrassed?

Because your debate opponent's stack of three-by-five cards was taller than yours?

You pussy.

save SEND delete

Friday 10:32 p.m.

No. Sorry. No.

Look – I thought you had some profoundly worthy reason for abandoning God. Like, you didn't win the lottery, or you published a book of exquisite haiku that the critics just couldn't appreciate, or you prayed really hard to be cured of acne before the prom and God didn't come through, so you abandoned the home team and moved over to Satan's side.

But you dumped God because in a one-on-one with a snot-faced kid you lacked a devastatingly quick retort. You've taken the safest of public positions: denying the existence of God and playing the role of your snot-faced tormentor. You didn't reject God – you rejected the socially vulnerable, manhood-threatening stance of public faith. You prefer the immediate power of being the know-it-all who embarrasses vulnerable others.

save SEND delete

Saturday 5:57 a.m.

I am NOT simplifying.

And, no, we never did agree to be *nice* to each other. We agreed to *see* each other.

Let me do some mirroring here. You stuck out – you didn't say this but it is my guess – because of your history – you'd just left a monastery – and because of your faith. Your uni pals egged you into a debate with the brash young atheist on campus. He asked you a question you couldn't immediately answer and you blushed and you stammered and for the first time in your life, you knew what it felt like not to be the smartest guy in the room, and you bailed on God *for that.*

Now that I know the details behind your departure from Christendom, I've concluded that our side is better off without you.

You're not just a pussy, honey, you're a big wet pussy. Good riddance. Have fun with Satan.

save SEND delete

Saturday noon

Well, first of all, maybe you don't hang around with enough Christians.

And, second, if my anatomy were, in fact, arranged as you describe it, it would be much easier than it is now for me to pee in the woods.

save SEND delete

Saturday 12:15 p.m.
That is the WORST joke I have ever heard! I'm dropping a dime on you to Amnesty International!

Listen, have you heard this one? Wait, you have to hear this spoken out loud to get the punch line. Can you phone right now?

save **SEND** delete

Saturday 12:36 p.m.
Groovy. I'm unplugging the computer. Talk to you in a sec. Looking forward to it. :-)

save **SEND** delete

Monday 7:57 p.m.
Dear Rand,
I want to let you in on what it has been like at my end to be receiving these queries from you. I sit myself down at the computer, in the dark, alone, dwarfed by my high ceiling and its massive, exposed beams. I conjure your face in the debate with the kindly Anglican cleric who insisted on dubbing you "Randy." Rand, I hunger for your most predatory face. You look at me – even just in my imagination – as I have, without realizing it, yearned to have someone look at me my entire life: as if my every move matters. Do humans want to step through forest inhabited by tigers because only the unseen tiger's eye confirms to us our worth, communicates the importance of our choices, and forces us to perform at our peak? Is that the tiger's true evolutionary niche – not to gnaw muscle and bone, but to define us fleeter, cleverer, strong? Only you, Rand, champion atheist, may force me to grow in relationship to my God.

I want so badly to say only what is true to you. It's not that I go around lying. I don't lie even when I could and "should" lie – when lying might advance my career or make people like me.

In relation to you, I discover within myself a whole 'nother standard that I had never even attempted to live up to before.

This standard is as stark and unforgiving as the light detectives use to extract confessions – at least in film noir. I feel as if – in fonts, in words, and in figures of speech – my number of choices shrinks, and yet also deepens. I use only the words a primitive might to convey the fundamentals. Justin van Peenen has no idea what I felt for him. You do. I report these tangents to you for no other reason than because they flit across my consciousness; they are the aurora borealis display on the screen registering the MRI of a stimulated brain. To think something in response to a question you ask me, and not to report that thought, would fail to live up to my commitment to exercise this new discipline of spiritual nakedness with you.

You are a disembodied conscience for which I want to perform with integrity, an obstacle course I pant to run. Simply speaking to you in a way that will meet with your approval might make me a better person.

I admired you. I know that sounds odd. That first time I saw you on Bill Moyers. I felt that I had more in common with you than with that sappy Irish poetess with the big, gray hair and the maudlin harp music, as she barely woke from her walking trance to rhapsodize about the Jesus of the fens, or the black liberation theologian sticking it to the man, on the man's paid sabbatical leave.

That was why I was so wounded when you knee-jerked into dogmatic atheism. I wanted you to live up to what I saw as the best in you. I wanted you to remain suspended in flight, hovering in air, not surrendering to the easy comfort of firm ground. You have wings, Rand. You soar. Moyers asked tough questions, and you asked questions that made Moyers' questions out to be sissies. You were so clearly beyond all care of risk. Your material wings had singed and fallen and your body had sunk to earth, below earth, into the shadow lands of Hades. You voiced pure spirit, the essence of curiosity unencumbered by ego, fear, or flesh, deathless defiance shaking its fist at comfortable enclaves and easy answers. You were out there in the desert, Rand, not being challenged by Satan, but challenging *him.* You dared. You double dared. Your body and your soul, in their circumference, encapsulated those acres of air an eagle commands beneath, and above, its wings.

I want my faith to be able to run the obstacle course you present, with your scoffing and your drive to go to the edge, and then, just, to keep going. If it can't, I'm ready to let my faith go. Because I felt I had more in common with you, Rand, not just than the Irish poetess, or the Black Liberator, but more in common with you than with anyone I have ever met in the flesh. You were like a character I'd dream of, write a story about, too good ever to meet in this face-to-face world. I think that that is why I fell in love with you

save send DELETE

Monday 10:03 p.m.

Dear Amanda,

I've begun to lie to him. How can I tell the truth about Jesus when, with every keystroke, I am hungering for Rand, and acting as if I were not?

save SEND delete

Wednesday 7:54 p.m.

Dear Rand,

Yes, I know it's been taking me a while to get this answer to you.

Look – it's fantastic: a carpenter in Israel two thousand years ago is crucified, and that fixes everything, everywhere, for everybody. Do I really believe that?

I have been obsessing on that question for days, and I have not come up with a "yes" answer or a "no" answer. Rather, I've come up with yet another story. Can you be patient and hear yet another story? Honestly, this is the best I can do.

Years ago I was a teacher in a tiny little outpost in Nepal. It wasn't inhabited enough to be called a village, but let's call it one. There was no electricity. No running water. No one had a radio. No planes flew overhead. It took me five days from the nearest dirt road to walk there. There were only about four inhabited houses, in a rough scrape of yellow dirt, on a tongue-shaped plateau hanging seven thousand feet in air.

On three sides, the earth dropped very steeply down through three thousand feet of zigzagging trail. First were pines and rocks. Rhododendron blazed up crimson in spring. As you climbed down through the thickets, careful not to get lost on woodcutter's trails that meandered into mazes of brush, you heard peacocks whose lovelorn cries rippled curtains of monsoon rain. You drank from waterfalls so pristine their exquisite beauty made you regret all of civilization. Up above you, gray langur monkeys shot the breeze. Their faces and hands are black because Hanuman, the monkey god, burned his face and hands while rescuing Sita from the fires of the Ten-Headed Demon. Wearying, you blessed chautaaras, platforms that pious souls erected around the base of pipal trees. Buddha achieved enlightenment under a pipal tree, a sacred fig, 2,500 years before, and travelers now rest at their bases. Chautaara platforms are built of stone and perfectly calibrated to reach just to the height of a load being released off of a weary traveler's back. I can feel right now the rearrangement of muscles and bones after I backed up to a chautaara, placed my backpack on the platform, released the waistband, shrugged off the shoulder straps, and stepped forward. Refreshed, and climbing all the way down, you reach the crashing white water and the foam of the Dudh Kosi, the river of milk, one of seven sister kosis. There is also the Sun Kosi, the river of gold, and the Arun Kosi, the river of the dawn. The Milky Way is a reflection of these seven rivers; they are so full of reflective bits of mica from the Everest range of mountains which they erode.

On the fourth side, behind the village, the earth rose in

wrinkles like a bunched-up carpet. This ridge blocked the sun; we always had an early sunset. Kids gathered firewood up there. Jackals ate one of the kids. His father wandered around, very sad, for days. People called out, "Hey! I heard a jackal ate your kid. I'm really sorry." And he shrugged.

Wildcats stole chickens. This happened even as you watched. You knew you were watching five chickens and you'd not see a darn thing – they were that fast – and suddenly there were four chickens. Tracks of cat paws and chicken wings traced in the dust, but the cats were the same golden color as the ripe grain out of which they materialized.

During the day, sometimes, I heard clack, clack, clack; a weaver weaving homespun. I heard one isolated bird's song. This was a wagtail, a small, gray, white, and black bird that patrolled the stream and ate its bugs. Some days, that bird's song was the loudest, most significantly patterned sound I heard. Wind. Rain. Every night, the jackals, yelping.

Every now and then, someone would go down to the center of the settlement, and start hollering for all she was worth. I theorized that this might be a form of mental illness unique to this village, or a religious ritual. After I'd been in the village for months, I heard, way off in the distant hills, another person hollering back. Previously, I had not been acclimatized enough to hear the other half of the conversation.

I slipped a lunghi – a tube of cloth – over my head, dropped my sari to the ground, and walked into the wagtail's stream. One day I washed my underwear before washing myself, and placed my underwear on a rock. By the time I was finished bathing, my underwear had frozen to the rock. I chipped them free with my Swiss Army Knife.

I had fleas. Everyone had fleas, but around me everyone had fewer fleas. Something about me was very attractive to fleas. When I slept next to others in tea shops, they would awake in the morning and bless Buddha for how few bites they had received in the night. My sleeping bag could practically walk.

For about a month in late winter, we could buy tangerines in the market. They were the best tangerines, ever, anywhere. I ate the peels. I can't say that the peels tasted good. I can say that I was hungry. As the days become milder and winter loses its grip, the old harvest's crops have all been eaten, and the new season's crops are not yet in. Spring's wild berries, fruiting from snow, tantalize your tongue, but cannot fill your stomach. I collected alien leaves along the path. My test: if they looked benign, I ate them. My neighbors warned, "Miss, that stuff is poisonous!" I survived.

I had a favorite student. He was dyslexic, and I am, too. One Friday he gave me a marble; a rare gift in that village. I still have that marble in my backpack. Monday he did not show up for class. "Stomach ache." Dysentery. He was dead.

In the United States, my brother became fatally ill. Within thirty-six hours of sleeping on a clay floor, under a wattle roof, where mice ran along unfinished rafters peeling bark, I was in the United States. I saw people so fat that they took up the space that two or even three Nepalis take up. People complained of headaches, took aspirin, and were well. Homes were outfitted with curtains and wallpaper and picture frames and slip covers and bed sheets. An American room had more to protect it from mere air than my students, who were, as often as not, barefoot, with just their one ragged garment, day in, day out, between them and wind and sun and snow and rain. Americans threw away more manufactured objects in a given day than most of my villagers would touch in a year.

I was looking out the windshield of a car driving through Pompton Lakes, New Jersey. Pedestrians crossing the street, shoppers on the sidewalks, everyone, without exception, was acting out dramatic unhappiness. Their faces and postures told individualized accounts of bitterness, disappointment, paranoia. Shoulders slumped. Parents jerked children by their wrists. I kept toting up all they had that most people in most places during most times in history never had: calories, choices, warmth in the cold, the ability to read, access to information; they could vote; they could drive; they could drink water from a tap; they could close a door and be alone on the other side of that closed door.

I didn't want them to be better people. I didn't want them to accept Jesus. I didn't want them to box their old clothes and canned food and bandages and send that package anywhere. I just wanted them to be grateful. The car moved on through Pompton Lakes, New Jersey.

My brother died. I flew back to Nepal. In Peace Corps, there is a story that volunteers tell each other; often an old-timer will tell this to a new trainee. I don't know if it is true. A Peace Corps volunteer comes back to the United States and goes mad in the cereal aisle of the supermarket.

I did not want to go mad. I wanted to be a good sister to my brother and daughter to my parents, and so I flew back to America when my brother was dying. I wanted to be a good teacher to Laxmi and Raj Kumar, and so I flew back to Nepal.

I feared that I could not hold those two worlds in my mind without going mad. I did not even try. I said to myself: "When you are in this village, no place else exists. Once you leave, this village does not exist."

Rand, don't you remember moments in your childhood when the adults around you were insisting that X was true, and every bone in your body said that X was not true? To fit in, you went along for the ride. I had no idea what adults were talking about when they said that this or that woman was beautiful. I thought that my Aunt Tetka was beautiful. She was a fat, gold-toothed woman in a black babushka. When one adult said to another, "I'll be over in half an hour," I knew that they'd invoked some impenetrable code. How could there be words that would exchange one person's time with another's? A perfect summer afternoon hovered, like a hawk suspended over a hot field full of rabbits;

she progressed with the languor of a preening swan. There was no word for that unit of time that could be understood by a businessman who spent that afternoon in an air-conditioned office cubicle. Time, beauty: I faked these concepts for years in my childhood before I finally got them.

Rand, I have had moments when I was as sure as I've ever been sure of anything that Jesus Christ is true man and true God, that he lived and died for you and me and that faith in him is all that is necessary. Those have not been moments of bliss. They terrify. Surety that God suffered and died for *me* defies everything that I mime believing so that I can survive consensus reality. Belief in Jesus Christ violently wrenches me out of what I've come to nestle into as moorings.

Yes, Rand, I do. At this moment, as I write to you, and I inhabit my left brain, and run my sharpened pencil down the inventory of things I believe and find plausible and things I find fantastic and too painful even to contemplate, I believe. I don't believe because it makes any sense in a world where rape and murder and war crimes and child abuse are rampant. I am as if a receiving clerk checking off a bill of lading against all my expectations of what a convincing deity should be and do. That receiving clerk finds this story pretty outlandish, and, frankly, full of holes. But, even at this moment, when I inhabit my inner receiving clerk, I know that, while walking down modern streets in modern cities, against my attempts to forget her, to sequester her behind an impenetrable ghetto wall in my mind, for no better reason than my own cognitive convenience, I remember Nepal. I remember hungry peasants who gave me their food, expecting nothing in return. I remember vivid joy and vitality in the faces of my students, filthy and barefoot though they were. I remember moonlight on that massive curtain of ice and rock, Nuptse Ridge. I remember the deafening silence and the blinding azure sky that became louder and more overpowering the closer I got to Sagarmatha. I know that that other reality exists. I know because

I was there.

save **SEND** delete

Thursday 9:02 a.m.

Are you back on that topic again? Are you just changing the subject because you can't refute anything I just said? Or is that the default mode of your brain: not atheism, not science, but sex?

save **SEND** delete

Thursday noon

Heh.

I'm just remembering that, in the "Canterbury Tales," the Wife of Bath is the only woman, and she's the only character who has to justify the fact that she's actually had sex.

Wait, no. She's not the only woman. There is also a nun.

Et voila.

save **SEND** delete

Thursday 12:03 p.m.

Dear Amanda,

Intimacy. The riskiest game. Our quarry which we hunt, which hides from us, which might die, is not just the other, it is also ourselves.

He and I are not tearing off our clothing to reveal our nakedness, but, rather, we are revealing something far more intimate – our souls.

Were we face to face, the moment would come when I would drop my clothing and he would accept my naked body or reject my naked body and that would be it. To achieve greater intimacy with Rand, it isn't enough just to expose a body I acquired readymade. This is e-mail. I have to type my next word. In discovering my next word, I discover myself.

I just want to hear from him, the sentences I keep trying to get him to say, are, "Expose yourself to me, Mira. I want to see you,

105

not to study you, or to intellectualize you, or to exploit you in my next book. I want to see you because I value you and getting closer to you is my desire. I will respect and cherish that which you expose, no matter how other it may turn out to be."

save SEND delete

INBOX
dinner with a potential patron last night ... o how wearying it is constantly to prostitute oneself for one's art ... almost burst into sempre libera over dessert ... if only art were always free ... pray that your yahweh god will smile upon us in the form of small unmarked bills ... or large marked bills ... not choosy about denominations ... bills or gods ... hindu goddess laxmi i've been told ... by you? ... showers her followers with golden coins ... it's for a good cause

Thursday 12:34
Dear Lord Court-Wright,
Okay, if we're going to have to talk about this, then let's just talk about this, and get it out of the way.

News flash: I am not a virgin. Film at eleven.

I'm a woman, I've never been married, and I've had sex. Does that make me unworthy to call myself a "Christian"? Some would say yes, absolutely. Virgin or whore: a woman's two choices. Men's misogyny, which has existed everywhere, at all times, from ancient Pagan societies to modern atheistic ones, often masquerades as Christianity, in complete contradiction to Jesus' career. Jesus told the religious leaders of his own day that prostitutes would get into heaven before they did (Matthew 21:31).

I am hardly the first since Jesus to notice the many ironies inherent in a Christian misogyny that identifies women with sex and sex with sin. I love this from Sor Juana:

Who is more to blame,

though either should do wrong?
She who sins for pay
or he who pays to sin?

Jesus famously broke up a gang that was using religion as their excuse to produce a ghastly scenario of S&M pornography – a stoning. Stoning is one of those institutions that, to a lot of modern Americans, sounds medieval, and, therefore, distant enough to have lost its edge of horror. The internet is here to teach us otherwise. I watched a stoning just before teaching a class on honor killing. Du'a Khalil Aswad was a 17-year-old Kurdish girl. That stoning is pornography was made very clear by the girl's murderers. Even as deadly stones flew thick, men's hands reached in to yank up her skirt, to expose her. Even as she was dying, she kept trying to pull down her skirt. An even more certain seal of stoning as S&M porn: the killers filmed their victim, and then, with pride, they shared their trophy videos on the internet.

I bring what I learned from watching that video to the story of the Woman Taken in Adultery in the Gospel of John. The misogynists' porn had begun with their apprehension of the woman. As they themselves triumphantly and shamelessly report, they had nabbed her even as she was having sex. You have to wonder – did they lie in wait? Hide themselves, and their mounting excitement, as the act began? You have to wonder what garment, if any, they threw over her body before they dragged her to Jesus. They further made her a spectacle by making "her stand in the middle" between Jesus and his followers, as Jesus was teaching. Men interrupted the Messiah bringing salvation to humankind. They thrust a woman, and sex, and their own sick proclivities, and their own warped concept of religion, a religion made up of self-righteous male superiority and dominance and female worthlessness, between suffering humanity and a saving God. They then used their warped concept of religion to challenge Jesus to abandon his mission of salvation and join them in their S&M orgy. If Jesus refused this poisoned invitation, they would exploit his unorthodox response as an excuse to lynch him. Satan is nothing if not an economic strategist and expert campaigner.

Jesus did not respond verbally. He squatted down and wrote in the dust. This is the only record we have of Jesus writing. John's gospel doesn't say what Jesus wrote. Some see the key in Jeremiah 17:13 – those who turn away from God will be written in the dust. If this is the case, these men, who get their kicks by persecuting women for their sexuality, Jesus equates with the damned who have chosen their own damnation by turning away from God. Other biblical scholars assume that Jesus was writing down the sins of the men who wanted to stone the woman. They assume this because of what Jesus said after he stood up, "Let the one among you who is without sin be the first to throw a stone at her." This is really interesting because Deuteronomy 17:7 stipulates that the ones to cast the first stones be the eyewitnesses of the crime. Here Jesus is saying that the eyewitnesses are themselves sinners. Is Jesus saying that peeping at women having sex, becoming aroused by that, and then wanting to punish women for having sex, is itself a crime? Whatever Jesus wrote, it so intimidated the bastards with the stones that, starting from the oldest and proceeding to the youngest, one by one, they simply walk away, leaving Jesus alone with The Woman Taken in Adultery.

Jesus doesn't take a radical Free Love stance with her. He doesn't say, "Hey, I'll be by later for the orgy, and I'll bring the goat grease." A second species of misogynist than those who wanted to kill this woman want to destroy her by hijacking and rewriting her story. This species of misogynist demands that Jesus and the woman had sex. This is the Dan Brown, "Da Vinci Code" style misogynist, who, like the stoners, insists that women exist to satisfy men sexually. Dan Brown tells us that Mary

Magdalene was Jesus' wife. First, Mary Magdalene was NOT the Woman Taken in Adultery. This is a common misconception. They are two different women. Second, Mary Magdalene was not Jesus' wife. She was his financier (Luke 8:1-3). She was the first apostle (John 20:18). But to the Dan Brown set, if there's a woman there, she's not a prophetess (Luke 2:36-38), she's not a skilled debater and loving mother (Mark 7:25-30), she's not a political wife of rare and steely courage and prophetic gifts (Matthew 27:19). To the Dan Brown set, a woman is just an anatomical item. It is impossible for misogynists on the right or on the left even to imagine that a woman presents anything of interest – an immortal soul, say – that is more compelling than a few inches of female flesh. Reminds me of a joke you hear on the street. "What do you call the useless meat surrounding a vagina? A woman." The Dan Brown set insists that the church censored Jesus' many New Testament orgies. This is idiotic. There was no reason to censor orgies in the Roman Empire. There were flourishing religions based on orgies. If Matthew, Mark, Luke and John just wanted to give audiences what they demand, that's what they would have given them. Orgies. What is in the New Testament is far more transgressive: Jesus sees something in the Woman Taken in Adultery that the misogynists armed with stones and the misogynists armed with K-Y Jelly can't see. It is the woman's individual soul that compels Jesus, that justifies his risking, and his sacrificing, his life.

Another story, also from John. Jesus approaches the Samaritan Woman at the Well. He initiates their brief, history-shattering encounter with a one-liner straight from a film noir: "Give me a drink." Jesus casually mentions that the Samaritan Woman has had five husbands, and that she is living with yet another man to whom she's never been married. She's impressed by Jesus' supernatural knowledge, but she doesn't fall at his feet to beweep her sullied state. In fact, at no point in the story is a big deal made of the fact that Samaritan Woman is a "tramp," that she "sleeps around." Jesus never berates her. She never dons sackcloth or ashes, or takes an oath of abstinence. Nowhere does John, the author of the text, demand that Samaritan Women deliver a sobbing, disgraced-politician, Oprah-style confession. Jesus mentions her many men for one reason: to inform her that he *knows* her. He knows the bare, biographical facts of her life. He knows her compromises; he knows her imperfections. He knows that she is not, by the standards of her society, perfect. He knows her in the sense that he loves her, and he wants her in his kingdom.

Samaritan Woman doesn't stutter or falter or go blank after Jesus brings up her many men. She immediately starts talking theology. She opens up a debate on the best place to worship. This is a mighty bold move and I can only wish I could have Samaritan Woman over for lunch. She is something.

Though Jesus often conceals his identity, he wastes no time with her, stating plainly that he is the Messiah. Jesus has singled her out for his greatest gift: letting her know that he is the way, the truth, and the life. She, too, is a woman in a hurry. She puts down her water jar, goes to her town's center, and preaches the Good News. Her testimony brought many to salvation. In the literal sense of the word, "one sent," the Samaritan Woman at the Well, this Woman of Many Husbands, is an apostle – one sent by Jesus to bring souls to God.

I am saddened that we don't have the names of these ancestral matriarchs, but I rejoice that we have their stories, and others like them: The Widow Who Donates Two Mites, The Woman Who Anoints Jesus in Bethany, The Woman with a Hemorrhage. The folk attest to their importance by applying names to them. In folk tradition, The Syrophonecian Woman is "Justa," Pilate's Wife is "Procula," and the Woman with a Hemorrhage is "Veronica." Other than the Judeo-Christian, I know of no other narrative tradition where common, often peasant, women from two, and three, and four thousand years back, take on individual life and importance that outlasts the renown of kings.

In short: Free Love and Puritanism: a pox on both these houses. I'm finding, in back-channel kinds of ways – this development is *not* something that has made the national news – that me and a bunch of other been-there-done-that women, women who came of age after the introduction of the birth control pill, after the modernizations of Vatican Two, and after the "War on Poverty" took much of the economic onus off single motherhood, are now saying, "If I had it all to do over again, I wouldn't." We're the same women who look at Britney Spears and other kiddie, soft-porn celebrities and want to cry.

When I was younger, I did have relationships I now wish I had never had. I had them because no one had taught me how to say "No." The puritanical rationale for teaching girls to say no was flawed. No feminist rationale replaced it. No one stepped up and said, "We don't want to burden our girls with misogynist religious images like the Whore of Babylon, but we also don't want to burden our girls with excesses of Free Love that tells them, not that they *can* have sex with whomever they want, but that they *must* have sex with anyone who asks, and if they don't, then they are prudes, or, worse, they are invisible. We reject a Free Love that says that the only use for a female is to please a male, and that the only way a female can please a male is by servicing him sexually."

But I don't want to ride the pendulum back to Puritanism, either, where the only possible relationship is a straight line. A looks to her left and starts walking toward B. B looks to his right and starts walking toward A. They meet in the middle at C and just continue from there, a straight line that, by definition, goes on forever.

Not all relationships plot like that. Some form a crucifix. A walks toward B, B walks toward A, but bearing down on them, unbeknownst to them, is Time. Time hurtles down from above, and when A and B meet at C, Time bisects them, and then just keeps going. They had to come together. But they are not meant to remain together. Their union was a point that existed only to be shattered. We humans find this hard to understand, impossible to accept. We want love to affirm our worth. Since we go on, we want love to. What good is someone who says "I love you" and then disappears? Cross-shaped love, like death, teaches us that the blessed moment is just as sacred as eternity.

"Brief Encounter." A 1945 British film. I think they made it on a budget of about a buck sixty-five. Black and white, no special effects, shot in train stations, cheap apartments and grassy fields. Britain was strapped for cash in those days. Fighting World War Two bankrupted the treasury. I say there were "no special effects," but the screenplay was by Noel Coward, the soundtrack is Rachmaninoff, the director was David Lean, and Celia Johnson and Trevor Howard star. You had the fireworks of real talent, real intelligence and heart, instead of exploding spaceships and comic book monsters.

The plot: a woman gets a bit of grit in her eye, and a stranger helps her, and they fall in love. They don't leave their spouses. They never have sex. But it *is* adultery. They have fun with each other. Moments sparkle with magic. Life becomes more exciting. They think about each other when they are apart.

Is what they did a sin? A terrible sin? Falling in love while a stranger helps you get a bit of grit out of your eye? Yearning for that stranger to touch you intimately? Going to a matinee on a weekday afternoon, giggling like a kid at a movie that, normally, would have bored you, and not telling your husband? Crying after you say goodbye? Is all that sin?

Yes. It is a sin. It goes against the Bible. It causes you and your loved ones pain. It rends your life and leaves you wounded forever. Grit in the eye – is that the perfect metaphor, or what? Our most cherished, sensitive organ, our sine qua non for perceiving and understanding, our eye, so powerful, so vulnerable, this, as Hopkins wrote, "sleek and seeing ball," that a mere "prick will make no eye at all." She got grit in her eye, and that tiny bit of flotsam comes close to toppling her entire, carefully crafted life. Aren't wounds like that what make us human, what make life, this miserable, biological exercise in morning excretion and petty quarreling over even pettier, emptier dramas, and jockeying to be first in line at the feed trough, worth anything at all? Aren't such wounds our sunsets, our spring grass, our baby smiles? Can we experience mystery or grandeur without these wounds? What kind of Pecksniffian robots would we be if, at that moment that fate dropped upon us like a spring rain, at that moment that a featureless stranger moved out of the gray, rumpled crowd, took on definition, and began to glow, and hum, and flush into full color and three dimensions, and reached for our hands, and said, "Here, let me help you," and our hairs stood on end, because we knew, we just knew, it's as if this moment had been scheduled for us long before we were born, if, at that moment, we turned away from the suddenly, breathtakingly beautiful stranger and from his glow, and from life, and from this, our sudden sensing of the music of the spheres, and coughed out a stiff, dead, "Don't talk to me. Don't be visible to me. Don't see me. I cannot walk this path with you." And turned, and marched away, and never looked back? What would the Psalms be had they been written not by the sexually broken David, but by the virginally intact Justin?

I applied for a job recently at a Christian school. I was intimidated by their guidelines. I wondered if they would not hire me because I am not a virgin. In their online promotional materials, they heavily emphasized their teachers' chastity. You have to wonder, if you are going to single out one Biblical theme, why sex? Why not emphasize the Biblical teaching on the ownership of more than one coat? "Whoever has two coats should give one to someone who has none" (Luke 3:11). I obey that.

In any case, they did not hire me because I am Catholic. I later noted that they hired a retired military officer. One would think that killing people would be more serious a matter than having sex. Christians have nurtured manly saints, going all the way back to that high-testosterone, confessed whoremonger, Augustine, who developed the Christian theory of "Just War." Might not we Christians nurture some feminine saints who would develop the theory of "Just Love"? If there are times when it is right for a Christian man to pick up a weapon and kill his fellow men, women, and children, is it not possible that there are also times when it is right for a Christian woman, fully alive to and functioning in her Christianity, to spread her legs and speak a fully engaged, "Yes"?

save SEND delete

Thursday 3:03 p.m.

My God, but you take my breath away.

After your silly, randy – strike that – horny schoolboy response to my post about whether or not I believe in Jesus, I thought, okay, he doesn't want God talk. But then you send me this, one of the most beautiful spiritual documents I have ever read.

Rand, ditch the physics. What more is there to say about the Big Bang? You should be writing theology. People who never read theology would want to read you.

You made me cry.

You are soul.

save SEND delete

Thursday 3:59 p.m.

You perverse weirdo! I just paid you the highest compliment I've ever paid anyone and all you can think about is some bizarro, imaginary competition between you and Justin!

Yes, Justin was a very pretty young man. Yes, his nose was more pert than yours.

And, yes, writing the best theology is way more –
Sheesh, I give up.
Men.

save **SEND** delete

Thursday 4:30 p.m.
Pervert.

pervert. pervert. pervert.
P E R V E R T

save **SEND** delete

Thursday 5:07 p.m.
Okay. I hope you have a terrific time. For now, good night, sleep
tight, and don't let the bedbugs bite.

Pervert.

save **SEND** delete

Monday 9:00 a.m.
Dear Rand,
Hi! Great to hear from you again. I'm so glad you had such a
good time. Yeah, I read that guy's book, too. I have to admit I
wasn't overwhelmed by it, or even whelmed. But since it worked
for you, I'm glad you got to co-present at a conference with him
and that you both enjoyed it so much. How lucky that he went
skiing in Gstaad same time as you. Synchronicity, eh? Huh?
Huh? Ah, never mind.

Not much to report at this end. Students driving me crazy.
You taught for a while – you know the drill.

I've sent you so many long e-mails. You send me a long one,
so I'll have something to chew on.

save **SEND** delete

Monday noon
Dear Rand

save send **DELETE**

Monday 1:01 p.m.
We're on marshy ground

SAVE send delete

Monday 1:14 p.m.
We're on marshy ground.

save **SEND** delete

Tuesday 9:00 a.m.
This is what I mean.

The Tao teaches that emptiness is as important as solidity. Isn't the emptiness that you and I, Rand, maintain and respect between us as valuable, and to be cherished just as much as the solid points where we make contact?

It was easier to fight with you before I came to like you so much, and when I thought you might disappear at any moment, so it didn't matter what I said. I think that that is why strangers can experience such a fierce intimacy unknown to people comfortable in long-standing relationships. The more comfort, the more to lose if one risks.

save **SEND** delete

Tuesday 9:37 a.m.
Well, aren't you the little kamikaze pilot.

Okay, what about this – we've all got sacred scripture. I know that you don't believe mine. I'm okay with that. But, Rand – I don't believe yours, either. Will you be able to handle my desecration of your sacred texts, my dissing of your saints? Or will you become enraged and stomp away?

The Gospel According to Rand: The Law of Large Numbers:

given enough events, anything can happen, including miracles. Confirmation Bias: humans focus on the data that confirms pre-existing beliefs. Pattern Recognition: humans are so driven to find patterns that we see old men's profiles in the rocks on a mountain, or Jesus in a grilled cheese sandwich. Cold reading: psychics toss out many vague statements and believers focus only on the "hits" that match their own lives.

In your church, you measure time BS and AS: Before Sagan and After Sagan. Your messiah, Carl Sagan: Scientist-celebrity, star of "Cosmos," seen by billions and billions of television viewers, author of "The Demon-Haunted World: Science as a Candle in the Dark." Before Sagan, humanity was bestial, and religious. After Sagan, humanity at least had the opportunity to put religion aside, and evolve ever upward, to be, in a word, scientific. Believers inhabit the Dark Continent. Atheists are the brave missionaries bringing us the light.

Your scripture is a hackneyed, comic-book version of the "White Man's Burden" myth. I don't believe that your saints and demons have any historicity at all. Your atheist saints are patched-together fictions, based on mythological figures like Prometheus. Your demonic enemy, the gullible masses, are straw men.

Atheist debunkings need to be debunked. Case in point: In 1917, three Portuguese shepherd children claimed to have seen the Blessed Virgin Mary. Mary promised them a sign. On October 13, tens of thousands of people, some skeptical and there to mock, some faithful and there to pray, claimed that they saw the sun dance in the sky. I bring this up because I have always doubted Marian apparitions. I don't understand why Mary would bother visiting just to tell us to pray the rosary. That is a message you can get in any Catholic church. I wanted to find an airtight debunking of the Miracle of the Sun. An atheist claims that the witnesses saw sundogs – the reflection of sunlight off of cirrus clouds. This is ridiculous. Portuguese shepherds, farmers, and fisherfolk, people who spend their waking lives out of doors, would not mistake a sundog for the visions described in the Miracle of the Sun. We're stuck with the confounding testimony of tens of thousands of people. I'm okay with waiting until an adequate explanation comes along. I have not encountered that comfort with not knowing in your camp, Rand. It's not your curiosity that puts me off; it is your rush to place a stamp of surety on events not easily tamed.

Your religion places left-brain skills like numeracy on an altar and makes them the object of worship, and denigrates right-brain skills like intuition, and makes those skills the object of scorn. How much damage has been done by men, highly rational, analytical, and scientific, who have contempt for "emotional" people, for women, for children, and for "savages"? And you know that foundational atheist thinkers like Freud divided the world up just that way, with rational, atheist men on the top of their hierarchies, and believing women, children and savages on the bottom. No set of statistics can ever tell us how much harm that worldview has done, but, for the moment, think of physicians, going back two thousand years to Hippocrates, who dismissed women as cesspools of feeling. Hippocrates gave us the word "hysteria" from the Greek for "womb." Emotions were bad. Women were emotional. Women had wombs. Emotions, women, and wombs – all bad, because not rational, because not male. In the nineteenth and twentieth centuries, physicians performed hysterectomies on tens of thousands of American and European women, because men found them too emotional. Tens of thousands of people, in the twentieth century, were lobotomized, some just because they did not color within the lines dictated by the rationalist worldview. When I worked with the dying, I met patients who received great comfort and wisdom from their spiritual lives, who were mocked, even as they stood at the doors of death, by doctors who lectured them to "grow up" and "get beyond all that." I know of doctors who accused patients who had had near death experiences of going mad, and prescribed anti-psychotic medication to the dying, to forefend their talking about their spiritual experiences. Yes, your scripture has done incalculable harm.

In the same way that you think that there are psychological explanations for belief in anything beyond material reality, I think that there are psychological explanations for belief only in material reality. The hardcore atheists I have met have all been gifted in one narrow set of left-brain skills, but they find social interaction challenging. Intuition, reading between the lines, getting the gist of a poem or a joke, hearing the still, small voice, seeing the starlight that is best perceived through peripheral vision: these are skills at which hardcore atheists often fail.

Often these men deal with their lopsided, people-unfriendly skill set by retreating to their own makeshift monastery – an academic job, a computer cubicle, for the unfortunate ones, poverty and eccentricity. From their island they can mutter imprecations against those humans who are never quite as smart as they, but who seem able to function in the day-to-day world with an elusive ease and success that they can only envy. Isolation and the combination of a sense of superiority and inferiority feed contempt.

Scientists' awkwardness at human interaction often shows. It's not for nothing that Carl Sagan earned the nickname "Butt Head Astronomer." Students at Cornell, where he was supposed to be a teacher, pulled pranks to highlight his arrogance and aloofness. There was the "I Touched Carl Sagan" contest. A six pack of beer was to be the prize for the first student to have any contact with this "teacher."

There's an interesting aspect to Sagan's atheist fans celebrating him as the Luminous Science Messiah who jousted with the Dark Side, a Dark Side identified by them as the primitive, intuitive, spiritual, and religious side. In 1961, psychiatrist Carl Jung wrote a letter to Bill W., the founder of

Alcoholics' Anonymous –

Pause. Do you know what Alcoholics' Anonymous is? I mean, do you know what it *really* is? This is e-mail, and I can't tell if you are nodding or shaking your head. I don't want to wait for a return e-mail informing me if you are nodding or shaking your head. If I do wait the point I'm trying to make will slip permanently from my head. I'm going to cut to the chase and provide a thumbnail history of AA.

The Twelve Step Movement was founded in 1935 by two Americans, a stockbroker and a physician. True to Twelve Step custom, which emphasizes anonymity, "friends of Bill" refer to these two men by their first names: Bill W. and Dr. Bob. Bill wrote the Twelve Steps, a record of how drunks got sober in AA. Alcoholics "Came to believe that a Power greater than ourselves could restore us to sanity," and "Made a decision to turn our will and our lives over to the care of God as we understood God," and, finally, "had a spiritual awakening" that enabled them to help other alcoholics. When Bill was writing those twelve steps, he wasn't telling needy people what to do, he was recording what successful people had done.

Carl Jung noted the burgeoning Twelve Step movement with interest. A spiritual movement was succeeding in the treatment of alcoholism, while medical science and psychoanalysis had had lesser success. Freud, the founder of psychoanalysis, had cherished Jung as his heir-apparent. In his fawning love letters to Jung, Freud not only referred to Jung as his "heir," but as "my successor and crown prince," and "spirit of my spirit." Freud was very good at loving others, as long as those others were young men like Otto Rank and Carl Jung whom Freud thought might help him cheat death and carry on his own name into immortality. Neither Rank nor Jung lived up to Freud's expectations. Both "sons" broke with Freud. One major fault line between Freud and Jung: religion.

Freud utterly disdained religion; he wanted it obliterated.

Freud's work is replete with the kind of white-man's-burden contempt for religion modeled by E. B. Tylor, the founder of anthropology. Influenced by Darwin's model of evolution, Tylor divided humanity into a hierarchy of three classes. "Savages," the most primitive humans, were on the bottom, "Barbarians" were above them, and "Civilized Man" was the most highly evolved, up at the top. Tylor, a Victorian English gentleman, placed Victorian English gentlemen at the pinnacle of the human pyramid. Any religious belief located the believer on the bottom, along with unevolved European peasants, and Africans. Women and children were at the bottom, as well. Science and atheism were at the top. If you wanted to get to the top, to advance, to *evolve,* you had to abandon belief in God.

Freud bought into this tri-partite hierarchy. His atheist tract "Totem and Taboo" is, in addition to being indefensibly absurd, one of the most imperialist works ever written. Any religion, any belief in God was comparable to mental illness, and was comparable to being a woman, a child, or a "savage."

Jung was the son of a pastor father and a mother who was visited at night by spirits. Jung himself had a dream that, he believed, foreshadowed World War I. Jung wrote to Bill W., the American alcoholic stockbroker who had applied spiritual insights in the founding of AA. In his letter, Dr. Jung spoke about a former patient, an alcoholic: "His craving for alcohol was the equivalent, on a low level, of the spiritual thirst of our being for wholeness, expressed in medieval language: the union with God." Jung pointed out that "alcohol in Latin is 'spiritus' and you use the same word for the highest religious experience as well as for the most depraving poison. The helpful formula, therefore, is spiritus contra spiritum": "spirit," or soul against "spirit," or drug. We hunger for a life of the spirit, and when we deny ourselves spiritual food, we fill the void by turning to drugs – legal, illegal, or prescription. What does Jung's letter to Bill W. have to do with presumptive atheist, scientist messiahs?

Freud, a user, praised cocaine as a "magical drug." And Carl
Sagan smoked a lot of marijuana. In a 1969 essay, Sagan identified
smoking marijuana as a religious experience.

It is poignant to read of Sagan's budding conviction – no pun
intended – in his mid-twenties, that "there was more to living
than science," and of the "euphoria" he enviously observed
marijuana-users exhibit. He tried pot and didn't get high, and,
because he didn't get high, he decided that it was all a hoax. This
sounds much like disappointed atheists denouncing religion: "It
didn't work, immediately and palpably, for me, so it must be
phony." Sagan kept trying, though, and eventually he did get
high, and began to experience "astonishingly harmonious,"
"exquisite," visions. These visions were not purely abstract;
"somewhere in them," he writes, there was "a symbolism significant to me which I won't attempt to describe here, a kind of
mandala embossed on the high." Attending to this mandala
"produced a very rich array of insights."

Under the influence of marijuana, Sagan gained a new appreciation for art. He was able to hear aspects of music he'd been
deaf to before. He gained a sometimes "awful" – from "full of
awe" – and a sometimes "playful and whimsical" sense of the
absurd. He gained a new awareness of human ego and hypocrisy,
including his own. He felt a sense of "communion" – his word –
with his animate and inanimate surroundings. "There is a
religious aspect," to marijuana use, Sagan concluded.

Sagan takes on the very role believers play in their jousts with
radical atheists. Don't belittle me for my belief in pot, he insists.
This is all real, he shouts. This is not just real, it is *important* –
he proselytizes. He makes the very argument religious believers
make. My paraphrase: "You can believe my testimony on the
difficult-to-measure matter of transcendent insights because my
testimony on more easily measured matters – the names of high
school acquaintances, for example – is verifiably accurate."

It is important to produce support for his judgment, Sagan

says, because marijuana provides insights unavailable to the mind of a man who is "down" – that is, a man not "high" on drugs: "there is a world around us which we barely sense ... we can become one with the universe ... [marijuana] helps produce the serenity and insight, sensitivity and fellowship so desperately needed in this increasingly mad and dangerous world." Marijuana, he says, teaches compassion. It made him aware of that which he and rational others had spent a lifetime "trained to overlook and forget and put out of our minds." There is good reason for this training and practice at filtering consensus reality; if we noted everything, including our own egos and hypocrisy, we would go crazy. "A sense of what the world is really like can be maddening; cannabis has brought me some feelings for what it is like to be crazy, and how we use that word 'crazy' to avoid thinking about things that are too painful for us ... I discovered that there's somebody inside in those people we call mad" Sagan writes.

It's a "myth," Sagan insists, that the insights that pot imparts are chimeras that crumble into the dust once the effects of the drug fade. In a line that any person of faith who has tried to communicate to an atheist can only applaud, Sagan wrote, "the main problem is putting these insights in a form acceptable to the quite different self that we are when we're down the next day." Sagan is talking about having two selves. One is left-brain dominant, the other right-brain dominant. One is open to the transcendent, and convinced of its importance, and one is threatened by, or contemptuous of it. That effort to communicate between the mind of a man high on marijuana and the mind of a man who is "down" is, Sagan wrote, "some of the hardest work I've ever done." In spite of his hard work, he had to admit that the moments when his perceptions were "of a religious nature," would never withstand the scrutiny his scientific mind would exercise in evaluation of them. "Listen closely, you sonofabitch of the morning! This stuff is real!" Sagan's high self harangues his down self.

As Jung said, getting high through drugs is an ersatz experience for getting high through spirit. The routes Sagan was interested in traveling: inquiries into unflinching yet compassionate insight into his fellow human beings, art, music, love and sex and into the ultimate nature of reality are best traveled through religious discipline. To paraphrase Paul Newman, "Why go out for a hamburger when you have steak at home?" Why settle for tetrahydrocannabinol's action on brain cells when you can do what minds like Buddha, Jesus, Teresa of Avila, Julian of Norwich, Pascal, Descartes, Newton, Thoreau, Tolstoy, Jung, Gandhi, Dostoyevsky and Edith Stein have done before you – pursue the ultimate questions with the ultimate guide?

save **SEND** delete

Tuesday 9:59 a.m.
Yeah, but I don't want to be humored.

save **SEND** delete

Tuesday 10:16 a.m.
I know you didn't say that in so many words.

I was using my intuition. Reading between the lines. Get it, get it?

save **SEND** delete

Tuesday 10:34 a.m.
Good grief, now you're talking about me as if I'm an insect on a slide. Am I going to be a case study in your next book? The very smart PhD who actually believes in transcendent reality?

save **SEND** delete

Tuesday 3:37 p.m.
Dear Amanda,
Hiya.

save **SEND** delete

INBOX
loya
tsup?

Tuesday 3:52
I finally get it, I think, why Court-Wright opens my heart and makes me flood. He's a glacier. I'm a blowtorch. His hyper-rationality and stunted emotional life provide scaffolding. For once in my life I can lean back. There is finally a methodical, cold and rational yang out there equal and opposite to my arithmetically retarded, ever-exploding yin.

Opposites attract. For a time. But what do you get when you combine a glacier with a blowtorch in a domestic setting? Wet and singed carpeting.

save **SEND** delete

INBOX
does it have to be that way pumpkin ... accentuate the positive eliminate the negative don't mess with mr inbetween ... remember the tarot card temperance ... an alchemical angel blends two mutually exclusive substances to create one superior and new made perfect by exposure to its opposite ... attraction to one's opposite is an invitation to be born again

Tuesday 4:58 p.m.
Yeah, but that's tarot, Amanda. Opposites blend beautifully, in the ethereal, imaginary city erected by a tarot deck.

No matter how close Court-Wright and I get, he will never know me as he does his own flesh. He will never be able to predict me. I am a different creature. My posture in relation to him will always be on tiptoe. I will always be reaching for, but never quite attaining, contact. That very element that makes my desire for him so sharp is that which will always keep us apart. Those blissful, unpredictable moments when I say something that touches him or when he makes me laugh quiver with so much life exactly for the same reason that a perfect summer afternoon shimmers under our eyes. Contrast defines. Death is the sine qua non, the without-this-nothing, of Life. It is that Death present in our every moment of life that makes this one of the most intense relationships I've ever had.

save **SEND** delete

Wednesday noon

Dear Rand,

Look – I'm going to tell you. At least some of it.

This is a risk. But what I value so much about you is that air around you, the air that surrounds an eagle in flight. If we can't launch into nothing but air, our relationship is not what I thought I valued.

Diving in. Or up.

Rand, I could never be an atheist like you because I live in both worlds. I live in consensus reality. I've always had to assess situations with the coldest of eyes and calculate benefit versus risk. The ciphers in my trigonometry: the knife in my backpack, the reaction of the crowd, the chances that a serial killer or merely a conventionally bad person would stumble across me if I dropped my pack and unrolled my sleeping bag on this desert floor tonight. Material reality? Been there. Done that.

I know that the non-material world exists, because I've always lived there, too. My mother was psychic. And when you go on TV and rant against psychics, you look like a judge at a witch trial to me.

I don't think anyone ever used the word "psychic" at our house. She used the word "feel," or "feelings," if she used any word at all. It was just how my mother and her house and her world worked. Some Sundays, about five times a year, after mass, we would drive to a bakery and pick up some jelly donuts dusted with powdered sugar. Otherwise, we never indulged in these luxuries; they were expensive, and we did our own baking. But baking takes time; these would be a last-minute purchase.

On those Sundays, a big boat of a car would pull up in front of the house, and Aunt Tetka and Uncle Strechko would get out, and begin their slow, old-boned parade up the front walk. They moved with the dignity appropriate to creatures going extinct; these were people who had been born, and who had shared their first kiss, under the Hapsburgs, the Hapsburgs of duels and Strauss waltzes, an extinct empire. Tetka and Strechko would burst into folksongs and not stop till they sang one hundred verses. They were old when I was born and they were old when I got my first gray hairs. They were the kind of people nobody makes any more.

Tetka and Strechko didn't phone. They just showed up. Why didn't they phone? Maybe because all three of them – my mother, Tetka, and Strechko – had grown up in tiny villages in Eastern Europe without telephones, and they got used to working with feelings.

My world, Rand. Low-rent details for you to tear apart. Relatives from the Old Country arriving without warning on a Sunday. My mother always prepared with jelly donuts to serve her guests. No one in my family predicted John F. Kennedy's assassination, or made a fortune on the stock market. We are small potatoes people. Kennedy is not a character in our story.

I know your question; it's mine, too. If people really do have psychic abilities, why don't they just purchase the right lottery ticket and retire on their winnings? Let me ask you this – if people really do have hands to manipulate the material world to our favor, then why do we screw up material reality as badly as we do? If science really works, why don't we just cure cancer right now and get it over with? Psychic ability may give you an extra telephone, but it doesn't give you a different fate. One of my childhood friends had test scores so high he was awarded a full scholarship to study neuroscience. For a kid from our neighborhood, that was like being handed a ticket to the moon. He's never done anything with his Ivy League science training. He moved back to our hometown where he works low status jobs. My mother's psychic abilities – something you insist does not exist – didn't change her fate, and my friend's proven science gifts – something that you insist provides all salvation – didn't change his fate.

Here's how it started for me. I was nine. I was walking down the street on a beautiful summer day. I was with Tommy Dahlgren, an older boy from next door. He was carrying a newspaper. He said, as a joke, I think, "So, pick a lottery number for me." He was checking the numbers from the day before. I had no idea what the lottery was. I said so. Impatient, he said, "Just give me some numbers." I rattled off a series of numbers. He huffed, annoyed, "You knew." Again, I had no idea what he was talking about.

"Knew what?"

We went inside and Tommy told my parents and it was declared, then and there, that, like my mother, I had this thing. Because the numbers Tommy bullied me into rattling off were, exactly, the previous day's winning lottery numbers.

My friend Sandy is a physicist, specializing in high-energy, experimental particle physics. He aggressively mocks all religion, and has no conscious relationship to any god. He says that when I experience an "anomalous event," I enter an alternate universe. He says that since there is an infinite number of universes, there is an infinite number of possible events. To me, Sandy's multiverse theory is as weird as anything any religion, or even Aleister Crowley himself, ever cooked up.

One morning I told Sandy to be careful; there would be an earthquake in Berkeley that day. There was an earthquake in Berkeley that day. I know that you are running the odds, Rand, so I'll tell you – that was the only time I ever told anyone that there would be an earthquake, and that was the only time an earthquake in Berkeley made the front page of the paper while Sandy and I were living there together. Even so, Sandy continues to insist that he does not believe in anything supernatural. He also believes that every story I tell him is true, beyond chance, and beyond his ability to explain. I asked him how he squares the two. He says that he does not. He is content to know that what he calls "strange" things happen. He has no need to know why, or to alter his purely materialist worldview. As for me, I want to know why, I want to know how, but I don't. That day of the earthquake, or after any of these "anomalous events," I can only be flummoxed, trying, again, to locate my coordinates in the four-way intersection I appear to occupy between conventional understandings of space and time and the alternate versions of these highways that announce themselves to me most articulately when I forget them.

I'm going to tell you some things I've never told anyone. Events, from long ago, on which I do not focus. These things happened so many decades ago, and they are so unlike anything I've experienced since, that I myself question them. My memories of them are as crisp as any memories I have. By what logic would I doubt them, and not doubt memories of the neighborhood candy stores I patronized in those days? The candy stores left no lasting imprint on my life. These experiences inscribed themselves into me; I strive to live out their truths to this day. I am who I am because of these experiences.

I used to speak at Twelve Step meetings for children who grew up in alcoholic homes. In those settings – surrounded by people who had been beaten and forced to sleep in their drunken parent's vomit and shuffled from foster home to foster home – my fellow survivors asked me how *I* survived, and how I did not become an ax murderer.

When I was a child, at home, I was beaten. I was sexually abused. I was told that I was not wanted, and I was treated that way in every aspect of my life. That I could show up in school, day after day, covered in bruises, unkempt, and that no one ever dare breathe the word "abuse" speaks volumes to me about the courage necessary for, and the vital importance of, calling things by their true names.

I read about people on death row. I read about bad things that happened to them in childhood that, allegedly, explain their committing the heinous crime that placed them on death row. I read of childhoods similar to mine. Often, not as bad as mine. Why am I not on death row?

I had spirit guides. I saw them and I heard them. They arrived in dreams, or while I was walking in the woods, or kneeling before the statue of Mary in an empty church – never a church with people in it. They spoke in unambiguous, English-language sentences I have never forgotten. A teacher about whom I used to dream said, "What is happening to you is not your fault, and it has nothing to do with you. It is wrong. You have what it takes to survive this." Before I fell asleep one night, angels said, "You do have a choice. The choice you make is the most important thing you will ever do. You can choose to be on the side of the right, or the side of the wrong." During a moment of terror so intense I thought the terror alone would shatter me, an unseen presence whispered, "You must have strength in your faith, and faith in your strength." After I heard that, I always knew that what got me through would not be of this material world.

These guides did not rescue me. They did not ease my pain. I suffered from colitis, eczema, migraines, hair loss, and just simple bad health. I despaired. I hated. I failed in school. I had few friends. I screwed up with boys. To the extent that I did survive, I credit the guides – nobody and nothing else.

It all stopped, with abrupt finality, in first grade. I tried to tell the other children that what they were telling us about God in St. Francis School was good, but not the whole story. Word of my schoolyard revivals got back to the nuns and I was forbidden to go out and play at recess. I didn't like that at all. I wanted to be like other kids. The visions stopped, and I was allowed back out to play at recess.

Small potatoes, Rand: a mother whose status as a seeress did not spare her a lifetime of cleaning luckier women's houses; encounters, not with a Cecil B. DeMille God who delivers laws on stone-hewn tablets, but rather with angels who do not deliver me from a childhood hell, and who sporadically provide Hallmark card road signs: is that how you will make fun of me, the way I've seen you make fun of believers like me on international television?

Go for it, Rand. Knock yourself out. All I can tell you is this: not in my childhood did any flesh-and-blood person, any media figure, any magazine or newspaper or school teacher, communicate to me that persons like me have any worth at all. I received audible, coherent messages that defied everything I knew of reality. In a world without choices, I was given a choice, and I put my puny, small-town-girl-in-dirty-clothes life on the line for that choice.

Decades later. I went to Bloomington, Indiana to get a PhD. Shortly after my arrival, the professor for whom I worked harassed me for missing four workdays to attend my father's funeral. I was asked to testify against her; I was told that she was a "sociopath," that she had ruined many, but that the school couldn't touch her, because she was black and female. Since I had "nothing to lose," it was assumed that I'd speak up frankly about her. Throughout my entire second semester at the university, I was summoned to secret meetings with the top officials on campus. I was housed here and there, in university buildings. Without my realizing it at first, the university's lawyers were reading all of my e-mails. All this while I was mourning my father and taking a full credit load of graduate classes. I got straight A's.

Suddenly I was finding it hard to walk down hallways, to see, to keep food down, to hear, eventually to stand, or even to move.

Without my realizing it, my inner ear had burst. Why? Perhaps the stress. Perhaps the tears. For the next six years, I would be relatively functional on some days, and, on other days, sometimes a month at a time, I couldn't move, I could barely see and I vomited constantly.

I lost thirty pounds. I lost my life savings. I lost my friends. I think they would have responded heroically if I'd gotten the diagnosis of a conventional disease, the kind you see on TV – cancer, heart attack, multiple sclerosis – anything with a familiar narrative. But this – crippled, blinded, vomiting, with no certain prognosis, no charity foundation, no celebrity spokesperson: it was too weird, too gross, not terminal enough. "Vestibular disorder": it simply doesn't have the same cachet as "cancer."

I applied for Social Security Disability Income. I was turned down. I went to social service agencies. Staff members informed me how many working poor Americans, like me, died every year before they could get medical care – 26,000. I wrote to everyone, from Oprah Winfrey to Deepak Chopra to Governor Bayh and Senator Lugar. Bayh and Lugar blew me off. Chopra sent me brochures for an ayurvedic resort and spa. For a mere $575 I could attend a weekend retreat. Oprah sent me a mass-produced post card with a mass-produced signature.

I wrote to Indiana State Senator Vi Simpson. State senators have relatively little power. Vi Simpson could have just thrown my letter away. Rick Gudal, Senator Simpson's legislative aid, was not handsome. He was not powerful. He was not rich. He was not young. He espoused no ritzy philosophy. He was the kind of a lumpy, stubbly, Midwestern, hard working, pickup-truck driving, Lithuanian-American who, half asleep and on autopilot, doesn't wake up during an hour commute to work until he quaffs deeply from a Styrofoam cup full of black coffee. With no medical training, no funds, no sanction, Rick took up my case.

Why? I asked one of Rick's colleagues. "It's his nature, his

Catholic upbringing. He'll never give up."

With Rick's urging, a doctor in Indianapolis injected gentamicin into my inner ear. This drug made me completely deaf in that ear, but it also destroyed any remaining vestibular function. Six years of uncontrollable vomiting, crushing vertigo, and nystagmus simply, immediately, ended. No complicated, expensive intervention had been necessary; the biggest cost was the anesthesia. I could read again, all the time, and not wait for "good days" to get my reading and writing, and my dissertation, done. I could walk down hallways. I could look both ways before crossing the street. I could put on weight, and my body started in on that with real enthusiasm. I may never again have the svelte thighs of a chronically ill woman.

Friends reappeared, like seasonal animals whose winter-hibernation had ended. I got a job. I was taken out to dinner. I went to parties. I went on dates. I was, once again, allowed to be a human being among other human beings. Not because I had become a better person. Because, overnight, I had switched from being unfortunate, to being relatively fortunate.

I don't spend a lot of time thinking about those years. There's no point to it. I can say this, though. One night, I was in the thick of the disease. It was right after ... oh, one of the big betrayals in the course of the illness.

My absentee landlady's house was well-situated for solitude: the most distant, affluent suburb in a Midwestern university town. A street only our few neighbors traveled was out front; a train track for twice-daily, eighty-car coal trains ran out back. I was ten minutes' walk from cornfields that stretched as far as the eye could see. In the yard, there were foxes and deer, and tomatoes and cucumbers I was growing – under deer-proof netting – and the occasional killer storm.

It was July. Moths were gathered on the screen. The refrigerator had just kicked on. Rusty, the geriatric dachshund next door, was barking out his hoarse, croaky bark. The crickets and katydids were as mad with vociferous passion as an opera chorus. I could hear the infrequent whoosh of a car approaching, driving past, receding. Somewhere out there, and I was grateful that it was not too close, there was a hint of skunk.

Before this particular attack struck, I had been at the kitchen table, penciling out a "list of things to do": "1.) Re-appeal SSDI case. 2.) Find a food bank." I had had to put the pencil down. The vertigo was overwhelming. I retreated to the couch. I was all balled up in a fetal position, pressing myself into the couch, because complete immobility and physical contact with another surface were the best ways to deal with the crushing vertigo. I would have to do this for days at a time, moving only to relieve myself or vomit, unable to stand something as simple as the stimulus from a TV. I was completely alone. In the depths of these attacks, it was as if I had plumbed the depth of a mine; beyond all distractions like civilization or hope. This night something different happened. Suddenly I felt, as certain as the chair beneath me now, hands on my shoulders.

I'm not the woman to come up behind unannounced. In high school, my more mischievous buddies, a couple of times, sent a new kid up behind me, only to watch me swing around and punch the new kid in the face. This time, though, I didn't have a problem with being touched in this way. The touch conveyed instant bliss. I suddenly felt seen, heard, cared about, embraced, supported, part of the glow that takes in all creatures.

Even as it was happening, I was analyzing it. I asked myself, "Am I imagining this?" I sort of declared, inside my head, "This can't be real." And I waited for it to stop.

Only it didn't stop. It became more insistent, stronger. I felt as if I could lean back, and this presence would uphold me, with love. My "list of things to do" was erased.

I began to become convinced that it, whatever it was, *was* real. I say "whatever" but I never doubted that it had the warmth and individuality of a person. It connected with me as persons do. And I decided that it was supernatural. *Not,* primarily, because of its sudden, soundless manifestation, but because these unseen hands on my shoulders communicated, to me, feelings so unearthly good.

I suspected that the overwhelming love and peace these hands, this presence, were communicating to my body would erase my tasks, amputate my plot, render my worries ridiculous. I'm a workaholic, a compulsive cleaner, a writer. I sort of felt, okay this can stop now. I need to get back to ... whatever it is I need to get back to. Slowly, it began to fade, and eventually, it was just me and the katydids, and the crickets.

Had anything like that palpable touch ever happened to me before? Heck no. Have I, in the years since that night, at lousy moments, hoped that that sensation would return? You bet. Has it? Nothing even close. Did I imagine it? I wasn't trying to. I was trying hard to do something else – erase consciousness of nausea and vertigo.

I'm not telling you this story to get you to believe. This is the point I'm trying to make: I asked for the bliss to stop. Don't get me wrong. I loved it. It was the best feeling I've ever had. But I was ready for it to be over. After I had fully basked in the complete pleasure, I consciously, gratefully, and humbly requested for it to stop. Mind – I had been ready for it to stop after I'd concluded that I thought it was false, and it didn't stop then, it just became stronger. But after I had concluded that it was possibly real, and after I had surrendered to, and enjoyed the sensation, I communicated, "I'm ready for this to stop." And it stopped.

I wanted to get back to even the pettiest, most niggling details of life: my ego, my ridiculous competitions, like whether or not I earned the highest score for my Amazon review of some movie, and the reward we humans get from not knowing the end of the story, from our lives being full of plot twists, a real page-turner. I wanted to gain the strength and mastery and sense of victory we gain from solving our own problems, and not having them solved for us. Yeah, sure, you can get the answers to the crossword puzzle from the paper, but you want to struggle and tease your brain and do what you do by figuring out those answers yourself.

save SEND delete

Wednesday 1:32 p.m.
I knew you'd try to explain it away. I tried to explain it away. The rationalization: that the presence came from within me. It was an elaborate reaction formation. I didn't want to sink into nihilism, and I wanted to cling to my religious faith, so I imagined a loving God. I conjured it out of my wounds and isolation. It was an evolutionary reflex to keep me going through tough times.

Only it wasn't. You know how I know? Because I have imagined a lot to keep myself going through tough times. When I was really sick, I would, in intimate detail, fantasize getting better, baking some cookies, and watching a good movie. I know two things about the imagination: "imagine" is an active verb; it is something we do, and I know what it feels like to "imagine." And you can't imagine something you've never been exposed to. As a kid, and then again when I was sick, I was visited by a love I've never known in life.

This sensation didn't come from a need to retain my faith because I've never had a need to retain my faith. Often this was my prayer: "Jesus, you come back here down to earth and I will crucify you again." Hell offered no terrors to me. I had nothing to lose; I was beyond consequence. I felt no need to imagine myself into Christianity, or even into humanity. I just wanted the vertigo and the vomiting to stop. The illness had stolen millions of years from me; I had been crushed down the evolutionary scale; I had the same agenda as a blind lizard in a cave: to know up from down.

My body was ruined and my mind was a jerking, staticky

series of ugliness and chaos. To that, a presence of pure love made itself felt. Not when I expected it. Not when I asked for it – there were nights when I lay on my mattress crying and shaking till dawn. I have had moments, before and since, where I wish I could, even just for fleeting, cheap comfort, conjure up a caring presence, or a sense of the divine, and I could not.

Rand, you must know these lines from T.S. Eliot's "The Wasteland":

Who is the third who walks always beside you?
When I count, there are only you and I together
But when I look ahead up the white road
There is always another one walking beside you
Gliding wrapt in a brown mantle, hooded
I do not know whether a man or a woman
But who is that on the other side of you?

Eliot's notes reference Shackleton's Antarctic explorers, who, "at the extremity of their strength, had the constant delusion that there was one more member than could actually be counted." Another possible allusion in these lines: two thousand years ago, two distraught men were walking to Emmaus, discussing the recent crucifixion of the man they'd hoped would be the messiah. A third man joined them and entered into their lively debate. He tossed in biblical interpretations of his own. They all sat down to dinner together, and when he blessed the bread, they recognized him as the risen Christ.

save SEND delete

Wednesday, 2:14 p.m.
No, no no no no no no. I mean, come on, Rand. Come on.

If that's all the Judeo-Christian tradition were, rainbows and puppy-dogs, we could all just buy warm blankets and New Age music and vanilla-scented candles and crawl inside our cocoons and eat raw cookie dough. My tradition blasts real life into my face, demands I confront the guts and bones of even the ugliest reality in an uncompromising way.

Listen. Listen. This is the photographic negative of the experience I described, above. This happened first. It was at this moment that I got it that I was "chronically ill" – I'd never applied that term to myself before this day. When I got it that I was going it alone. This was before Rick took up my case. There was no hope of rescue on the horizon.

I was walking parallel to Third Street, across the grassy lawn between St. Charles Borromeo R. C. Church and a strip mall. It was June. It was a period of wellness. I could move and not vomit. As was usually the case during these periods, I was rushing around Bloomington, frantically doing errands, stock-piling groceries, picking up or returning specially ordered library books, in anticipation of the next time I would get sick and not be able to move for days or weeks. I suddenly realized I was helplessly riding an avalanche into hell. Life, just, the condition of being alive, of being, like a blue-green algae, like a gazelle, like Stalin, like a homeless drunk, just a living thing, was something that had slipped from my hands; I had exited; my body, now encased in some special glass, now moved in this zero degree parallel to life. I just, suddenly, did not know how I could keep my body moving across the green lawn. I thought that that was it, for me. I did not have to complete the day's errands; I was, for all intents and purposes, a corpse. At that moment that I hit that awareness that I was already dead, I heard a voice. "I'm not here to argue with you. It is all very bad. Before you succumb under the avalanche, if it is the last thing you do, go to the Borders bookstore in the strip mall, pick up a Bible at random, and read a passage. Go."

I had nothing to lose. The Borders bookstore was on my route. I did think that I would open the Bible to a significant passage. It would be something like "Awake and sing, ye that dwell in dust"

– Isaiah 26:19. It would be the kind of inspiration that would make me want to ram the goddamn Bible down the throat of a televangelist who smiled like a ventriloquist's dummy.

I trudged into the Borders bookstore. When I entered the Bible aisle, I crossed my eyes so that everything would be a big blur, so that I wouldn't pick an edition I knew well, or any predetermined passage. I was trying to follow instructions and be as random as possible. I closed my eyes, waved my hands – the one holding the Bible and the one that would open to a passage – wide apart. Eyes still closed, I ran my finger over the unseen page and stopped it at a place that seemed right. I opened my eyes to see that my index finger had landed on the opening to Psalm 39, a psalm unknown to me. I know it now. Psalm 39 is the lament of a seriously ill person asking God when his life, and his suffering, will end.

> Lord, let me know my end, the number of my days … my life is as nothing before you … Lord, what future do I have … Take your plague away from me; I am ravaged by the touch of your hand … you dissolve all we prize like a cobweb … listen to my prayer, Lord, hear my cry; do not be deaf to my weeping! I sojourn with you like a passing stranger … turn your gaze from me, that I may find peace, before I depart to be no more.

The Bible in my hand cross-referenced this to Psalm 88:

> I am reckoned with those who go down to the pit…
> My couch is among the dead, with the slain who lie in the grave. You remember them no more; they are cut off from your care.
> You plunged me into the bottom of the pit, into the darkness of the abyss.
> Your wrath lies heavy upon me; all your waves crash over me.

Because of you my friends shun me; you make me loathsome
to them; Caged in, I cannot escape...

Do you work wonders for the dead? Do the shades arise and
praise you?

Is your love proclaimed in the grave, your fidelity in the
tomb?

Why do you reject me, Lord? Why hide your face from me?

I am mortally afflicted since youth; lifeless, I suffer your
terrible blows.

Because of you companions shun me; my only friend is
darkness.

Commentators say that of all the psalms, 39 and 88 are unique in
that they lack any positive resolution. No matter what depths the
psalmist traverses, he always ends on good terms with his
creator. Witness the brutal Psalm 22 that begins, "My God, my
God, why have you abandoned me?" but concludes with a declaration of God's righteousness. Not in 39 and 88. They have no
happy ending.

I know your questions; they are mine, and they are more
pressing to me than they could ever be to you. If God could steer
me to a powerful poem that stated *exactly* the horror I was
living – right down to the waves, my metaphor for how it felt
when the vertigo came over me – why oh why didn't he just,
simply, heal me? I don't know the answer to that. This is what I
know: I heard acres of words during those years. I lived those
years on a major university campus. I heard many words from
PhDs: "The power of positive thinking; Think yourself well; Eat
wheat grass; Go organic; Stop trying to get a PhD; Read this book
by Louise Hay; Live in a house without formaldehyde; Those
cold, greedy, bastard Republicans; Those lying, conniving,
bastard Democrats; Lousy America; Lousy doctors; Lousy luck;
Lousy karma; Fill out this form; Check off these answers; Are you
dizzier in the morning or at night? Can you hear this high-

pitched tinkle? Can you hear this low-pitched moan? Do you vomit immediately after eating or does it take several hours?"

In all those years of illness, in all the years since, that moment was the first, last, and only time that anyone spoke the truth to me about what I was going through. Those two psalms told, not some proximate truth that I interpreted to fit my situation in the recent past or distant future; they told the *exact* truth of what I was experiencing at the exact moment that I heard the voice telling me to go to Borders. Standing in that Borders bookstore, at the behest of a disembodied voice, was the first, last, and only time anyone confirmed to me what was happening to me. First. Last. Only.

I wrote about this experience in my diary right after it happened. The entry shocks me. "Someone is aware of the hell I've been going through. Ever since then I have felt, maybe I can make it. Even if I can't, that's okay. I have felt a certain peace. I think everything is going to be okay. And that doesn't mean anything except I feel in the presence of God." I ask myself why I was willing to let God off the hook so easily. He did not meet my demands. What I most craved was to be healed. I was not.

Perhaps this is one answer: Being heard was as astounding as being healed. A cure could be interpreted as the result of blind chance, skilled surgery, powerful pharmaceuticals or impersonal time. Only a heart, only a soul, only one who loves hears. That moment was one of those moments I've told you about, when I am one hundred percent certain that there is a God, and that he is in intimate contact with me, contact more intimate than my own breath. I wasn't cured. I was *known.*

save SEND delete

Wednesday, 9:02 p.m.
Yeah, but, you know that that is not true. You know it's not just me, and you know it's not just people like me.

I heard this story in Nepal, a quarter of a century ago, and I've never forgotten it. I just Googled and e-mailed the man who told it to me, whom I have not seen since. I asked if I could share his story with you. He said yes, but he didn't want his name used; at his request, I'll call him "Lamjung," the district where he worked. Back in Peace Corps days, even behind his days' old beard and the rags and fleas that we all wore as a uniform, Lamjung was unmistakable as a scientist. He was one of those people who divides reality up into discrete units and analyzes them with dispassion. He missed the points of jokes and right-brained people like myself. His identity as a scientist did not protect him from the numinous.

Here is the story Lamjung told me twenty-five years ago, and that he just told me again in an e-mail. This happened about thirty years ago, on the campus of a US research university.

I was a cartographer. My work combined visual creativity with careful measurement and the mathematics of perspective, scale and proportion. I also did classified work for the defense industry, in the construction and design of nuclear facilities. I was doing well financially. I owned a sports car. I was teaching cartography at a major US university, where a great deal of my time was taken up by my study, research and instructional requirements. I was seldom at home and had grown somewhat distant from my wife and son. I did not take as much of an active participation in daily family activities as I should have, and was very much wrapped up in my own personal concerns.

One night, as the last lights on campus were going out and I was headed to my office, to shut down my work activities for the day, I had the sudden and overwhelming sensation come over me, that something was about to occur that was very significant – life-changing, in a traumatic sort of way.

At that moment I looked at my wristwatch and now recall having mentally attempted to halt the sweep of the second hand – to halt the advance of time itself, were such a thing even possible. How long this sensation lasted, I cannot now recall. At that period in my life I had very little comprehension of altered states of consciousness, or of ineffable experience – epiphanies, etc. It did not then occur to me that my perceptions and internal reflections might account for the unusual sensations and feeling of trauma.

Whether from an external source, or from my own internal perceptions (I know not which, if not both) – I now recall the very strong impression that the world around me had suddenly, fundamentally changed. "Something overwhelming is happening," was my reflective response, as the experience began to fade a little.

Perhaps there was an audible voice – or perhaps it was only the very unusual coincidence of my own imagination – but "Something overwhelming has happened," echoed in my ear, as I entered the building where my office was located, and made my way to the door. The phone was ringing – an unusual thing for that late at night. I finally got around to answering the repeated ringing, and found that it was my nearly estranged wife on the other end of the line, informing me that our son had died a few minutes before.

This was the closest I've personally come to a paranormal experience. I had not previously felt much interest in the supernatural or the paranormal. I tended to be a pious skeptic.

This event was a life-altering occurrence – at the most basic level of my being – at the most basic level of my interconnection with others. It was the first event in a series of circumstances which eventually brought me to the most significant spiritual realizations in my life. It increased my honesty, sense of wonder, and willingness to be open and to listen to others.

"Why should I believe these stories?" you may be thinking. Rand, these stories are not for sale. I don't tell them to convince you. This is yet another reason why I don't proselytize. These are my stories, and these are why I know that there is more to life than the material.

I'm telling you these stories partly for myself. When I write to you, Rand, I imagine you here, sitting in the chair next to my desk. I measure every detail of my narratives against your metrics of mathematical probability, psychological necessity, and verifiable veridicality. In recounting my tales to you, I retest them for myself; I attempt to plumb their depths. Casting my stories into the ruthless, desert wilderness of your ear is my latest pilgrimage.

Rand, you may be right. Maybe there is a very basic mathematical equation that explains away the stories I've told you here. If that is indeed the case, I'm much worse at math than I thought.

save SEND delete

INBOX
plz frwrd attchd flr ...

"'Shamlet' is a Shmash! Amanda Clitheroe and her band of merry players bring colors and dimensions to the greatest play ever written that would astound the Bard himself!"

"Who would have thunk it? Hamlet as a black woman played by a white actress. Amanda Clitheroe, that's who, and Prince Hal will never be the same."

"Clitheroe's delivery of Shamlet's 'To Be or Not To Be, Mothafucka,' soliloquy is a theatrical tour de force."

Tickets on sale at the box office or through Ticketmaster.

---

otherwise pumpkin how art thou?

Thursday 2:02 p.m.
Shamlet?

save **SEND** delete

INBOX
focus group tested "thelma" … anagram of "hamlet" …
unwashed masses did not get it

Thursday 2:16 p.m.
I hear that Ophelia is being played by a Tupac Shakur lookalike.

save **SEND** delete

INBOX
standing ovations last night … not dropping any names but
oliver stone was in attendance … could "shamlet" make it to
hollywood???

Thursday2:23 p.m.
I don't see why not.

save **SEND** delete

INBOX
how goes it with your atheist?

Thursday 2:25 p.m.
Fine. Everything is fine.

save **SEND** delete

INBOX
the sex is fine?

Thursday 2:29 p.m.
We're not having sex.

save **SEND** delete

INBOX
for now it is only verbal?

Thursday 2:41 p.m.
No, we aren't having sex verbally. I've been very chaste. There was an outbreak of … banter, but that was all on his part, in response to my mistakenly mentioning a crush I'd had on a kid named Justin. I wasn't even trying to be provocative. I was attempting to be scathingly self-exposing. I ain't no blessed Virgin.

save SEND delete

INBOX
a woman cannot be honest without being provocative … describe banter outbreak plz … should i get myself vaccinated … will outbreak reach left coast?

Thursday 2:45 p.m.
Nah. It's passed. He got all competitive, as men do. So, he sez, Justin was so handsome. How can he *measure up*? Wink, wink, nudge, nudge. Why do they think it's all about meat? Men are so materialistic.

See, Amanda? I can talk about this with you and not expect a sexually competitive e-mail in return. Because you are a woman, and you acknowledge the existence of the soul.

save SEND delete

INBOX
i don't want 2 have sex with u

Thursday 2:50 p.m.
He doesn't want to have sex with me. No sign of that. He wasn't so much bantering with me, as locking horns with Justin. I was just there on the sidelines, with the rest of the does, hanging out

146

at the salt lick, gossiping about what a tramp Bambi's mother is.

save **SEND** delete

INBOX

if a man is spending his free time with a woman he wants to have sex with her ... no chance of sex or sex has already happened ... he moves on ...

Thursday 2:55 p.m.

Is that true? All the time? Have we really not moved past high school? What does that say about the chance of a genuinely spiritual conversation between a man and a woman?

save **SEND** delete

INBOX

have been on my own since i was sixteen ... one insight has stood me in good stead ... with men all life is a high school cafeteria and i am on the menu ... need to keep my wits about me & keep them off balance & never forget who the grown-up is ... and never forget my game plan ... i offer these gifts to you mira ... gotta go matinee

Thursday 3:01 p.m.

Break a leg!

save **SEND** delete

Friday 6:02 a.m.

Dear Rand

save send **DELETE**

Friday 6:07 a.m.

Rand

save send **DELETE**

Friday 6:11 a.m.
Dear Lord Randolph Court-Wright, Marquis of Alnwick
save send DELETE

Friday 6:15 a.m.
Amanda,
I hate Them. I hate Them all.
save SEND delete

Friday 11:04 a.m.
Dear Rand
Forget it. Just, forget it.
save send DELETE

INBOX
wwbwd?

Friday noon
Amanda,
Even before my conscious mind understood your message, I broke into tears. My soul immediately grokked "wwbwd?" "What would Bill W. do?"

You understood, Amanda, from the slim clues in my last e-mail, that I was writing you about a Twelve Step issue.
save SEND delete

INBOX
is nine a.m. here in people's republic of berkeley the sole significant site of consciousness remaining in the inhabited biosphere outside of stonehenge on summer solstice sedona after tourist season and the burning man festival before the ecstasy addicts show up ... was checking e-mail first thing this morning ... considering a money-spinner script that has dropped into my lap ... district attorney in the latest batman

... once met christian bale on a fox hunt ... he is british you see in spite of convincing gotham city accent ... advised juice fasts to him as he seesaws between skeletal / buff roles ...

yes miroswava hudak yes i know ... small t "them" like last time equals men ... capital T "Them" equals civilians

u & i did meet at a twelve step meeting after all

what did the scoundrel do? do not be kind show no mercy take no prisoners ... i'm in no mood for Them myself right now ... why have some civilians been born to families easy and smooth while we friends-of-bill live our entire lives executing every stunt prima ballerinas do but with our minds and souls and on the edge of an abyss They don't even see?

Friday 6:06 p.m.

Yes, Rand, I received your reply. No, I was not planning on sending a response. In your most recent e-mail, you directly requested a response, so here it is.

You importuned me – and this is one of those moments when the fusty word "importune" is entirely appropriate – you importuned me to tell you why I could never be an atheist.

I complied with your request. I told you why I could never be an atheist.

Your response addressed none of my points.

You changed the subject. You changed the tone of the conversation. You changed the rules.

save **SEND** delete

INBOX

r u getting enough chocolate ... just checking ... shall i dial 911 and send in the emergency medical theobromine technicians ... it IS the food of the gods ... or should i not mention god/s ...

Friday 6:32 p.m.

Well? Will you do the new "Batman" movie?

save SEND delete

INBOX

no need pumpkin-ette no need to pretend you are interested in my stuff ... anyway yes i shall ... see myself more as catwoman than district attorney ... o well can't have everything ... am definitely past the babe phase of an actress's career ... at least i'm not yet in "driving ms daisy" phase ... so tell me how goes it with the civilian?

Friday 6:59 p.m.

How does it ever go with civilians? People who have never had to camouflage a bleeding wound underneath their work clothes.

We can only ever fake it around them, because the second we say anything real, they write us off as crazy. They control the press. They control the dictionary. They define us.

People like you and me, Amanda, meet in our little Twelve Step meetings in church basements and only there can our story be told.

I'll never forget the first time I met you. It was the Adult Children of Alcoholics Twelve Step meeting in the basement of Berkeley's All Souls Episcopal Church.

This Goddess sashayed into the room. I was certain that she must be lost; no way *she* belonged at a Twelve Step meeting. We Friends-of-Bill repeat this over and over again, but it never sinks in: "Do Not Judge Your Insides By Other People's Outsides." This woman's outsides had stepped from the pages of Vogue. Her long hair was so thick you could moor a ship with those night-colored strands.

You were the speaker. Your parents were Hollywood; they had money, but it was all the same. They were drunks; they raised you to be insecure; they toyed with you, terrified you. You left home at 16, but you took home with you: the bad relationships; the insecurity about your art; the long struggle to become a successful actress. Finally, you came to Twelve Step, in designer clothes, clothes designed expressly for bodies like yours. Our rooms were full of reformed drunks, the battered and the batterers, and losers like me. There were no professional "therapists" – no Jungians, no Freudians, no psychoactive compounds, legal or ill. All we had was this slim promise: "Came to believe that a Power greater than ourselves could restore us to sanity," and this no-frills discipline: "Made a decision to turn our will and our lives over to the care of God as we understood God." And it was all free. Yet you found a healing in the rooms that had eluded you in pricier and more rarified celebrity health spas. We were all in this together: "together we can do what we could never do alone."

I committed myself to you that night, Amanda. It was partly your beauty. You taught me that being a woman as beautiful as I am ugly can be its own burden. Before you ever knew I existed, I walked forward, out of the shadows in the back of the room, and very self-consciously thrust out my hand, took yours, and shook it vigorously. "Hi, my name is Miroswava Hudak, and I just want you to know that whatever happens, from here on out, I am on your side." I could see it, beyond your sheen and sophistication, even beyond your fear, you didn't just shine, you glowed. And we two very different women became friends.

You are my family. The rest? Civilians.

save **SEND** delete

Saturday 5:04 a.m.
Dear Rand,
I do not want your pity.

save **SEND** delete

Saturday 5:30 a.m.

Dear Rand,

That's a mere technicality.

And you still have not responded to any of my arguments for a reality transcendent of the material.

save SEND delete

Saturday 5:47 a.m.

Dear Rand,

I hear your frustration.

I'm up this early – it's early here – to get to Corrado's produce market before the jostling, multilingual throngs have absconded with the last of today's shipment of blemish-free, cheap, red bell peppers.

Rand, give me a day. Give me a day to think about why you assess that e-mail as so beneficent, and why I found it so cringe-inducing.

I was really touched by the frustration in this, your most recent note. Your frustration tells me that maybe you wrote that e-mail differently than how I read it. Or maybe you are reading me differently than who I am. Or I you.

Let's keep talking.

Give me a day.

I'll get back to you.

Meanwhile ... xxx ooo xxx. Do they have that system of shorthand in England?

save SEND delete

Sunday noon

Oh – What you just wrote is so incredibly touching.

Listen, are you sure that you are a world class scientist? Are you sure that you are not a poet? You'd have to be a starving poet – you're *that* good.

Reading what you just wrote makes me see everything we've

said to each other over the past few days totally differently.

I understand, now, how troubled you were to read, not so much of the abuse in my childhood, but that no bystanders intervened. You didn't want to be one of those "sinners by omission" – quite the phrase from my atheist friend. No matter how late it came, you wanted me to know that someone saw, really saw, and objected, and held out a hand.

That's a sonnet you wrote there, Rand.

You humble me. I'm in awe of you.

I'm so glad you let me know that you weren't pitying me – that's what I suspected and what drove me away. But – and this isn't a "but" in the sense that it cancels out anything you said, because it does not – I was that person, once. I was someone who was waiting and hoping for someone to see, and to intervene. To, at the bare minimum, call things by their true names. I waited and I hoped for a long time. If for no other reason, I wanted someone to make me feel okay about being a human being among other human beings. I didn't want the condition to feel so damn smarmy.

When it didn't happen, that part of me iced over. It's gone, Rand. I'm no longer someone who sits around waiting, needing or wanting my fellow human beings ... even to be.

But, anyway, yes, I'd love to talk at seven my time, midnight yours. I'll be right next to the phone. I'll lift the receiver in the middle of your first ring.

save **SEND** delete

Sunday 3:07 p.m.

Dear Rand,

I know we're going to be talking in a few hours, but I keep thinking about that e-mail you sent me this morning.

Rand, are you such a scabrous asshole on TV, not because you *are* a scabrous asshole, but because you are truly a tender heart? Of epic proportions? Kind, feeling, easily moved, easily hurt? Is it a coconut husk kind of thing? The harder the outside, the sweeter the inside?

And does this have anything to do with ... well, with ... God? When God let you down, he really let you down, and you don't want, no matter the promise of rewards no matter how sublime, to risk contact with the God, in whom you once believed? Because no matter how good reunion could possibly be, the disappointment with which you are already excruciatingly familiar overwhelms, indeed poisons, any potential heaven you could possibly imagine?

But how did God let you down, Rand? We've been talking a lot and you've never so much as alluded to that kind of hurt ...?

Am I treading close to your boundaries here? Should it wait for me to say something like this? Or is saying something like this the next step?

SAVE send delete

Sunday 3:19 p.m.

SAVE send delete

Sunday 3:28 p.m.

SAVE send delete

Sunday 3:40 p.m.

SAVE send delete

Sunday 5:01 p.m.

save send DELETE

INBOX
well?

Saturday 10:02 a.m.

He and I have talked on the phone every night this week.

save **SEND** delete

INBOX

good?

Saturday 10:19 a.m.

Scary.

save **SEND** delete

INBOX

do i have to pull your teeth

Saturday 10:45 a.m.

Oh, come on, you know what I'm thinking.

save **SEND** delete

INBOX

just for fun go ahead and spell it out for me … like annie sullivan spilling letters into helen keller's palm … we aren't all psychic children of psychic transylvanian moms

Saturday 11:09 a.m.

He has a wife. He has a wife, Amanda. And one of these days he is going to bring her up in an e-mail, and share how happy they are together, and that he gets issued, unlike the rest of us, twenty-nine hours in a day, which is why he can spend so many hours writing e-mails to me, even though he has a wife. He has a wife. He has a wife.

save **SEND** delete

Friday noon
Dear Rand,
It's nice to *read* you again. It's been a while! But I love how what
we say to each other in phone conversations differs from what we
say in e-mails.

Listen, Rand. I have a request for you.

Convince me that there is no God.

save **SEND** delete

Friday 12:47 p.m.
Nope, not kidding; nope, not speaking in code; nope, no ulterior
anything. Just what the message said.

save **SEND** delete

Friday 1:01 p.m.
Yeah, I do. I do have a reason.

save **SEND** delete

Friday 7:03 p.m.
How about this. How about, first, you convince me that there is
no God, or at least try, and then I tell you why I asked?

save **SEND** delete

Sunday 9:00 a.m.
Dear Rand,
Well, to be honest, I didn't want to say anything. Because I did
ask you to do this. But I think that that is a fairly weak argument.
Please don't be offended. You were only acceding to my request,
and I appreciate that. But it just doesn't rock my world.

Please don't be mad at me.

save **SEND** delete

Sunday 9:15 a.m.

Oh, come on. I mean, really. Seriously?

save **SEND** delete

Sunday 10:04 a.m.

That's not fair. You're the professional atheist! You make your living doing this! You're supposed to have the bulletproof arguments! And *that* is the best you can do?

save **SEND** delete

Sunday 10:17 a.m.

I most certainly could. With one hand tied behind my back.

save **SEND** delete

Sunday 10:31 a.m.

Yeah, but I'm not a professional like you. I haven't written books on this topic. It's not like I can – oh, merde. Oh, all right. Give me some time. I'll go for a walk and … or maybe not. Let me at least go take a shower, and I'll come back, and I'll do my feeble best to refute you.

Although I don't know why. Cuz I asked *you* to convince *me.*

Sheesh.

Woman's work is never done.

save **SEND** delete

Sunday noon

Dear Rand,

No more splashing around in the kiddy end of the pool, eh? Shall I do what my students do when they are tackling a big theme? Announce my gravitas by typing "Theodicy: The Problem of Suffering and God" in the center of the page, in a fancy font, in italics, AND boldface AND underscore AND ALL CAPITAL LETTERS?

Since I'm Catholic, let me immediately make something clear. I am not a member of the church of the cilice. In fact, I don't even know how to pronounce "cilice." It's one of those words that I've only seen in print, never spoken or heard. I encountered it in Dan Brown's "Da Vinci Code." Opus Dei is a Catholic cult listing 87,000 members, worldwide. Its members wear cilices, spiked metal belts, on their thighs, under their clothing, for two hours a day, in order to cause themselves pain. Josemaria Escriva, the founder of Opus Dei, said, "Blessed be pain," and "It is so beautiful to be a victim!" These are the kinds of Catholics who give Catholicism a bad name. To damage oneself only for the sake of damaging oneself is masochism.

You'd have to be blind to miss the strain of masochism in Catholic art. The prime examples are found in the Baroque. But Catholic art from the Gothic is very different. Rand, are you near a computer? What an idiotic question! Of course you are. Do a Google image search and have a look at "The Crucifixion," painted around 1400, by the anonymous Master of the Berswordt Altar. Most Gothic artists were anonymous. We don't know who created those magnificent cathedrals. Their art was not about earthly glory, including personal fame. In lieu of a personal name, we call this artist, "Master of the Berswordt Altar."

Jesus hangs on the cross in the Berswordt altar. Jesus' arms and legs, his torso, and the placement of his head on his neck are all slack. As far as his muscles go, Jesus could be napping. He does not assume a dramatic posture that highlights his wrenching anguish, the deviousness of Roman torture, or the painter's mastery at capturing agony in an eye-popping, dynamic pose. Jesus' limbs are straight and unmuscled; you could not teach an anatomy lesson from this depiction of the human form. You could have taught such a lesson from Classical Pagan sculpture; in Christendom, you have to wait for the Renaissance to be able to do that again. But this is 1400, when Jesus' naked flesh glows pale, like the wax wall of a white candle cupping a subtle flame. Though Jesus is on the cross, his mouth is not open in a howl, or grimacing in pain. His eyes reflect no torment. Rather, the crucified Christ's facial expression is that of a kindly priest who has just heard a not-very-funny joke from a second grader; he doesn't want to give offence by not laughing, or by laughing in the wrong way. Mary, at the foot of the cross, is plainly unhappy, but not, from her facial expression, because her son is crucified; rather, she's upset because, try as she might, she can't remember where she left her keys.

This painting is not the product of a Baroque, masochistic Catholicism, but, rather, one from centuries earlier, one focused on the spiritual, and on transcendence. If you would fault it for anything, you would fault it for being too ethereal, too divorced from concrete reality. My guess is that peasants who prayed before this altar had their fill of concrete reality, from the bedbugs that bit them as they slept to the manure they trod through to milking their masters' cows before morning mass. A little transcendence was probably a very much appreciated quality circa 1400 A.D.

From six hundred years ago, the anonymous Berswordt Master assures me, "Yeah, the world is a pretty tough neighborhood – you got that much right. The best man who ever lived is hanging on a cross, after all. But let not your heart be troubled. The light shines on in the darkness, and the darkness has not overcome it. Have a nice day, dear one. Don't go away without a smile. All this shit surrounds us, but we are so much more."

Compare the gentle, ethereal affection of Gothic art to Il Sodoma's 1525 painting, "Martyrdom of St. Sebastian." In the third century, Roman emperor Diocletian was persecuting Christians. Sebastian was a captain in the elite Praetorian Guard. Given that he was a captain, he had to have been a man of some years, and he is depicted as a graybeard in the earliest mosaic. When Emperor Diocletian discovered that Sebastian was a Christian, he ordered his execution. Sebastian was shot until his body was "as full of arrows as a sea urchin is full of spines"; then the Romans clubbed him. His mangled corpse was deposited in an outhouse. A painting depicting Sebastian's true martyrdom would be grim beyond aesthetics.

Giovanni Antonio Bazzi was a bad-boy Renaissance painter who lived more than a millennium after Sebastian. Bazzi embraced his nickname, "Il Sodoma," "The Sodomite." Il Sodoma's Sebastian is a pouty-lipped, naked hunk of a boy, twenty years younger than the Sebastian of the story. He is lashed to a tree, and writhing against it, tilting forward from the waist, assuming the position for the act referenced in Il Sodoma's nickname. Two arrows penetrate Sebastian, but they are nothing more than fashion accessories. Plainly, he is eager to be penetrated again.

Masochists, in and out of the church, with or without church sanction, would produce many such works of art perverting and exploiting St. Sebastian's, and other Christians', martyrdoms. They had plenty of material. Pagans were not just ruthless, but also inventive. Nero illuminated garden parties by dipping Christians in tar, lashing them to poles, and setting them on fire. He had Christians sewn into leather bags and doused with water. As the bags dried, they shrank, and squeezed the Christians inside to death. However you feel about masochism as a kink, to me Il Sodoma's painting, and others like it, are comparable to turning the Holocaust, or slavery, or child abuse into porn. And, yes, people do those things, too. One of the odder aspects of suffering is that it can always serve as someone else's entertainment.

For every ogling eye sweeping over a similarly masochistic and well-muscled martyrdom, there are many more Christian masterpieces that say something about suffering that all humans, of any faith, need to hear. My favorite of all time is Caravaggio's 1601 painting, "Conversion of St. Paul." Saul was on his way to Damascus to rout Christians and drag them to Jerusalem in chains, where Saul could stone them to death. A bright light knocked Saul to the ground; a voice cried, "Saul, Saul, why are you persecuting me? I am Jesus, whom you are persecuting. Now get up." Saul did get up. He became Paul, the second most important figure in the founding of the church. Paul's conversion on the road to Damascus changed the course of history.

Thanks to his conversion, Paul would himself be martyred by Nero. Paul's companion, Peter, was crucified upside-down. Paul, a citizen of Rome, was exempt by law from crucifixion – what Cicero called the "servitutis extremum summumque supplicium," the "extreme and ultimate punishment of slaves." Paul was merely beheaded.

How does Caravaggio choose to depict Paul's earth-shattering conversion? If you could turn the painting upside down, your focus would be the eerie light of the supernatural, Paul appearing to levitate, weightlessly, on that light, and the look of the time-out-of-time on Paul's overwhelmed face as he, a mortal, confronts God. But if you look at the painting as we normally do, head-on, Paul is foreshortened, rumpled on the ground, nothing more than something you might trip over, like a piece of recalcitrant carpeting. The focus is the horse, and the horse is nothing special – sway-backed and dun colored, it looks as dumb as – a horse, and it assumes no heroic pose that dramatically highlights its musculature. An anonymous, barefoot old man, with sturdy calves, supremely humble, grabs the horse's reins, perhaps to protect Paul. Is this dutiful peasant Christ in disguise? Is he thinking, "I wanted the clumsy oaf to found Christianity, not be trampled by his horse. C'mon, Paul, get a grip." Even as Paul is talking to the risen Christ, life goes on. We all are, our fascinating narratives notwithstanding, mere footnotes.

"Conversion of St. Paul" is one Catholic expression of the Zen proverb, "Chop wood, carry water." Zen Buddhists say, "What do you do before you become enlightened? You chop wood and you carry water." Chopping firewood and carrying water are, of course, two never-ending tasks of peasant societies. "What do you do after you become enlightened? You chop wood. You carry water." Reaching the spiritual heights does not exempt you from the sheer plod of day-to-day life. The greatest saint, even after he has achieved enlightenment, even after he has conversed with God, must still perform the most humble of tasks, tasks everyone, the enlightened and those not so lucky, must perform: chopping wood, carrying water, and avoiding getting stepped on, or pooped on, by a horse.

"Christ Crucified Between Two Thieves: The Three Crosses: Fourth State" is a 1653 Rembrandt etching, made during the usually flamboyant Baroque era. It is as unassuming as a black-and-white news photo, and as quiet and as spiritually right as a prayer. There are no gleaming, naked musculature, no prettified youths, no blood. You make out a rocky outcropping, three men on crosses, a crowd, its jostling, and, utterly shocking in this hell – assertive light. Rembrandt's "Christ Crucified" pulls me in. It demands – it absorbs – my time. I "hear" it. I don't "hear" other paintings. I gaze at the scene, very spare in details, not at all naturalistic, and I enter it. I hear the awful silence, interspersed, intermittently, with muffled sobs, cruel taunts, triumphal snarls emerging from imperial trumpets and lips, the buzzing of flies. Then, again, I hear, and I feel, like the weight of an anvil, the silence. The awful silence. It is the light in this etching that declares that suffering, as profound as it is, and it is profound, exists to be overcome. Rembrandt included just enough – and that is not much – of the cruddy, earthly details of a crucifixion to communicate how in his crucifixion, even for those who torture-murdered him, Christ achieved transcendence. I have to believe that if you presented this etching to a thoughtful person from a distant culture who had never heard of Jesus, he would under-stand that something very big was happening here, and he would want to discover what that something was.

Though I am not a member of the covens that sacralize

masochism, I do adhere to the same creed as Buddha, in this, his first noble truth: "All life is suffering." I recognize the same truth as M. Scott Peck, who opened "The Road Less Traveled," a record-breaking bestseller, with the sentence, "Life is difficult." I am especially fascinated by Mary's statement to Bernadette Soubirous, the peasant girl to whom Mary appeared in Lourdes, France, in 1858. "I do not promise to make you happy in this world, but in the next." If you decide to avoid all suffering, you don't want God, you want heroin. If you think you or anyone else can make suffering disappear with the power of your positive thoughts, you don't want God; you want to hand $14.37 – today's Amazon paperback price – over to the author of the latest bestseller to peddle that shameless, shopworn drug.

"I do not promise to make you happy in this world, but in the next": Mary's statement to Bernadette haunts me. Mary could have given sickly, dirty, illiterate Bernadette, who had had cholera, asthma, and would die of tuberculosis, Bernadette, who lived in a one-room hovel with her parents and five siblings – Mary could have promised her, what – heck – indoor plumbing. Enough food to fill Bernadette's little stomach. But what was Bernadette's reward for having face-to-face conversations with the Immaculate Conception, the Theotokos, the mother of God? Bernadette was mocked, criticized, poked, prodded, given the Third Degree, by mayors, lawyers, doctors, and priests. They treated her no better than they would have treated an accused witch. Finally Bernadette was wrenched from her family and packed off crying, to a convent. There the Mistress of Novices, Mother Marie-Therese Vauzou, scorned and doubted her little, lumpen seeress. Even so, Vauzou trotted Bernadette out to meet important visitors to the convent. Bernadette was a fund-raising cash cow. Bernadette's fellow nuns circled, as if she were a freak, either worshipping or pestering her. Both approaches probably tormented the lonely Bernadette. One clergyman's prank: a bishop bent low over the ill Bernadette's bed, just so that his skullcap would fall on it, and she would have to hand it back to him. Bingo! He just scored a priceless relic! Bernadette couldn't even mend her underwear without relic-hunters grabbing her clipped threads. She died a long, slow, painful death, at 35, of tuberculosis of the bone.

There is one element in Bernadette's fantastic account that I find it hard to dismiss. I am skeptical of her brief, eighteen visions, over the course of six months in 1858, of a "beautiful lady." It is her final thirteen years that confound me. Declared a living saint, she had the world on a string. Bernadette could have told Vauzou to go sanctify herself. She could have set herself up as her own money-spinning traveling show. She could have been powerful. She could have been rich. She endured Vauzou's malice. She lived a humble, miserable existence, and was devout until the very end. If Bernadette were just a con artist, or crazy, how do you make sense of those years? For the sake of argument, let's say that Bernadette *did* see Mary. Why could Mary not give Bernadette any happiness in this world?

Or take David Prueitt, a 42 year old Oregonian logger who was dying of lung cancer. In January, 2005, under Oregon's Death with Dignity Act, Prueitt's doctor prescribed a lethal dose of Seconal: one hundred capsules. Newspaper accounts report that Prueitt swallowed the entire dose, but woke up three days later. His wife, Lynda, says, "He told me that he was in the presence of God. He told me that the bright lights and everything around him was so beautiful, that there were no words to describe it." God allegedly told Prueitt that suicide was not the way to heaven, and that he had to live until he died a natural death. Lynda says that Prueitt commissioned her to tell others this. She is in favor of Oregon's Death with Dignity Act – she's not telling this story to change the law.

Prueitt had so very little time to live. Did God urge Prueitt back into his body with the promise that he had a mission to fulfill? Prueitt wasn't going to perform any of the feats we associate with a word so grand as "mission." He wasn't going to create a work of art, invent electricity, discover a cure for cancer, or father a child. Prueitt's life until his death was guaranteed to be suffering – and zero "accomplishment," as we understand "accomplishment." He died sixteen days after taking the Seconal. If the Prueitt story is accurate, God returned a virtually dead man to a rotten body – Prueitt had shrunk to less than one hundred pounds from a formerly two-hundred pound lumberjack's frame; Prueitt was so weak he needed assistance to sip juice. God insisted that the disposition of Prueitt's eternal soul depended on Prueitt's lying in bed in pain for sixteen days. Pain not just for Prueitt, but for his wife and family. WTF?

Perhaps this is TF: We Catholics are wary of being labeled masochists, of wallowing in suffering for suffering's sake. Some Catholics do: the cilice crowd, the fans of St. Sebastian. When Catholics are asked in this twenty-first century about suffering, we tend to take an antiseptic, addition-subtraction, logical approach: In order to enjoy free will, you must have suffering. God did not invent suffering for its own sake, but it is an unavoidable byproduct of what we most value: the freedom that is the sine qua non of our identities.

Bernadette's tuberculosis, or Dave Prueitt's chat with the Supreme Being, invite us back to an ancient concept we secular moderns would just as soon jettison as being too dangerous for contemplation: suffering for suffering's sake. Am I a believer? If Bernadette were here, I'd give her the Third Degree. Ditto Dave Prueitt. Even if I could find no evidence to repudiate their accounts, I don't know how to cozy up to a God, or to a universe, that demands suffering for suffering's sake.

On the other hand, I don't believe in a God who, the moment you cast your lot in with him, or read that bestseller about the power of positive thoughts, makes you happy, pretty, and rich. I do believe that there is a supernatural entity who can make you feel 100 % better instantaneously, and his name is Satan. Feeling angry? Smash in someone's face. In pain? Inject heroin. Poor? Steal. All sins provide quite the rush. Nine out of ten hedonists and ten out of ten cowards recommend Satan as their deity of choice.

I've got to take a break here, not because I'm running out of things to say, but because about ten thousand things are pressing against my fingertips, begging to be typed. This is kind of scary. I never realized I had so much to ask, by way of attempting to assert, about suffering.

So, Rand, rate what I've written so far, on a scale of one to ten, one meaning you are going to quote it extensively in your next book as evidence of faulty logic, and ten meaning you now acknowledge the existence of God and see no alternative but to return to the Carthusians, which would mean of course that I shouldn't expect any replies, because Carthusians aren't allowed to talk to gurlz.

save SEND delete

Sunday 9:59 p.m.
Manda, you there?

save SEND delete

INBOX
kinda ... pesto calls ... aren't you usually asleep at this hour?

Sunday 10:12 p.m.
I'd never want to stand between a Berkeleyite and her pesto.

save SEND delete

Monday 3:59 p.m.
Rand,
I need to talk to you about something.

save SEND delete

Monday 4:04 p.m.

Gosh, that was fast.

Look, Rand, we've kind of built up a rhythm here. We have a way of talking to each other. Which, I guess, constitutes our relationship.

I want to talk about something that is different than what we've talked about so far, and I want to talk about that something in a different way...

Rand, suppose I were to tell you, for no other reason, but just to tell you, that I am afraid of thunderstorms? And that we were having a big one, here, right now? And, I wanted you to respond to me, not as a debater, not with a masterful science lecture demonstrating that fear of thunderstorms is irrational, but suppose I wanted you to respond the way you would if we were both in the same room, and the thick, black mammatus clouds were prowling across the sky, and mugging the sun, and the very air were bruising into a sickly green shade, and the electricity snapped off, and the thunder crackled, and, whimpering, I bugged out my eyes and stared at the sky as if it were about to crash onto the roof?

save SEND delete

Monday 4:30 p.m.

Oh my God you are so sweet you are a human puppy in the Halloween costume of a rational scientist no wonder I adore you.

save send DELETE

Monday 4:37 p.m.

Dear Rand,

I never used to be – till I lived in Indiana. Indiana is in the Midwest, the cauldron weather goes to when it wants to boil over and frighten mere mortals. But I'm weirdly addicted to them, too. The tornado siren would go off and I'd not be able to tear myself away. I'd stand out there watching aluminum siding and roofing tiles skitter down the street and the transformer boxes bursting into flames.

Rand. I'm afraid. I'm afraid of religion, Rand. And that I can state that to you plainly, now, means something really wonderful has happened between us. Way back when it all started, I never would have had admitted that to you. I would just assume that you'd steamroll me, "Of course you are! Religion is evil!" But now I have faith that you will let me talk about all the nuances chasing each other around my brain like cats and mice and ... more cats and more mice.

You know why everybody was obsessed with Scott Peterson? I don't know if American tabloid news makes it across the Atlantic. Peterson was this handsome, thirty-something businessman. He murdered his wife, eight-months pregnant, and dumped her from his fishing boat. Everybody obsessed on the Petersons because everybody wanted to marry, or wanted their daughter to marry, Scott, or someone like him: movie-star looks, manly, charming, a good provider, excellent teeth. Laci looked so radiantly happy in her wedding photos, and her pregnancy pics. What rots our joy?

I think of the Peterson story – the scary side of love – and I want to retire to the lesbian separatist compound that, according to legends circulated by disgruntled heterosexual women, nestles happily somewhere among the Redwoods of Northern California. When I think of the scary side of religion, I want to be the purely rational, Enlightenment scientist, as gleaming and white as the inside of my refrigerator. When you crap out a roundworm, you never want to eat again. Look, I know that that's a gross image, but I'm not being cheap. In Peace Corps, volunteers used to talk about these incidents and how they made food so unappealing. If you eat again you might swallow more parasites. But hunger drives us. Hunger for food, no matter how tainted, for love, no matter how risky, for ... God? "Life is like licking honey off a thorn," said Louis Adamic, a great Bohunk writer.

When I was a teenager, I read Nikos Kazantzakis' "St. Francis." I felt as if I were in a different, better world. I didn't feel like I'd entered a fantasy address like Middle Earth. Rather, I felt that my own connection with God was heightening by the book, and that that heightened connection so altered my perceptions that I felt as if I'd entered a parallel dimension – one of forgiveness, and love, and eternity and meaning. When I was reading the book, I didn't want to stop. After I put the book down, I didn't want to pick it up again. I felt that the book was inviting me to something, something big, and I had no idea what it might be, if it were safe, or if it were dangerous, or if I were ready.

Once I finished it, I did not read a single other Christian book for the next twenty-five years. I read scholarly books of comparative religion and mythology, analyses of Judaism, bashing of Christianity. But nothing ecstatic like Kazantzakis' "St. Francis." This was a very conscious choice.

I wanted to kiss boys. I wanted to learn to experience satisfaction the way everybody around me experienced satisfaction: by shopping at the mall. I wanted to master material reality. And I didn't want to go crazy.

Decades later, I consciously broke the glass and began, again, to read overtly Christian books. I felt that I was old enough, grounded enough, to handle any ecstasy that might ensue. I selected authors whose photos and bios depicted clean, productive, reliable citizens. Their resumes had to include some success in the secular world; I wanted to know that they could and did chop wood and carry water. I was careful of the time of day that I read. Midday, and its bright sun, offered the safest conditions. An hour at a time seemed a safe interval. No reading under the bed sheets, late into the night, with a flashlight.

At one point, my guard down, I picked the wrong book: "My Soul is Full of Troubles" by Brenda Bent. Just skimming the first few pages, I shrank back in horror.

In Twelve Step meetings, I'd gotten used to recognizing the language of delusional self-dramatization. It is a language that is heavy on interpretation and scant on facts. The folks who speak this language will not say to you, "I spent the day mainlining heroin," though they did. They will not say to you, "I blew the rent check on cocaine," though they did. They will not say, "I hit my wife," though they did. Rather, they present you with *their interpretations* of facts they will not confront, even by so small an act of courage as speaking with concrete nouns and action verbs. Rather than reporting, "Today I sobbed uncontrollably and my kids went without dinner," they report their self-dramatizing interpretation, "Today I was on the verge of a breakthrough with God."

Bent's book begins with a claim of intense, spiritual experiences. It's a series of metaphors without referents. "I was at sea ... there was a storm ... I saw a lighthouse." Oh, baloney, Brenda. Unless you were *literally on the bleeping ocean* stop telling me you were "at sea." Unless the atmosphere produced nimbocumulus clouds, low air pressure, and lightening, don't tell me there was a storm. Tell me what you did with the rent check, Brenda; tell me what your kids ate for dinner. Was it macaroni and cheese or paint scraped off windowsills, while Mommy went crazy again?

I'm thinking that you are with me on the whole "Is religion madness?" question, Rand. You won't be with me, I suspect, on this next fear. Satan. I've been convinced that by being a mediocre Christian, I've been flying under Satan's radar. Why would Satan mess with me? But here I am now writing to the world's most famous atheist about my faith.

Since you and I have begun writing, I have had – what – maybe three moments where I could, I think, feel Satan trying to get to me. These moments have felt different than anything I've felt before. Satan is boredom: "Why bother talking about this? A new Adam Sandler movie just opened. Go see that." Satan is carnivorous despair: "How could there be a God in this horrible world?" Satan is reality: "Your life sucks. How is it possible that God loves you? That you have any authority at all to speak as a member of the club?" Satan is self-protection: "When you write about the moments of your life when you have felt most in touch with something transcendent, you feel vulnerable and exposed. Don't go there. Keep up your guard." Satan is wisdom: "Religion is all a bunch of hogwash. Do you want to go crazy like Brenda Bent?"

You and I are transcending. We're being our best selves. We're using the big words. We're focusing on the eternal. Can't we just tell dirty jokes and drink to oblivion and fall asleep with our heads in the toilet and our sweaty arms about each other?

save SEND delete

Monday 9:01 p.m.
My dear, Dear Lord Randolph Court-Wright, Marquis of Alnwick,

I love the e-mails you have been sending me lately, you know it? Warm and funny and inviting and supportive.

Thank you so, so, so very much, Lord Randolph Court-Wright, just, for reading me. For allowing me to be. Do you know that just by being there, by reading and responding, you make me larger? You provide borders for my spirit that are so much vaster than those others provide. You let me expand. You let me breathe and follow my stars. You make me kinder, more patient, because I don't have to rely on others for anything. I can come here and I can have you. You make me more the self I remember being, from before I got sick. More the self I want to be, when I live up to dreams I've had since I was a little kid, and dreams I never even knew I had.

I'll never forget any of this, but for this, especially, I'll never forget you, and I hope never to stop being grateful.

And, yes, I will send you my next installment on God & suffering. And I promise I will never again mention to you ... that particular adventure in parasitology I mentioned in a previous e-mail. But I'm glad you saw my point. :-)

And, just, thank you.

SAVE send delete

Monday 9:02 p.m.

save **SEND** delete

Tuesday 4:00 p.m.

Dear Rand,

A bright and sparkly good afternoon to you. I'm ready to step up to the plate, if you are ready to man the mound and pitch another one of your no-hitters. Does any part of that metaphor translate to cricket, which, as I understand it, is what you Brits play? Or soccer, or rugby, or snooker?

Who am I trying to kid? Enough with the sports metaphors; I'm a girl and you're a geek.

I just got in from work. Every time DuQuayne talks to me, we talk for at least an hour, and every time we talk, he sobs. Given what American pop culture and academia command young black males to be – tough, criminal, political correctives to everything pop culture and academia despise about America – it is something to see a teenage black male be what he is – a boy – doubled over in tears, snot and mucus smearing his face, his fingers limp and drooping as his teacher hugs him. His auntie died this semester. He is a member of the Crips and fears retaliation for distancing himself from the gang. He can't enter his own home; his late aunt's boyfriend appears to be taking it over, though the house had been willed to DuQuayne. Even his losses are non-standard; DuQuayne was abandoned at birth by his biological mother, no one has a clue who his father was, and DYFS – the Division of Youth and Family Services – shuffled him through a series of foster homes for most of his life. This recent death, significant as it is, is just the death of the woman he most recently called "auntie." Recognizing his intelligence, his teachers have pressured him to be a high achiever. He can't get a job at McDonald's – he says that they hire only Mexicans.

Tanisha dropped by after I told her that her weak proposal for a research paper would earn her an F. She drooped. I asked her what was up. She was hesitant to speak. I pound it into my students that I won't accept whining in place of schoolwork. Tanisha didn't want to whine in place of schoolwork. Tanisha's schoolwork is stellar. I pressured her to speak. She's pregnant. I made the mistake of immediately beaming and congratulating her. At least I didn't go all the way and say what I was about to say, "You'll make a wonderful mother!" Tanisha started crying.

"You don't want the baby?"

She shook her head.

Again, I did not think quickly enough. "You can put it up for adoption – "

Tanisha cried harder. She's 17.

"You made the right decision. Don't give it any second thoughts. You are doing the right thing. I have complete faith in you." I don't believe in abortion. I believe in Tanisha.

"If there is anything I can do ... if you need someone to go with you ... "

She shook her head.

"Money?"

"I've got enough. I won't be in class Wednesday," she stated flatly. The first time she's missed class all semester.

Peaches and Krystal, both teenagers, are dealing with having been raped by fellow students. Juan is addicted to marijuana and wants to stop, but hasn't found anything else that takes care of him like pot does. Ahmed is far from home; he's been in this country for only a few months, and he is the only Muslim in a class of American students who have some chips on their shoulders against Muslims. Blanca has been erased by campus bureaucracy. She's filled out all the proper forms and paid her tuition on time; her name just doesn't appear on any of the lists it ought. When she calls the dean to ask why, she is put on hold and, after a lengthy wait complete with elevator music piped in to the receiver, she gets cut off.

No set of details constitutes the worst narrative. Rape is not the most punishing event my students have come to me with. Death of a loved one is not, nor homelessness nor drug addiction nor exile. This is the worst: the sufferer without words to name what is happening to him. Jesus also reached this degree of amnesiac, apparently meaningless suffering. On the cross, he asked, "My God, my God, why have you forsaken me?"

DuQuayne is from Newark, into which many regions of the spectrum of light simply never penetrate. There were riots in Newark forty years ago, and a lot of business and culture just closed up shop, left for the suburbs, and never looked back. Nature abhors a vacuum. Power groups have experimented on DuQuayne: Nation of Islam, the Crips, Limousine Liberals, Ebonics teachers, Black Liberation Theologians – every door-to-door salesman with some shoddy tchotchke for sale, every recruiter seeking warm, young bodies for his army, every megalomaniacal would-be messiah who needs worshippers. These bloodsuckers were very careful never to give DuQuayne a hammer, or a flashlight, or a shovel, or any other neutral, multi-purpose tool DuQuayne might wield to advance in a direction he might choose himself. Thus, he has only the flimsiest grasp, if any grasp, of personal responsibility, of hope, of possibility, of the Declaration of Independence, of Shakespeare, of Freud, of the Sermon on the Mount, of Bette Davis, of Frederick Douglass.

DuQuayne is having a nervous breakdown, and he doesn't realize it; he has never heard the phrase "nervous breakdown" and comprehended it. All he knows is that every time he talks to me, he can't stop talking, and then he can't stop crying. He has no clue that there are entire industries built around, publications dedicated to, young black men like him and their heartaches. All he knows is that he needs to start selling crack again, or his gang brothers will beat him again. All he knows is that his muscles are sore from sleeping on a park bench.

That is the most painful witness: someone suffering, and unable to name what is happening to him, because he has no context, no vocabulary, no ability to turn what is happening to him into an abstraction, a narrative, an organism built of words that he can operate on, take apart and put back together, with a toolkit made of other words. I watch the pain spread throughout DuQuayne's dumb soul, turning his being into a voiceless bruise.

When confronted with suffering in my students, I have learned that it is my job, not to produce an essay, but to be quiet, to listen, and, when it comes time for me to speak, to ask questions. By being quiet and attending, not judging, not rewriting, not exploiting, not rushing, but just by listening and attending, we create the space necessary for wounds to morph to wings. I offer my presence as a blank sheet, and their words stitch into me their quilt, their meaning.

I don't stop at silence. I offer silence until the student is spent. When he or she has not spoken for about ten minutes, when I've gotten the answer to the who, what, when, where, why, how questions, and I've learned everything I can about his burden, and when she has had the opportunity to turn her bruise into a story, only then I speak. "What do you want me to do?" is the fundamental question. If I can do something, I do it. If I can't, I don't. I couldn't hug Tom, about whom I told you. I couldn't hug him because his shirt was off, and, at that moment that he'd taken his shirt off and begun to cry about his scars, I began seeing him as something other than a student. I could not betray him by forgetting my status in relation to him. I've only ever seen DuQuayne as a child, and so I can hug him, and I do.

I offer money. I offer time. I offer muscle. I offer presence. I offer knowledge. I offer words, "What you are experiencing is not unusual; there is a name for it; you can get the band-aid one needs in this situation, at this address. C'mon, let's go."

At times, when I have been in pain, I have attempted to read essays on God and suffering. This is what I read: "Blah blah blah blah blah blah blah." Suffering is so immediate, so pulsing, so real, and documents about suffering are often as dry, crumbly and lifeless as dust. The worst kind of writing or talking about suffering is the kind that exploits the details of others' narratives to prove the author's pet theory. Often this theory is an expression of hatred the speaker wants to justify. Often people don't respond to suffering by saying, "Let's help the people who are suffering." Rather, often people respond to suffering by saying, "Let's punish – even if only verbally – those we identify as the perpetrators."

When a horrible illness was crucifying me, and people tried to lecture me about my miserable state, I hated them and I hated their words. The lecturers had some agenda they wanted to drive home, and they exploited the details of my crucifixion to advance their own worldview. I was living proof of their pet theory. They could say, "Those damn Republicans and their resistance to national health care!" or "I blame Global Warming!" They did not understand that they were not doing me a favor by insisting that, because I was sick, they would, on my account, hate the Republicans, or fear Global Warming, all the more. What do I wish they had said? "I am so sorry that this happened to you. Let me hold you while you cry. Here's fifty bucks so you can buy groceries this week, instead of shoplifting them."

One night, I had not been able to stop vomiting for the previous seven days, and I had not even attempted to eat any food during that time. The crushing vertigo was beginning to let up just enough that I thought I would risk a bath, although I feared I'd dissolve in the water. I had checked a CD out of the public library, and I absentmindedly slipped it into the CD player. I wasn't even trying to resurrect. I just wanted some background music to distract me from the dizziness and nausea as I stepped into the tub and sponged off the crud of seven days of vomiting and inertia. The CD was Frank Sinatra's "Songs for Swingin' Lovers," which I'd never listened to before. The symmetry of Cole Porter's lyrics, the exuberance of Nelson Riddle's arrangements, the "I've been around the block, and I ain't stopping now" thrust of Sinatra's delivery: an angel rolled back the rock on my tomb. I could go on for another day. Frank Sinatra. Nelson Riddle. Cole Porter. I promise you.

I'm not trying to avoid your question, Rand. How can I believe in God in a world of suffering. That's a fair question – that's *the* question. But I don't know how to answer it without adding to the already overflowing toilet of blah blah blah blah blah blah blah. And I don't know how to answer it without exploiting the details of someone else's crucifixion to prove my petty point. And I know I'll never achieve the altitude or velocity of Sinatra's "Swinging Lovers."

There is a temptation to put the grand, glorious theory first, and then to manipulate the intimate facts of real people's real lives to serve the theory. People want to believe in an omnipotent, omniscient, and all-loving God – or they want to believe in a beneficent Universe or Tao – or they want, simply, justification for their desire to sit at home in their comfortable leather lounger and watch their big screen, color TV, and not devote a second's concern to a world raising howls of misery. For a lot of people that comfortable squat in that comfortable chair in front of that big screen *is* God. Believers make central the idea of a benevolent universe – benevolent primarily in that it justifies their comfortable ass in that comfortable chair. They place the insistence that "it all makes sense" as their North Star that all other truths must serve, and then they manipulate others' narratives in order to serve that truth. They do it because they can't allow themselves to internalize how much incoherent pain there is in the world. If suffering's tackiest theorists allowed themselves to think of all the innocent, abused children, screaming, raped women, betrayed, destroyed and crushed men, they fear they would go mad. So, as if wielding knitting needles, they refashion the details of others' suffering in order to make it more sensible, less horrible, smooth and neat.

The "incoherent" part is every bit as bad as the "pain" part. It's not only the existence of suffering that troubles us. What really gets us is the suffering that throws a monkey wrench in the way we make sense, that crumples our maps, that makes chaos of pattern, that, like some devious computer virus, renders our hard-wrought, spelling- and grammar-checked narratives, gibberish. We need meaning to prove our own value to ourselves more than we need our bodies – that's why we humans are compulsive storytellers. Meaning and pattern, as much as benignity and power, are our definition of God. Atheists are as eager – as desperate – to create, by any means necessary, a sense of meaning as theists are. I know atheists who say that they didn't let go of one life raft – God – until they latched on to another – Darwin. They could not handle being adrift in sheer sense-lessness. Others select from the gospels according to Nietzsche or Marx, Freud or Einstein.

When suffering comes along that pulls the rug of meaning out from under us – when a bride dies in a limo crash on the way to her wedding, when a soldier falls off the ship carrying him home from war, when a baby contracts a terminal illness – we give up on God, because we can't wrap our minds around any concept of God that transcends our concept of meaning. We don't even think of giving up on God when a fisherman falls off a ship, or an old man contracts the same illness, or if the woman never married and died a spinster in a fifteen-car pile-up during a snowstorm. She'd been at a singles bar before she got behind the wheel of her car. All of that is okay; God gets a free pass. Our sense of meaning is not violated.

But our sense of meaninglessness is an essential part of God's plan, our plan, because we create it with him, by eating that apple, anew, everyday, by stepping away from God, logos, meaning.

Preston Sturges was an American filmmaker from Hollywood's Golden Age. He made a 1941 movie, "Sullivan's Travels," a screwball comedy, with a pretty blonde, chase scenes, and pies-in-the-face style humor. John L. Sullivan, the lead character, is a successful Hollywood director. He's ashamed of making silly comedies like "Ants in Your Plants of 1939." He yearns to make a profound work of art, "Oh Brother, Where Art Thou." It's the Great Depression, World War Two; Sullivan wants to honor the suffering of the impoverished masses. But he knows he is too sheltered and shallow to do his dreamed-of masterpiece any justice. He decides to don a hobo's attire and hit the rails, as American men were doing in those tough economic times. They'd go down to a rail yard, and hop on any train, hoping to find work. Sullivan's efforts to experience human suffering are futile. He knows who he is, and he knows he can return to his Hollywood mansion anytime he likes – until, one day, when a rail yard bull beats him senseless. He has amnesia. He's arrested and sent to a chain gang. His life becomes one great confusion of pain. That's when he learns something. Only when he forgets that he is a prince of Hollywood, and can return to his little Hollywood heaven whenever he likes.

People fear an absence of meaning and rush in to provide any meaning, no matter how tawdry. In my case, New Agers insisted that I had brought my illness on myself, by not thinking positive thoughts. Rape victims, these types will insist, ask for it. Abused children ask for it, as well, by picking bad parents before they are born. Cascading rationalizations follow one on the other, until the rationalizer creates a world in which there is no real injustice, no deep pain, and, therefore, no need to feel sad, or act with compassion, or get up from that well-upholstered chair in front of the TV. Atheists do the same thing. They insist that they alone are ethical, and that their rejection of God is the only possible response to a world of pain, and that any other response is unethical and morally blind. Disclaimer: not all New Agers do this. Not all atheists. Some.

I don't want to do that to anyone. I do not want to harvest the details of others' pain to prove my superior intelligence or ethics or to justify my approach to God, or to reassert my own theory. I resolve not to do it to my students when they come to me in pain. I did not say to Tanisha, "Well, the positive aspect to unwanted pregnancy is that you've learned a lesson about the critical importance of prophylactics." A refusal to put a tidy bow on suffering – any tidy bow – the "We've all learned an important lesson here" bow or the "God chastises those whom he loves" bow or the "Everything happens for a reason" bow or the "There cannot be a God" bow – any refusal to put theory first and the human being in front of you last leaves the witness in a jail cell full of senseless agony.

Here's my position: I'm willing to be a witness in a jail cell full of senseless agony. During high school and college, I worked as a nurse's aid. I held the hands of human beings I had come to love who were dying in a nightmarish institution that violated minimal standards. I didn't chirp, "Oh, what a blessed thing it is that you are tied to a mechanical bed, that you urinate and defecate into diapers that, if you are lucky, get changed twice a day, that your adult children have betrayed and abandoned you, after making sure that you signed your house over to them, and that your only human contact is surly staff who cannot be bothered to learn your name and who spoon-feed you lukewarm slop from Styrofoam."

I did not distribute answers. I did not harvest my patients' stories to support my theory. I did not justify God. I held hands, and I listened, and I attended. I stroked faces. I told them – Etta, Mr. Greenburg, Jadwiga – how very much I loved them. And I showed up on time. I worked the entire time I was there, without sneaking unscheduled breaks. I couldn't rescue every nursing home victim in North America. I could, and did, change forty diapers a night.

One of my first jobs after I got my PhD was as a telephone interviewer for the university's survey research firm. It paid two dollars over minimum wage. I had been so lonely while I was sick, and here I was phoning stranger after stranger, asking highly intimate questions. I had not landed the tenure-track professor job for which I had trained and hoped, but I loved this work – I was once again in touch with the human race.

Any misplaced syllable might contaminate data. We could not sway our informants by, for example, saying "Good" or, heaven forefend, "I agree." Like robots, we had to ask each question of each new informant using the exact same mechanical script we had used to ask the previous informant. Our supervisors listened in; the number of times I said something so simple as "Uh huh" was tabulated. Even so, I discovered that there is an intimacy that can occur between two humans during encounters through virtual barbed-wire.

In one survey, we assessed the level of satisfaction of recipients of mental health services. I remember a man who was, like several others, plainly deranged, but he was close to me in age, and exceptionally intelligent. He was able to provide pertinent replies to my questions – his data would count – but his manner and his tangential comments revealed a man condemned to a life sentence in a very ugly cell – his own diseased mind.

"On a scale of one to six, with one being strongly disagree, and six being strongly agree, how would you respond to the following? 'My health care bills are paid in a prompt and timely manner,' Remember. There are no right or wrong answers." Even as I was asking survey questions like that, I began, silently, to pray for the anonymous madman. My heart was breaking, selfishly. Constrained by our conversational boundaries, I could do nothing to reassure myself that I had done all I could, or to be sure that he'd be okay after we went our separate ways – after we hung up our phones. I suddenly realized how lucky I was, lucky and privileged and blessed. My body had broken, yes, and I had spent many years paralyzed and vomiting, but I could inhabit, run with, and rejoice in the fine mind that God or chance – through no effort or deservingness on my part – had deigned me. I began to question God. How could God do this to this man, and the hundreds of other mentally ill persons like him we were interviewing? I despaired.

At the end of the interview, if my supervisor had not been listening in, I would have said, "I am so sorry" or "I hope you can get the help you need" or "God damn the God who has done this to you." I would have done that for me, not for him. I would have done that to place some bow on this man's story. I would have done that to provide some moral or sense to the chaos and pain he had exposed merely by speaking, I would have done that to reassert my own meaning – a meaning that certified me as the superior victor who had dodged this bullet, and him as the inferior victim, whose lousy, crappy, pathetic life could never have any worth at all. Because my supervisor was listening in, I could not say any of the things that my instinct and sense of propriety instructed me to say. Instead, something remarkable happened.

At the end of the interview, my anonymous informant's voice completely changed. Previously, he had sounded herky-jerky and unhinged. Suddenly his voice was rich and warm and his timbre stable. He said – and he broached this, not I, I could have been fired for doing so – he said, as if he had been reading my mind, "My life is very hard, that is true. And I face a constant struggle against this disease. I haven't been able to accomplish any of the things that a normal person accomplishes. I can't hold down a job. I'll never have a family. My mind torments me. But I know that I am in the hand of God, and I know that Jesus Christ has a plan for me."

Small potatoes, Rand: an insane man's disembodied voice at the other end of a telephone line, in a monitored conversation in which I could not even state what was simply true, "As I've been talking to you, I have been praying for you fervently; you have moved me, taught me, and humbled me; I will never forget you." But hearing that man say those words at the end of that conversation with a sense of conviction, strength and integrity, emphasized for me that I cannot be the one to apply meaning to someone else's narrative of suffering. Rand, as a graduate student I sat for entire semesters in the same room with world-class scholars and, with some of those classes, I cannot repeat to you a single sentence that those world-class scholars uttered. The words from the insane man in the phone survey, I remember verbatim.

Atheists like you say that you can't believe in God because there is so much suffering in the world. That's imperialism. You presume to speak for others, others who do not want you to speak for them. You start with the Holocaust. Fair enough. Corrie ten Boom was a Dutch Christian who rescued Jews. Not only was she still a Christian after her imprisonment in the Ravensbruck concentration camp, she prayed for, and received, God's gift of forgiveness when one of the cruelest camp guards approached her after the war. Oswald Rufeisen, a Jewish survivor, became a monk. Elie Weisel, who survived Auschwitz, believes.

You live a long time and you think you've heard all there is to hear about how one human being can cause another pain. Then a news story comes along and manages to shock because it takes the elements of torture, mixes them up and repackages them so that you gasp and say, "That does it. I cannot reconcile the existence of God in a world where this new horror could have happened."

I try to pray, and I can't. I am addressing my prayers to a vast accountant in the sky. His office walls are pastel clouds; his long white beard threatens to overrun his desk; his attire is a white robe. This accountant God has made a terrible mistake with his abacus. He was supposed to allow evil to go only so far, and he let one abacus bead slip, and evil went too far. I study this God and the only character I can see is too absent-minded about his own creations to have rescued that victim, or someone who is so callous that he could let himself become distracted by other things while his beloved creation, that victim, cried out in agony as God did nothing to intervene. I remember that humanity reflects this God – Genesis 1:27 – God created humanity in his own image – and I see humanity, after a news broadcast of some new, unbearable torture, as an army of glorified cockroaches. Roaches find what pleasure they know in humble food crumbs, in recycling our garbage, not from the screams of their fellows: roaches are our superiors. If humanity reflects God, God is a Kafkaesque insect.

And, so, I let go of my belief in God. I don't fight it. I just let it go.

And this is what happens. I am reminded – I'll leave it to you to decide who reminds me – of those spirit guides I encountered as a child. I am reminded of Stefania Podgorska, who risked all to help Jews during the war. I am reminded of Rick Gudal, who received my letter begging for help, and responded. I have to erase my calculations. There is good in the world, even if it does not fit on my balance sheet.

And so again I pray. I pray to the good that I know exists in this world, and what lies beyond it, that my mind can never encompass. I struggle against my always self-regenerating image of God as a vast accountant who slips up in his figures, thus cheating us out of our pleasure allotment. I release, I let go, I realize I cannot encapsulate God in my mind, and I pray to the source of that goodness of whose existence I am certain.

I am not alone in this process. Avrom Sutskever was a Jew

living in the Vilna Ghetto, under Nazi occupation, when he wrote:

> I think I just thought of a prayer,
> But I can't imagine who might be there.
> Sealed in a steel womb
> how can I pray? To whom?
> Star, you were once my dear friend,
> come stand for the words that have come to an end.
> But, dear, deaf star
> I understand you're too far.
> Still, someone in me insists, pray!
> Tormenting me in my soul: pray!
> Prayer, oh wildest surmise
> I still babble you till sunrise.

If material reality insists that suffering is so great that there can't be a God, why bother obeying that inner urge to pray? But why apply more value to the material reality that tells us that there is no God, than to the eternal, inner voice that prods us to pray? Psalm 42: "As the deer longs for streams of water, so my soul longs for you, O God. My being thirsts for God." You may tell me that a yearning for God is just an evolutionary tick, and that we should just ignore it, but what would happen if we ignored our other evolutionary ticks, yearnings for food, for exercise, for love, for self-expression?

When I decide to allow suffering to knock my belief in God out of me, and I stop praying, I do not experience that as a neutral event that has no impact. Rather, I feel things change in my life for the worse. I act on my belief in the worst. Immediately, everything becomes darker and coarser. I do cruel things and enjoy doing them. I push on public transportation. I am surly with cashiers. (There is a special, as yet unnamed, patron saint who looks after cashiers. They have to take so much punishing unpleasantness from unending throngs of customers only conscious enough to be rude. And they do it all while wearing polyester uniforms in kindergarten colors, and plastic first-name-only nametags. It's one of the toughest jobs in the world, and every time I encounter a cashier who takes the trouble to bestow a genuine smile, I know that there is a God.)

I live a small-potatoes life. My Satanic acts will never earn me a slew of tribute webpages like those fans dedicate to serial killers. But that I push on public transportation, or speak subtle, clever putdowns to my students, or snap impatiently at cashiers who have strived to smile at me while handing me my change, or blind myself to the good in the world, tells me that my rejection of God creates a vacuum, a vacuum that Satan is happy to fill.

Satan is not a mustachioed trickster with horns and tail in a tight, red, vinyl jumpsuit. My best conception of Satan is this: in a human being, a religious certainty of one's own personal importance, combined with a cultivated conviction of one's own unjust victimization, and a refusal to see God, and good, in one's fellow human beings. That recipe left to percolate in the human soul has been the justification for an infinite amount of pain.

I haven't reached any kind of a conclusion here. I'm going to press "send" anyway. I so wonder how or if any of what I've written has affected you at all. Or will affect you – though I imagine you in real time sitting at my side as I write, you have not read this yet. I could save myself embarrassment by pressing "delete" instead of "send." Pressing "send" is, to steal the title from a prayer, an "act of faith." And one of love.

save SEND delete

Tuesday 5:01 p.m.
Manda,
Still attending to pesto's siren call?

save SEND delete

INBOX

mira darling how lovely to hear from you at exactly this moment ... was just thinking of you ... plz view attached photo of me in district attorney attire ... sexy enuf ... too ... not enuf ... ???

Tuesday 5:15 p.m.

I *love* that photo! My God but you look beautiful. I want to show it to people and say, "I know a woman who looks like *this.*" Really. I'll get raises and boyfriends. Wow. No worries, Amanda. You look *so* great. When does this new Batman start filming? Can I visit you on the set?

Listen, Rand and I are talking about the problem of God and suffering. I keep ping-ponging from anecdote to anecdote but I'm finding it hard to master what I want to say.

Have I ever said anything even vaguely coherent to you about God and suffering? If so, can you e-mail it back to me so I can cut it and paste it and send it to Rand?

save SEND delete

INBOX

can't help ... don't like those kinds of stories ... maybe you could finally read rhonda byrne's "the secret" ... really mira why not choose happiness ... it really is that easy ... no need for all this suffering you create with your belief system

Tuesday 5:37 p.m.
Dear Amanda,
Okay. Thanks.

save SEND delete

Tuesday 7:14 p.m.
Rand,
This is it. This is what I want to say about God and suffering.

There are three things that suffering people do not want to hear. From the New Agers: "You create your own reality;" from the monks manqué: "Suffering is good for you," and from the oh-so-clinical mathematicians: "You can't have freedom without suffering." Of course, what I have to say next is, "You create your own reality." "Suffering is good for you." And, yes, "You can't have freedom without suffering."

Years ago I was participating in an online discussion. A chronically depressed woman, Becca, mentioned that she had genital herpes, and that an uncle told her that she gave herself the herpes, in order to justify her chronic depression. The discussion had been a good one previous to this, because it was peer-to-peer. No one was the guru. No one needed to feel the shame and inferiority of being the suffering person speaking to someone who was not suffering.

That changed. Ted, a man identifying himself as an American Buddhist, posted in reply to Becca. He was not chronically ill. He wasn't there to speak as a peer. He was there to teach. Ted taught us that he could "clarify" Becca's dilemma. Becca *had* given herself herpes, Ted "clarified," and chronic depression, as well, because of past life karma. Karma's math was impeccable, Ted emphasized. Genital herpes? Becca had been a bad mother in a past life. (In New Age circles, you often hear about women giving themselves breast cancer. You never hear about men giving themselves baldness.) Ted was no dummy – he added a proviso. If readers had been "brainwashed by Christianity and Western, White-Male dualism" we wouldn't understand the just and compassionate functioning of karma, and we would be tempted to disagree.

I made no attempt to resist that particular temptation. "Ted" left the group after reading my point-by-point refutation of his nonsense. A week later, a poster using the internet handle "NotBrainwashed" showed up and began insulting me at every turn. NotBrainwashed's posting style was identical to Ted's. Then another poster showed up, one named "Siddhartha." Siddhartha's posting style was also very similar to Ted's. Siddhartha mostly just posted messages adamantly agreeing with NotBrainwashed.

I love dinosaurs. It's one of my dirty little secrets. I was in line for the very first, 10:30 a.m. showing of "Jurassic Park." Me and 1,500 guys. "Sue," the most complete tyrannosaurus rex skeleton ever found, shows signs of arthritis. Did Sue give herself arthritis because she was a bad mother in a past life? Chestnut blight and elm disease, both inadvertently imported from Asia, killed off American elms and chestnuts in the early twentieth century. Did the American chestnut develop "shame of being a chestnut" and is that why these trees sickened and died?

"The race is not won by the swift, nor the battle by the valiant, nor a livelihood by the wise, nor riches by the shrewd, nor favor by the experts; for a time of calamity comes to all alike." So says Ecclesiastes. I also like this from John 9: "he saw a man blind from birth. His disciples asked him, 'Rabbi, who sinned, this man or his parents, that he was born blind?' Jesus answered, 'Neither he nor his parents sinned.'" I'm not saying that I have a coherent argument that synthesizes all Biblical teaching on suffering; I do not. I'm saying that I like these two verses exactly because these two verses specifically reject the notion that all suffering is exact punishment for and proportional to sins the suffering person has committed. And I still think that we create our own realities.

After my first meeting with DuQuayne, I called everyone I could think of to call, to make sure that every one of his needs was cared for. A lawyer volunteered to work with DuQuayne, pro bono, to make sure he received his inheritance of his deceased aunt's home. My congressman connected me with a detective who has gained fame for liberating members of street gangs. A university dean provided DuQuayne with a free room. A government agency provided him with tuition money. A counselor contacted him repeatedly, offering free counseling.

DuQuayne stopped attending classes completely. Rather than focusing on the sources of free, professional help, he focused on all the ways that society had betrayed, hurt, and abandoned him. He hurt his knee while playing basketball. UMDNJ would not provide him with free medical care. DuQuayne went on and on about that. I told him that he would fail class because he stopped attending. He said I should not be so hard on him. He couldn't make it to class because his knee hurt. I reminded him that, in spite of his hurt knee, he had walked to my office. DuQuayne refused to meet with the lawyer, the detective, or the free counselor. He told me he has to go back with his gang, and, as much as it hurts him, start selling drugs again.

"You're a young African American male, and you talk about how drugs hurt your community, and you have decided to start selling drugs again."

As aggressively as any actor auditioning for a plum role, DuQuayne adopted a gangsta pose. "I got no choice," he insisted. "My life is very haaaahd" – "hard."

Of course DuQuayne has a choice. He has many choices. But DuQuayne's choices aren't obvious *to him.* That DuQuayne does not fully, consciously acknowledge how he is sabotaging himself, that DuQuayne insists he is an innocent, helpless victim, that DuQuayne justifies his spreading his pain around, and victimizing others, by selling drugs, should prove instructive to those of us who are not DuQuayne. Maybe we, as blindly as he, are choosing all the wrong things. Maybe we, also, without realizing it, are rejecting help. Maybe we, also, without realizing it, are focusing on how others have betrayed us, and not on how we have betrayed others, and maybe we are also attempting to justify our victimization of others. Maybe we, as desperately as he, need to reject the bitterness our own minds have cooked up for us, and need to place our faith in the Higher Power our souls urge us to pray to.

The Nazis sent Viktor Frankl to Auschwitz. He was separated from his parents, wife, and brother, all of whom died. The Nazis, sneering, confiscated the coat into whose lining Frankl had sewn his prized manuscript, his life's work. In Auschwitz, Frankl generated the spiritual experience that produced "Man's Search for Meaning," one of the greatest books ever written; no Auschwitz, no such masterpiece. "We who lived in concentration camps," Frankl wrote, "can remember the men who walked through the huts comforting others, giving away their last piece of bread. They may have been few in number, but they offer sufficient proof that everything can be taken from a man but one thing: the last of the human freedoms – to choose one's attitude in any given set of circumstances, to choose one's own way."

Ninety percent of the suffering people I know choose, not to work their way out of the Hell to which fate has condemned them, but to upholster it. My students, my friends, visibly, actively choose to exacerbate the most hated features of their lives. Dating an abusive man? Heck, why not up the ante and get pregnant by him. Working a dead-end job? Here's a great idea – start drinking. That will really improve things. Lost everything in a flood, fire, war, and brokenhearted over that? A suggestion – don't, whatever you do, move on; don't enjoy the present moment. Cling to your memories of what is gone, and your sense of yourself as a victim.

Humanity in the macrocosm recapitulates humanity in the microcosm. Just as individuals worsen suffering, societies worsen suffering. War, famine, plague: we, as a species could stop or lessen the suffering caused by all. We don't. We go to war. We rape the earth, making famine inevitable.

Like Adam and Eve, we are free to choose. Like Adam and Eve, we make the choice that educates us, and that causes us suffering: we chose away from God. Like Viktor Frankl, we can make the choice that turns our suffering into an opportunity for transcendence:

The way in which a man accepts his fate and all the suffering it entails, the way in which he takes up his cross, gives him ample opportunity – even under the most difficult circumstances – to add a deeper meaning to his life. It may remain brave, dignified, and unselfish. Or in the bitter fight for self-preservation he may forget his human dignity and become no more than an animal. Here lies the chance for a man either to make use of or to forego the opportunities of attaining the moral values that a difficult situation may afford him. And this decides whether he is worthy of his sufferings or not.

I hate to say this. I hate it that it is true. Many of the qualities in myself that I value most are rooted in the vile mud of suffering. It wasn't until I lost every hour of every day that I came to value time. It wasn't until I lost my body that I became dedicated to my body. It wasn't until nothing I did mattered that I realized that what I did mattered to God, and I devoted myself to choosing rightly, even in something so simple as wearing clean, matching, and pressed clothing on a day when I'd never leave the house. It wasn't suffering per se that made me a better person. It was my response to it. I had two choices: to be sucked under, to become a monster from which my best self would recoil, or to strive to keep my head above water. As best as I was able, I chose the latter – I strove. I approached every feature of my suffering: loneliness, pain, paralysis, despair, terror, rage, waste, poverty, as an obstacle on a course I was running for my own spiritual growth in the eyes of God – and, nobody else. That choice is what made all the difference.

I have found it impossible to communicate to anyone what happened to me in Bloomington. I have tried, but people do not hear me. Their refusal to hear is itself evidence that suffering is very big mojo. Suffering is powerful, and its power trumps our rationality; thus we experience it as supernatural. Maybe suffering is supernatural. Maybe it is mojo. That, in the face of suffering, people become deafened to the voice of the sufferer, guarantees that suffering is solitary confinement.

Individual people and trusted institutions betrayed me in ways I did not realize was possible. In a courtroom, a nun who knew me, the Social-Security-appointed-physician and the Social Security vocational expert testified, under oath, that I had been handicapped by illness and could not work. The judge called the nun a liar, rejected the Social Security experts' testimony and, with finality, denied me Social Security Disability Income, and access to Medicaid. I would not be able to go to a doctor. I would be sick forever, because of the decision of this judge. This judge was just returning to the bench after defending himself against charges of discriminating against female plaintiffs. He was knowingly turning down desperate women who might die. He was making a good living thereby. Though his superiors knew what he was doing, they returned him to the bench.

I posted my story online. In a distant, exclusive suburb, a wealthy, older man who did contract work with the Defense Department read my posts. He e-mailed an offer of help. He showed up in Bloomington shortly thereafter, suggesting that I become his mistress. He and his wife had an understanding. "She's having an affair with her yoga instructor!" For about a year afterward I practically made every man who so much as opened a door for me sign a form stating that he would never insist that because he had opened that door, I owed him sex.

An attack hit when I was trying to walk down the aisles in the library on the IU campus. Library shelves, supermarket aisles, high-contrast floor tile, rotating ceiling fans, films shot with handheld cameras: all present challenges to someone with a vestibular disorder. I started to weave, and to hold my head with my hand. Finally, I dropped my books. A man, white, late twenties, in neat blue jeans, a work shirt and a baseball cap, had been in the other aisle the entire time. No sooner had I started to show vulnerability than he crossed over from his aisle and pushed me hard against the shelves, ran his hands over my body, and then rapidly walked away. You are poor. You are sick. You are female. You are alone. You are the obvious target.

Before I got sick, I had not realized that there is a species of vulture whose enzymes digest the flesh of afflicted humans. I hadn't been wary of the traps that these vultures presented. Unaware of those traps, I fell right into them. I was hurt in ways I did not know it was possible to be hurt. Since getting better, I haven't had any encounters even vaguely like those I had when I was sick. No man has pushed me against a library shelf. It's as if that type of vulture has ceased to see, in me, a likely target, and is now feasting on some other victim. Or, without my conscious mind realizing it, my instincts just keep moving me rapidly past anyone like this, or are giving out warning signs to this type to give me a wide berth. "You seem tougher," an acquaintance said to me, "less easy to push around."

How to communicate any of this to people leading healthy, even marginally empowered lives? They have never met any of these people. They know that judge. He's a respected elder. With them, my self-identified benefactor is charitable – always talking about the needy females he's helping. That guy in the work shirt? A decent neighbor. Quiet, keeps to himself.

I was always taken aback when I met people who voiced affection for Bloomington. A soul-dead nightmare of monsters, thugs, perverts, and thieves: the Bloomington I inhabited. Tree-lined, cobblestone streets, quiet nights of fireflies, low crime rates, the values of a proud, heartland university town: the Bloomington where healthy, strong, young people and world-class scholars and musicians resided.

Psalm 30 says, "weeping comes for the night; but at dawn there is rejoicing." In John 16, to promise us that once we are triumphant, former tribulation will be of no consequence, Jesus harnesses the powerful metaphor of a woman suffering through labor and then rejoicing at giving birth:

She is in anguish because her hour has arrived; but when she has given birth to a child, she no longer remembers the pain because of her joy that a child has been born into the world.

So you also are now in anguish. But I will see you again, and your hearts will rejoice, and no one will take your joy away from you.

On that day you will not question me about anything.

The night of one very bad day, I was lying on my mattress on the floor. I decided to fix myself, as I had done so many times before. I projected myself into some point in the future. At that point in the future, I would no longer be in such pain. I'd performed this exercise before – when I was a kid getting beat up, or after a bad break-up with a boyfriend – and it had always worked. The future me would be older, healthier, happier, more powerful, with more resources, both inner and outer. That future me would look back on the past with a warm wisdom, compassion, and no regrets. To all the questions I was asking in the present, the future me had worked out all the answers. Imagining this didn't give me the answers, but it gave me the confidence that they would come with time. All my current problems were her interesting memories.

This dark night in Bloomington, I imagined it being ten years in the future. To my surprise, the exercise didn't work. I was still in pain. I advanced the clock. It was fifty years in the future. It was a hundred. I was released and dead. No luck. The exercise still did not work. It was a thousand, a billion, twenty billion years in the future. The sun had expanded, enveloping the earth in fire, and then contracted into a black hole. My constituent parts had long since been buried, crumbled, and those crumbs had, in turn, been incinerated, and wandered the void as interstellar dust. Even then the atoms that had once been me were still vibrating with pain.

Look, I've worked as an editor and I know damn well that the above paragraph reads like purple prose, like some amateur straining to come up with a metaphor that will convey a character's torment. I know that any writing teacher would not conclude the final lines before crossing the entire paragraph out, and scrawling an impatient, "Delete! Write me something *true,* not grandiose." In survivors' memoirs of atrocity, I've read more times that I can count, "You can never know what it was like. There are no words." In fact, there *are* words. There are no ears.

When I was sick, I spent hours, days, weeks, without any human contact. No one spoke my name. No one touched me. No one saw me. It's funny – being sick and poor in an American college town sentenced me to a solitary confinement as total as that of a pirate marooned on a desert island. I remembered a Joseph Campbell book that had been one of my inspirations to go to graduate school. Campbell wrote of Igjugarjuk, an Eskimo shaman. "The only true wisdom," Igjugarjuk said, "lives far from mankind, out in the great loneliness, and can be reached only through suffering. Privation and suffering alone open the mind to all that is hidden to others." I had always been attracted to the big truths – that's why I was reading that Joseph Campbell book. But I test as a pure extrovert. I am the only person I know who revels, during the holiday season, in being in the midst of a crush of harried shoppers in a frenetic, tinsel-bedecked mall. I can't think a thought without wanting to speak it to someone else. I have always yearned for the truth that emptiness promises; I just didn't want the emptiness. Maybe God was giving me the desert's truth the only way I could acquire it. Too social and hyperactive – not to mention perpetually horny and hungry – for a monastery, God blighted me with a repulsive illness that drove everyone away, turned eating into a curse, and paralyzed me, granting me the solitude and stillness I certainly did not want. Or maybe I was being tortured pointlessly by mere chance. Inhale as a believer; exhale as an atheist.

I was more alone than it would seem possible for a human

being living in a city of tens of thousands. I could have done anything, and it would not have registered with anyone else. It was then that I began to pay attention to my appearance. I purchased some make-up, and occasionally wore it. I took scrupulous care never to wear clashing colors. Before eating, I set the table as if for a guest. I had never done this before.

I began to pay a great deal of attention to time. I had healthy episodes. During those episodes, I was unstoppable. I read furiously, and wrote my dissertation, often, from five in the morning until ten at night. I did not put anything off. I could not afford to.

I learned to be kinder. Constant pain taught me. I'm not saying I'm a kind person. I'm saying that after I got sick, I became kinder than I had been before.

I was on fire with rage. I received repeated invitations to become a random sniper, to exact revenge on society for what it was continuously doing, to me. I consciously resisted that invitation. In that effortful struggle played out against emptiness, I turned to my teacher, and, absent any distraction, I worked to apply his teachings as best as I could. That effort was the single best school I've ever had.

My prayer life changed. I could no longer do what I had been doing all my life: pray for God's intervention, and for "our daily bread." I had daily bread because I had stolen it from Kroger's supermarket. Jesus said, "Ask and it will be given to you …Which one of you would hand his son a stone when he asks for a loaf of bread?" I guess Jesus wasn't thinking of me when he spoke those words. I had asked for bread, and he had handed me a stone. The recipients of his promise were yet another group for which I was not fit to be a member.

I walked into St. Charles Borromeo R. C. Church, the church where, when I had asked to speak to a priest, the secretary had turned me away – she was the plump woman in the parish who "helps" everyone; her main role, though, was as father's surrogate wife. To get to him you had to go through her, and she saw no value in letting me see father. I walked into that empty church and kneeled down in front of the statue of the Holy Family. Joseph was teaching Jesus to use carpentry tools; Mary looked on. I prayed these words: "I am here, and I am listening." I had no other words. In the years since, that has been my primary prayer: "I am here, and I am listening."

My prayers for others changed, as well. When I prayed for the village women in Darfur, beset by genocidal Arabs on horseback, who killed their husbands and sons, burned their homes, and raped them, I didn't pray for strangers. I prayed for my kin. I prayed for people who, I knew with a blinding suddenness, were every bit as smart as I, as valuable as I, as unique as I, and disintegrating under a crushing wave. Before, when I had prayed for such women, I had imagined them – without consciously realizing that I was doing this – to be less intelligent than I, less worthy, featureless. Surely God would not allow people exactly like me – people with just as many memories of heartfelt pasts as I, and just as many plans for significant futures, blameless people who had done absolutely nothing to deserve this fate – surely God would not allow such people to perish so viciously, to be exterminated without so much as a commemorative plaque.

The recognition of my spiritual sisterhood with the women victims of Darfur informs me of much about the spiritual world that I came to understand in no other way. I get it that fame is just … fame. Nothing more, nothing less. It is no signifier of worth. I get it that I have done nothing to deserve the pleasures I have enjoyed. I have done nothing to deserve the hot shower I had this morning, or the abundant, hunger-erasing calories in my refrigerator right now. I get it that the divine is as present in the life of an anonymous woman living in a straw hut, eating aid porridge, as he is in the person of the pope or a rock star; the divine is as present in what looks like pointless suffering as he is in that moment that the winner picks up his Nobel Prize. I "believed" all this before, of course; I "knew" all this before. Just as everyone else "believes" this and "knows" this. But now I really believe this, and I really know this. And I see that divinity in people, all the time, and I feel a new awe that, as far as I know, completely eludes fortunate people.

Confronted by nothing but my own pain, minute by minute, hour by hour, day by day, week by month by year, I realized that the only reality I knew – my own pain – stood between me and God.

I decided that God was more important than my pain. I let go of the idea that I was worth anything. I let go of the idea that my work was worth anything. I let go of the idea that my hopes and dreams and plans were worth anything. I let go of the idea that my need to serve was worth anything. I let go of the idea that I had any understanding of God at all. I let go of my need for meaning.

My temptation was to decide that since I had suffered, since God had "betrayed" me, I could walk away from God, into the arms and service of Satan. I had permission to be cynical, to be cruel, to despair, to generate darkness. That was my most formidable obstacle. Letting go of that permission, and, with it, any sense of personal entitlement, was my commission.

"My dissertation, my life's work, has just been rejected by a publisher who'd previously accepted it; 'too controversial.' Those wild forget-me-nots clustering in the grass are the same shade as the sky in heaven. Thank you, God, for that blue. I'm living off, and losing, my life savings. These melting icicles capture light and fascinate. Thank you, God, for weather and seasons, for water and their effect upon it. I can walk today, but in a few days, I won't be able to walk. This apple is so crisp and so sweet. Thank you, God, for my teeth and my tongue and for the fruit of the tree. I will never marry, never be a mother, never have a home. This student is so eager for knowledge. "Thank you, God." That's how, to my best ability, I do it. I struggle to let go of what causes me pain, because I don't matter. I am the seed that, Jesus said, must die. I am the shoulders that, Jesus said, must take up a cross and carry it. This is the day that the Lord has made. I work to rejoice and be glad.

I'm not going to ask you if you've ever chosen to suffer, or if suffering has ever contributed to your growth, because I already know that the answer to both questions is "Yes." You climbed Mount Everest, Rand. I didn't climb Everest, but I trekked enough in the Himalaya to know that ninety percent of the time, the trekker is at least uncomfortable, and there are plenty of moments of real agony. You push your body up, and up, and up, and the uphill never stops, until you crest the pass and then you experience the very different pain of managing a strategic collapse downhill for thousands of feet, struggling to spring, not squash, your ankles and knees. Your thighs and calves cramp and your socks fill with blood, the blood dries and abrades your skin; the resultant sores fill with pus; you can feel the fleas crawling over your knee beneath your clothing; you can see the blood stain your lunghi; you can't feel the leeches as they attach themselves to you, leech saliva is anesthetic, and numbs, but you can feel blood gush once they, sated, drop off of you; you crap outside and, occasionally, you see worms wriggling in your stool – no wonder your butt had been so itchy; you yearn to be clean, and well-fed, and warm, and you are, simply, bored out of your mind. The mountains are beautiful, but so is a soft chair. After ten or twelve hours of thousands of footsteps, nothing is more appealing than fantasies of a pizza – eaten in Kansas, a very flat state – followed by a warm bath. I used to trek with a guy who spoke of nothing – not the grandeur of the mountains nor the richness of the culture – but the first, and then the second, and then the third, and then the fourth, all the way up to the twentieth, meal he would eat once he got home to Fox Island in Puget Sound in the good old U. S. of A. His first meal was to be a turkey sandwich on sourdough bread with melted Swiss cheese and iceberg lettuce. He chose to trek. He chose to go without turkey sandwiches.

You chose to suffer, Rand, and you then bragged how much of a better man that suffering made you. You courted death. You slept on cold ground. You experienced a taste of altitude sickness – the often fatal swelling of the lungs and the enfeebling of the brain. You forced your calves and your thighs to work past the point where they were groaning for you to let them quit, past the point where they did quit and you had to work your hands over your thighs to pump out a hobble. You chose, not to step over sidewalks past lovely plate glass windows full of juicy consumer goods; you chose, rather, to step over ice where, if you slid just six inches, you'd fall thousands of feet into a crevasse and to your slow death from internal bleeding and a cracked neck. You say you can't believe in God because of all the suffering in the world; how do you climb Everest – to climb is to suffer – in your ideal, Godless, suffering-free world?

If I were God, pussy that I am, I would not have created suffering. I would have created a cotton candy world, sweet, without any calories, even, in which everything worked out for everybody all the time. Given my fear of bugs, I wouldn't have created ants. Ants give me the creeps. Pretty much anything with six legs and compound eyes gives me the creeps. I think an ideal aerobic exercise routine for most women would be to put them in a room and tell them that there is a bug in their hair. That will get them jumping around. Scientist Edward O. Wilson calls ants "little creatures who run the world." If I were God, I would not create suffering, and I would not create ants – and my antless creation, in no time, would be a non-functional slop.

God wants a relationship with us, and to have a relationship with him, we have to be given a choice. To choose God, we have to be able to recognize God. There is no recognition of anything without contrast. We would not recognize tall people without short people. We would not recognize God without the Godless. In order to be able to be given a choice, we have to eat from the tree of Knowledge, and separate from God. No suffering means no freedom. We are all Adam, we are all Eve, and we have all chosen suffering, because we have all chosen the freedom to choose. We chose this chance to be ourselves, because to have any identity, we needed to separate from God. God gave us that, and that is love. Those who want, but do not love, do not allow those they want any freedom, or any separation.

save SEND delete

Tuesday 10:08 p.m.
Dear Rand,
I am so sorry! I just realized that I mentioned to you that ... parasitological phenomenon that I'm not supposed, ever, to mention to you ever again.

Never again. I promise. Will scour every outgoing e-mail before pressing "send." I'll be as diligent as an East German border guard.

save SEND delete

Wednesday. 10:11 a.m.
Dear Amanda,
How goes it?

save SEND delete

INBOX
you are pretending interest in moi in order to bank some hours you can withdraw later to talk about your famous atheist ... n'est-ce pas?

Wednesday 10:34 a.m.
Amanda, ma chere,
Is it really possible that any mere mortal would have to *pretend* interest in *vous*?

save SEND delete

INBOX
touché my little cabbage touché … must remember that when
i fence with you i fence with a master

Wednesday 10:37 a.m.
So, are you going to update me or do I have to pull teeth?
Remember: I am a master. I've got my pliers at the ready.

save SEND delete

INBOX
the troupe is doing sophocles' "antigone"

Wednesday 10:55 a.m.
Dear Rand,
Wait! Wait. Approach a problem from its conceptual opposite
and one sees so much. Rand, Why doesn't anyone frame the
question THIS way???

You ask me to justify my belief in God in a world of suffering,
but not to justify my belief in God in a world of pleasure. Before-
and-after crime-scene snapshots often attest that pleasure, rather
than suffering, was the culprit, the thief in the night, the worm in
the apple.

Even suffering theorists seem to agree that an absence of
suffering is the norm as well as the ideal. It is suffering, and the
sufferer, that is other, that attracts and deserves dissection. Our
focus on what suffering does to warp us, but not on what getting
what we want does to warp us, reveals our prejudice against
those who suffer. We humans believe that suffering is a taint that
only the fortunate can cleanse, that sufferers are not just unfortunate, but the punished, and that only the fortunate can, with
the right theories, reprieve them. Suffering is a blight from
karma, chance, or God, and, as such it calls out for schools of
thought. Good fortune is normal; there is no need to study it.
People demand of the poor, "Why are you so poor?" Who swings

round and asks the real question, "Why are you so goddamn rich?" In a world where millions of children die yearly from malnutrition, isn't the question not, "Why are you so thin," but, rather, "Why are you so fat?"

Each sufferer has an idea of who he would be if he were not suffering: "I would be a fulfilled mother if my child had not died;" "I would be an accomplished athlete if my legs had not been amputated;" "If I were a rich man, I'd build a big, tall house with a fine tin roof and real wooden floors below."

In Bloomington, I had a doppelganger, a secret twin, an imaginary non-suffering self. My ideal, non-suffering self was healthy, of course. She was a successful scholar who had published the important works in her field. She had lots of lovers with whom she had lots of fun. She had a kitchen with a vast, butcher block table, Sabatier carbon steel knives, the kind of oven that does what a baker wants it to do and never scorches your fingertips as you struggle to work around its ill-fitting racks and seesawing thermometer, and a graduated selection of copper-bottom pots, from one small enough to melt two ounces of chocolate to one large enough to heat water for a bath. My doppelganger had a dog – an old-fashioned, snowy-day, fur-forever dog. She lived in an Arts-and-Crafts bungalow, on an acre of land, and wowed the adoring crowds at her many speaking engagements. A funny thing happened around the time that I finalized this fantasy. I met her. Only in my case, it was a he.

I was homeless. I was using up hours everyday trying to organize food and a horizontal surface for sleep. Professor Dante needed a dog sitter. I began selling myself over the phone. "I'm a non-smoking, Bohunk spinster who is about to finish a PhD. I love dogs:" who wouldn't want that woman sitting his house? Dante demanded references. No problem – my worst enemy would testify that I could clean a house in my sleep, and that I can get a dog to purr. Dante told me he'd have to check my references. He called back. "You really do love dogs, and you are very clean!" he gushed, awestruck. To this day I wonder what blessed soul supplied him with that recommendation. "I'd love it if you could house-sit for me," he said.

"I'll be able to take a bath!" was all I could think.

When Professor Dante and I met, we talked, non-stop, for two hours. We laughed. We cried. We had so much in common. We knew some of the same people back East. My old roommate worked with his mother. Dante had gone to the same school as an old boyfriend, blocks from my old apartment. We were both children of immigrants. His CD collection looked like the CD collection I would amass if I had money to buy CDs. The difference between us, of course, wide as the river Styx, was that he was a huge success, and I a complete failure.

Dante was at that stage of a world-class academic's career where every time he walked into a room, a greeting committee would intercept him with a bouquet of rosebuds and baby's breath and a chilled magnum of champagne. He was always going important places, meeting important people, and doing important things. I was to look after his house while he was away. He told me to sleep in his bed. I had a total body orgasm the first night. I rolled my body around on his high-thread-count sheets, and did not crash to the floor, as I so often did when I slept on chairs in the public library. His property included a black walnut tree, an English walnut tree, and a grove of apples. I wanted to write poems about his yard. I could not wait to bake a German chocolate cake in his oven. I could not wait to walk his dog – a St. Bernard!!! I could not wait to swing in his hammock, do a load of wash in his laundry room, mow his lawn, pull his weeds, dust the frames around photographic evidence of his meetings with the high and the mighty. Dante was the non-suffering Mira.

There are many unexpected routes to contact with another human being. A limited intimacy can occur during a survey phone call. A choked kind of intimacy can occur between a house-sitter and her client. My mother cleaned houses. My grandmother cleaned houses. I always worked to maintain discrete distance between myself and my employer, as did my mother and my grandmother before me. It was a question of propriety. And, yet, I couldn't help but continuously "meet" Dante, in, for example, the food in his refrigerator – Styrofoam containers of high-toned leftovers from fancy restaurants – sushi, prosciutto, tapas – and half-drunk bottles of wine. No fresh fruits, no fresh vegetables, no whole grains, no food at all that it would take more than five minutes in a microwave to reheat: tsk-tsk.

The affairs limned themselves in the form of haggard and enraged women arriving at Dante's door at all hours, pounding on that portal, and hurling consumer items at me at high velocity. One threw an espresso machine, another, a hand-held massager – heavy personal possessions Dante had left at their domiciles. I had to dodge quickly. The affairs unraveled in the Bloomington Farmer's Market, where grad students pulled me aside into the hay and reported, sotto voce, "So, you're house-sitting for Dante. Has he tried to fuck you yet? Don't believe his eyes. He's not a good looking guy; it's the eyes. They pretend interest. It's all pretense. Believe me. Ask my housemate Sarah. She was stupid enough to fall for it. She was his student, get it? His *student.* He started seducing her before he handed out the syllabus that first day of class. And her whole career is hanging in the balance on how he assesses her work, right? Well, guess what. He assessed her first between the sheets."

The affairs peeked out at me, like a kitten's eyes from under a dresser, in Dante's asides about himself. This was not a man celebrating his status as a great lover or even just an average player. "Well, I can't do anything right, apparently. Just ask any of my exes," he whimpered, after getting Anselm, his St. Bernard, entangled in the leash when handing him off to me. "So, you are single? A blessed state. Stay single. That is best," he would pronounce, shaking his head. "Anselm," he told me, "has a very high IQ. He's the smartest dog on the block. He's also the loneliest. His intellect interferes with his ability to achieve intimacy." Dante gazed into my eyes after that last comment. I didn't know if he wanted me to nod heavily, burst out laughing, clutch his head to my bosom, or slap my hand on his crotch. Good Catholic Bohunk girl that I am, I froze, remained poker-faced, and, later, got the line down in my diary. Paraphernalia left visible on the sink-top in a bathroom he knew we shared were the most explicit: condoms, K-Y Jelly, hair dye, Viagra, anti-dark circle under-eye cream, anti-bag under-eye cream, anti-depressants.

I dutifully took phone messages about missed professional opportunities and missed financial boats. I noted his asides about how much easier life would be if he could just give it all up, adopt a life of poverty and obedience, and enter a monastery. Failing that, he said, he'd like to go back to his old Catholic grammar school, and be the school janitor, the old deaf guy, who, uncomplaining, did all the nuns' chores, and never missed daily mass.

This shadowy, unsought, intimacy grew to vex me. The sense of Dante that began to bleed through me was of a man in pain. From my perspective, Professor Dante was my non-suffering doppelganger. From his perspective, he was one of the wretched of the earth. He didn't appreciate his house as a shelter from the cold; he bemoaned it as a burden that demanded his time in constant, handyman fix-ups. He didn't celebrate his fame as a blessed channel for his ideas to the wider world; he condemned academic celebrity as a pestilence. He didn't embrace his lovers as teammates in the greatest game; he cringed from them as if they were piranhas nibbling away at his peachy flesh. If only he could just be a janitor. I wanted to do something to assuage his pain, which was now reflected in me, but I couldn't. I couldn't because any intimacy I was experiencing was unilateral. I was in Dante's house; he was not in mine. I don't think he was even aware that when I wasn't house-sitting for him, I was homeless.

I guess I never took his pain as seriously as it warranted until the suicide attempt. This man who had everything that my non-suffering doppelganger wanted, wanted to die, or at least he wanted to scar himself for life, and cause his circle of lovers, students, colleagues and admirers crushing worry, or perhaps merely disgust. Failing that, Dante wanted what I had in abundance: poverty, obscurity, labor, isolation, and prayer.

In the same way that I experienced an intense vein of intimacy with the surveyed madman, and could never transcend that vein – having spoken to him only over the phone, I'll never know, for example, what he looked like – I had no context for my intense, but fleeting, impressions of Dante. I never interacted with him, or even observed him, in a room with other people in it. I got the impression, though, that he was not a nice guy. Nice teachers get it that having sex with students is nasty. Nice guys don't repeatedly inspire former girlfriends to throw heavy appliances at house-sitters.

What made Dante such an unhappy asshole? Suffering? In that glorious house, on that Eden-like property, with all those fans tossing their panties at him? I think that getting just about everything a scholar could possibly want is what drove Dante to attempt suicide. When people worship you, it is easy to mistreat them. When you are surrounded by people you've mistreated, who cannot openly retaliate, you are surrounded by bitterness and resentment waiting for their opening to make their vengeful move. When life holds nothing back and throws itself at you in all its flavors, your mechanism for registering joy fatigues. Tonguing every surface, your burned-out tongue tastes nothing.

I spent my time in Bloomington suffering, and I ended up being a person I am proud to be, a person I like, one with no regrets. If I had not suffered there, if I had gotten everything I wanted, I think I would have ended up exactly like Dante. His traps had my name all over them. Like him, I would convince myself that I was a special, charming, Bohemian genius to whom the normal rules of sexual decency did not apply; I would whine about the burdens of my fame till my tears blinded me to suffering as proximate as my house-sitter's homelessness. Though "an author of fierce compassion" (New York Times Book Review) I would not feel the pain of the students I slept with, and those I did not sleep with. Those traps would target my ego, intellect, libido, and self-pity as precisely as they suited Dante, as snugly as a shell suits its snail. I, too, would have been warped, not by pain, but by pleasure, a pleasure too addictive to push from my lips. Would I have enjoyed the pleasure to which I was addicted? All of that comfort would have stood between me and the awareness necessary to have recognized and enjoyed all of that comfort.

There is a trompe l'oeil feature to our desire to live in a world without suffering. The closer we get to the most precise non-suffering world we can imagine, the further it retreats. In the end, the non-suffering world, rather than solidifying into a concrete realty that mirrors our definition, disappears. All along, it had been an optical illusion. The bumper is always in front of the car.

So that's the best I can do when it comes to the blah, blah, blah, Rand. But I won't close with blah, blah, blah. I'll close with this, from James: "If a brother or sister has nothing to wear and has no food for the day, and one of you says to them, 'Go in peace, keep warm, and eat well,' but you do not give them the necessities of the body, what good is it? So also faith of itself, if it does not have works, is dead." All my blah blah blah, above, is about why I believe in God in spite of suffering. But God says that belief is not enough. We believers must also stand with others who suffer, and do what we can to meet their needs. In this world of suffering, God, the God who demands that we love the sufferer, is our very best map.

save **SEND** delete

Saturday 11:00 a.m.
Naked? On stilts? She wears a kaffiyeh and is a member of Al Qaeda?

save SEND delete

INBOX
pshaw

Saturday 11:17 a.m.
You're telling me you're doing Sophocles' play "Antigone" straight? With none of the effects that a less sophisticated theatergoer than myself might find pretentious?

save SEND delete

INBOX
swear on mother's ... scratch that ... on my brother's grave that is what i am telling you

Saturday 11:32
I'm impressed. And very happy. I love "Antigone." She's the only woman I've ever met who's more difficult than I. I'd definitely go gay for her, though she would reject me as not good enough for her, and she'd be right. I wish I could catch the show. Amanda, show kindness to a wayfaring e-mailer. Describe to me the first scene.

save SEND delete

INBOX
with pleasure my favorite wayfarer ... opening scene ... antigone ... your humble servant ... hangs suspended from a noose center stage ... lighting very dramatic ... stark black and white ... audience gasps ... music swells ... swollen music ... where's my ice ... creon sobs ... his hubris has doomed his son ... a kettle is whistling ... not onstage ... will return ... with a cup of early grey ... it IS early here even for british earls

Saturday noon

WAIT! Antigone doesn't commit suicide at the beginning of the play. She commits suicide at the END of the play. What gives?

save **SEND** delete

INBOX

old wine in new skins sweetums ... we're doing "antigone" in reverse chronological order ... just like "memento" flick about the guy with amnesia ... ending comes first

Saturday 12:46

Antigone didn't have amnesia?? And, with this reverse chronological order approach, you ruin the suspense. The audience will know how it ends!

save **SEND** delete

INBOX

IT'S A GREEK *TRAGEDY* SHERLOCK HOW DO YOU THINK IT ENDS? anyone coming to see this will know how it ends ... must keep audience on toes ... speaking of toes ... how much longer will you keep me in suspense ... have you started licking each other's yet?

Saturday 1:03 p.m.

I'm waiting. Just waiting. Sent him a long e-mail. Usually he'll e-mail or call with the most quotidian question. And I'll think, "Why did I send him all that?" thinking that all he cared about were the most trivial aspects. And then he'll write back later, or call, with something huge, and I'll just be all a dither, and think, Geez, this guy is really special.

Speak of the devil. A message from him in my inbox this very second.

save **SEND** delete

Saturday 1:05 p.m.
Dear Rand,
Like "Duke Wayne," not like "Duquesne."
save **SEND** delete

Saturday 1:11 p.m.
Amanda,
Bingo. Wanted to know how to pronounce one of my student's names.

He's throwing me off guard. He's concocting a bulletproof refutation of my arguments about God and suffering. I'm ready.
save **SEND** delete

INBOX
wake me when the toe sucking starts ...

Saturday 2:02 p.m.
Dear Rand,
Ecstasy? I wouldn't have thought that that would have presented such a large occupational hazard to a physicist?

I'm glad, though, that you see us as having something in common. I think?
save **SEND** delete

Saturday 2:33 p.m.
Dear Rand,
Yeah, I did say that I guard against ecstasy. Funny you picked up on that. But I'm religious and you're not. Are you referring to your days with the Carthusians? They're not an ecstatic bunch. I guess when you are very hungry even porridge can excite, but does it provide enough calories to support ecstatic states?
save **SEND** delete

Saturday 2:59 p.m.

I wasn't trying to be off-putting in my sarcasm. I guess I'm just missing your point. Okay, let me be very straightforward here. How does ecstasy relate to science, to physics, to cosmology?

And how is it that that is something that we have in common? Can you also not afford to lose control? Why?

I'm familiar with many images of saints losing any connection to their flesh and being taken up into other realms – Bernini's "St. Teresa of Avila," Murillo's "St. Augustine in Ecstasy." Both Giotto and Caravaggio did a "St. Francis in Ecstasy." Same title, but very different paintings.

You don't really come across artworks depicting physicists in such a state, although a Jackson Pollock of "Einstein in Ecstasy," if discovered, would fetch the highest price of any painting on record, no doubt. I'd like to stumble across that at a yard sale.

FWIW, here's the etymology of the word, which I just looked up: from "ek," "out" and "stasis," "stand." So, ecstasy is to stand outside. I can't say that I really get that.

save SEND delete

Saturday 3:01 p.m.

Amanda-Ananda,

He's writing me about ecstasy. Is this a ploy? Is he setting me up to accept some atheist argument? Or wordplay? I write him about agony and so he writes me about ...?

save SEND delete

Saturday 3:02 p.m.

Dear Rand,

Wait! I just remembered something. It's Jan Matejko's painting of Copernicus discovering the heliocentric system. Copernicus looks ecstatic. In fact, he is in basically the same posture – leaning back, arms wide – as St. Teresa in Bernini's statue.

Is that what you are talking about, then? The joy that you

experience, as a scientist, in discovering new things? But why would that be something one had to guard against?

save SEND delete

Saturday 4:00 p.m.

Rand,

Have I pissed you off? Just checking ...?

save SEND delete

Sunday 6:57 a.m.

Dear Rand,

Of course I see your point. And of course it is a good point, and an important one. Of course.

Of course as a scientist you need to guard against any force that lures you away from your objective. I can see how important it is to proceed from verifiable fact to verifiable fact, without imaging anything between the facts, and not ever to allow anything other than facts to interfere with the discovery of the truth.

I admire that about science, and I admire that about you, really I do.

And thank you for the cloud metaphor. It helps me to understand what you are saying. Just as our "pattern seeking" function allows us to see locomotives or Christmas trees or maps of Spain in the clouds, that doesn't mean that those realities exist outside of our own imaginations. Our brains don't focus on the individual details, but create details between details that don't exist in objective, verifiable reality. Yes, a kid daydreaming on a beach can do that with clouds and no one gets hurt. I agree with you. (Were you thinking of N. C. Wyeth's "The Giant"?)

And, yes, I deeply admire your courageous interrogation of your fellow scientists who see a cluster of facts and then plug imaginary material in between the facts to "create" a God, or to give the lay public the impression of God. It must frustrate you, as a cosmologist, to see other cosmologists and physicists speak *as* scientists and say that evidence indicates that there is a God. After all, as you say, they should be looking at facts, no more, no less, and not imagining and creating stuff that isn't there. I can see why book titles like "The Mind of God" and "The God Particle" upset you – they're irresponsible. They mislead the lay public into thinking that society's intellectual leaders have bought into Christianity.

I'm sorry if anything I said upset you so.

If I may, Rand, I'll mention just this one other thing. Imagining or creating stuff between the facts may not be what scientists are supposed to do. But it certainly is what some scientists have done.

Rand, you know the famous story about Archimedes jumping out of his bathtub and running down the street naked shouting "Eureka," after the concept of displacement suddenly hit him while he was bathing. You know about Frederick Kekule discovering the structure of the benzene molecule after dreaming about a snake swallowing its own tail. And about Otto Loewi's dream that won him a Nobel Prize in medicine. In other words, intuition blesses scientists as well as poets. Scientific discoveries may indeed come, usually, from a step-by-step, fact-by-fact process, but sometimes they come the same way a poem comes: "Aha."

Is that really something against which we must guard?

save **SEND** delete

Thursday 3:42 p.m.

Drear, Amanda, drear.

He's stopped talking to me.

save **SEND** delete

INBOX

he's inhaling

Thursday 7:56 p.m.
?????

save **SEND** delete

INBOX
we must do both my darling ... we must inhale we must
exhale ... we all have our own rhythms ... there are giant
tortoises in the far distant realms of every~when~land who
inhale for ten long seconds and don't exhale again for one
hundred and fifty years ... these are very long-lived tortoises
... resist the temptation to stop watch ... live your life ... enjoy
the sweet zephyr next it descends ... if it does not ... do not
blame ... any more than you blame yourself for the rhythm of
your own breaths

Friday midnight
Dear Lord Randolph Court-Wright, Marquis of Alnwick,
You are a breathtakingly intelligent man.

I'm supposed to know that because of all the books you've
published and your appearance with Billy Moyers and your
lunch with the queen.

But you know that's not me. I don't believe in bees because of
bee textbooks. I believe in bees because I've been stung.

I am in awe of your intelligence because Rand, you just figured
out something about me that no one before you – not Amanda or
Justin or Imre or Sandy the physicist or anyone, as far as I know, has
so much as a clue about. That you had this insight and that you
mentioned it makes you either smarter or more capable of intimacy,
at least on this one matter, than anyone else I've ever known.

H o w   d i d   y o u   k n o w ?

Did you work it out verifiable fact by verifiable fact?

Or did you color between the lines, and did it swoop down
upon you in one, big, intuitive leap?

save **SEND** delete

Thursday 8:59 a.m.

Hail, Go Dess!

I'm not even going to pretend interest in Antigone.

He exhaled. Big Time. And then retreated back to the enchanted realms of every~when~land.

save SEND delete

INBOX

what happened just previous to disappearance therein lies the clue ... antigone is a bitch ... couldn't she just let sleeping dogs ... her dead brother ... lie ... why wasn't the first burial adequate ... why did she have to bury polyneices twice ... my guess: antigone suffered from obsessive compulsive disorder ... probably a compulsive housecleaner ... always doing things twice, tidying things up ... trying to work that into script but with amnesia and reverse chronological order may be overload for average theatergoer ... am now wishing i had taken role of creon ...

Thursday 11:00 a.m.

I much prefer the obsessive compulsive angle to the amnesia angle. I hope you can change it before the play goes into full production. I imagine a complete line of Antigone cleaning products to accompany, and perhaps to fund, your play. "Get your house tidy enough to satisfy the Greek Pantheon." I'd buy those.

What happened before Rand disappeared this time? He made an amazing observation about me. Amazing because it's as obvious as the nose on your face, and yet nobody's ever made this observation before.

He intuited, or pieced together – or he took a damn lucky guess.

save SEND delete

Wednesday 9:42 a.m.

I Googled him. Is it against the girl code to Google a man who is ignoring you? Is it clever and Nancy Drew or "Fatal Attraction" and stalker-creepy? I don't even like that I'm asking these questions. I vow never to Google him again.

He's been in Washington, DC. Meeting with Al Gore.

I cried.

Because I really had convinced myself that the Atlantic Ocean was implacable and the reason we were restricted to e-mail. But, lo and behold, it appears that new technologies have been invented, and one may cross the Atlantic by zeppelin, and other vehicles, and he crossed it. Though, on a wall map of the US, I'm the width of a pinkie-tip north of Washington DC, he did not invite me to meet him there. Or feel any compulsion to come here to New Jersey.

Amanda, I am a deluded idiot. Only because this whole thing has been so utterly impossible – me, this non-entity debating with a bleeping *lord* – have I allowed it to myself. I keep reminding myself how impossible it all is, but part of me insists on taking it seriously. It's been like class. I've got neat rows, attentive students, all whipped into shape, all heads dropped, toiling over their assignments, and this one bad boy back in the last row, against the wall, staring at me, making eyes, refusing to obey, defiantly brandishing his crush on the teacher. I need to kick that son of a bitch the hell out.

save SEND delete

Tuesday 4:47 p.m.

Dear Lord Court-Wright

Hi. Something to hear from you after – not hearing from you.

I understand that a while back you were in Washington, DC. An interesting – and verifiable – fact. While Paterson and England are 3,498 miles apart, Paterson and Washington are a mere 233.

Do the math.

And then tell me why I should write to you again.

save **SEND** delete

Tuesday 6:52 p.m.

Why? Why have you had my fantasy?

Are you just telling me that as some pathetic lure to get me to write to you again?

save **SEND** delete

Tuesday 7:30 p.m.

But it makes no sense. There are obvious reasons why someone with my bio would fantasize that I wake up and that all other human beings on the planet have just disappeared over night, and that I get to have the place all to myself. There are lots of details that you didn't get. I like imaging going into super-markets and purchasing – and walking out with – whatever I want, and never being hungry again. And I like finally being allowed to have a dog. And to go swimming. And moving into a big house with a big yard and a big bed. But why would you have such a fantasy? Your life has been nothing like mine. You carry yourself like a civilian.

save **SEND** delete

Tuesday 7:59 p.m.

Okay.

save **SEND** delete

Tuesday 8:14 p.m.

No. Not a trick. Not a code. I said "okay." I mean, "okay."

save **SEND** delete

Tuesday 8:48 p.m.

Amanda. She said that I should let you exhale when you are

ready to exhale. If you aren't ready to tell me why you have that fantasy, you can tell me when you are ready.

save SEND delete

Tuesday 9:00 p.m.

She has her moments. That's why I keep her around.

save SEND delete

Tuesday 9:16 p.m.

Making up for lost time? Paging Monsieur Proust.

save SEND delete

Tuesday 9:30 p.m.

Well, just that you haven't written me in so long, and yet in the past – what – four hours? You've sent me a book.

What time is it over by you, anyway? Two o'clock in the morning? Three? Somewhere in there? Why not get some sleep? We can talk in the morning. I mean, at a decent hour. Not this "dark night of the soul" hour. Paging F. Scott Fitzgerald.

save SEND delete

Tuesday 9:42 p.m.

Because I care about you.

save SEND delete

Tuesday 10:00 p.m.

Yeah, I know.

save SEND delete

Tuesday 10:11 p.m.

Because you are wrong, Lord Randolph Court-Wright, Marquis of Alnwick. Because you are wrong.

Attending to discrete, verifiable facts is *not* the only way to get to the truth. Intuition, and its grandma, faith, are also routes.

If I attend exclusively to the discrete, verifiable facts, I see that you are – you will forgive me for this, but it's past my bedtime and I'm not at my most scrupulous – you are an asshole.

I'm not trying to be mean. I'm trying to do what writers do; I'm trying to use le mot juste. I'm trying to do what scientists do; I'm trying to offer a verifiable diagnosis based on objective facts that could be ascertained by another researcher running the same experiment.

You show up. You make intense statements that make me want to – . You act all intimate and engage with me in a way that is way out of bounds for what is really happening here. And then you disappear.

But you are more than discrete facts. You are a whole. A whole I see because I connect the dots, just like that damned, pattern-seeking, holy fool who insists on perceiving a detailed street map of downtown Barcelona in a sunset cloud. And the whole I see is, ultimately, a human being. A temple of the Holy Spirit – 1 Corinthians 6:19. Made in the image and likeness of God – Genesis 1:27. Christ in disguise – St. Francis and the leper.

I have *faith* in you. And I *love* you – and I mean "love" here in the sense that Jesus used it in the tale of the Good Samaritan. I'm not saying that you are a scabby, beaten up lump by the side of the road. And I'm not saying that you are not. And I'm not saying that I'm the charitable Good Samaritan who is taking you in, and I'm not saying that I'm not. It's too late at night to be editing all this to make it kosher.

You're a human being, Rand. I have faith in that. Although the discrete facts, like pins recording known, verifiable data on a chart, create the unmistakable profile of an asshole, the coloring-in between those pins that my imagination – and my faith – perform, renders you another, lovable, child of God.

save SEND delete

Tuesday 10:27 p.m.

You're not going to take my advice and go to sleep, are you?

Of course I forgive you. Seventy times seven, remember?

save **SEND** delete

Tuesday 10:46 p.m.

That is an excellent question. A really excellent question. I look forward to answering it. Tomorrow morning.

Sleep, my friend. Sleep.

save **SEND** delete

Wednesday 3:08 p.m.

Dear Rand,

So, I did not live up to my promise of last night and write to you this morning. I'm very proud of myself.

Rand, this business of your being very intense with me and then disappearing has been going on since our first encounter. It's hard on me. Eventually, probably, this will come between us terminally and things between us, like all things, will end.

I'm not asking you to be predictable. I'm not attempting to precipitate, right now, an end to our interaction. I'm just saying. It's been said. Let us, for the moment, move on to other things, like these fascinating e-mails you've sent me.

Rand, you wrote – in one of the many e-mails you sent last night – I'm not going to go through and find it right now – if I remember correctly you wrote that immediately after you read one of my e-mails, you were in an airport lounge, a common experience for you, and that you felt something that you'd never felt before. You scanned the crowd and found yourself asking, what dark secret of sadism, or child abuse, or simple indifference, lurked in each heart. You studied an attentive father, and wondered how far from society's eyes he'd have to be, or how hard life would have to kick him for him to become a molester. You eyed an elder statesman, and you wondered what decisions, behind closed doors, he had made that destroyed the lives of the voiceless poor. You saw people in a whole new way, and you didn't like it. It took a conscious effort on your part to see people in a benign way again. That felt phony, like pasting a smiley face on a skull.

Don't we all go through something like that after we learn one of the big, scary, horrible things that young people have to learn to become adults? Like when we learn about the Holocaust? I think most people just let that horror fade, and go back to not thinking about the dark reaches of the human heart.

I want exactly what you described wanting: I want to think, but I also want the simple ability to walk through an airport waiting lounge, view other human beings, and not be haunted by images of what secret crimes these human bodies smuggle behind their apparent niceness. Hate and resentment are heavy baggage. I'm a lone traveler. I can't afford their weight.

Here's what I do. I remember that no one is righteous, not a one, Romans 3:10. I remember that that "no one" includes me. In the same way that I have been betrayed, I have betrayed others. In the same way that I have been hurt, I have hurt others. In the same way that I hope to be loved in spite of my flaws, others hope to be loved. In the same way that I am convinced that there is something lovable in me in spite of my flaws, I am convinced that there is something lovable in others in spite of their flaws. I remind myself that God lives in everyone. I pray for the gift of forgiveness.

You think I'm just being *nice* in saying all this? Believe me, my friend. I am *not.* This is how not nice I am.

Almost as soon as I arrived in Bloomington for grad school, I joined PFLAG, or Parents and Friends of Lesbians and Gays. I became involved in gay rights because of the homophobia in town. I was from the coasts, new to the Midwest – I'd never seen homophobia like this before. The homophobes used Christianity as the excuse for their hatred. I knew that as a Christian I had to speak up for love. I wrote letters to the paper, broadcast essays on the radio, and marched in picket lines.

In PFLAG, I met David, an adorable, carrot-topped Hoosier, college student, and Eagle Scout. One day, after we had watched the movie "Bent" together, I for the first time, he for the fifth, David mentioned that he didn't feel well, and that he'd not been feeling well for some time. I exhibited the exact same bovine stupidity and mundane mean-spiritedness that others had shown me in my own illness. Friends had jumped at my illness as a happy opportunity to lecture me about any resentments they'd been storing up. "Oh, so you're sick, are you? I told you not to get a PhD ... eat dairy foods ... practice Catholicism ... be a bitch." I fell into the exact same trap. When David told me that he'd been feeling under the weather, I was blinded by gratitude. Finally I had an opportunity to lecture him. I brought up aspects of his life of which I did not approve. He had Midwestern eating habits and Neanderthal politics. David was a big fan of Mississippi Mud Pie, which he made himself. He was also something of a right-wing conspiracy theorist. Confession: I loved David's Mississippi Mud Pie, and I loved it that whenever he and I did anything together he fed me bad food that I never allowed myself. You'd never find Mississippi Mud Pie – made of equal parts chocolate, sugar, nuts, and heavy cream – under MY roof. When he told me he wasn't feeling well, I urged him to eat a better diet and assume a better attitude. David nodded at my sage and caring advice. He resolved to eat more fresh fruits and vegetables and reconsider his vow to always vote the straight Republican ticket. I was confident that I'd done a good deed. I never suggested that he might want to see a doctor.

David finally did go to a physician, who informed him that he had not been feeling well because he had leukemia. David used to phone me from the hospital. He cried. He described the terror of waking up blind. He talked about his fear of death. He talked about growing up in a Midwestern town, in an actual log cabin his ancestors had built, hating himself because he was gay, attempting suicide, being rescued by a gay Lutheran minister, working hard at loving himself, and then, before he'd ever had the chance for an intimate relationship, being told that he had cancer.

I could not drive to the hospital, fifty miles away; I did not own a car. I could not visit him, anyway; his immune system was weakened and they allowed him few visitors: his minister and immediate family. I could not even pace the room while agonizing over his plight; any strong stimulus, including worry over David, or even just crying, often brought on overwhelming vertigo; I could only press the telephone receiver to my ear, hunker down and ride out his calls for their duration. I pressed my body into the couch, squeezed my eyes shut, struggled against the vertigo, paralyzed, unable to reach out to him, unable to comfort his pain.

You would think that because I myself was ill, and because I loved David like the little brother I never had, I would have offered him special wisdom and compassion. Think again. During those phone calls I confronted shocking ugliness in myself: I envied David. He was receiving medical attention. For myself, without SSDI, I was convinced that once I'd exhausted my life savings, I'd end up on the street, vomiting and unable to move. I had learned that no friend, no family, no priest, no community would stand in the way. Everyone was rallying 'round David: his parents, his minister, doctors, siblings, fellow Boy Scouts, the gay rights community. Since he was getting medical care, and community support, he would get better, and I never would. For David, illness would be a way station, something he passed through on the way to the rest of his life, a heroic, character-building episode. He would pass me by, and I would remain there, alone, plastered to that couch. Some small but intractably evil sliver of me insisted on clinging to that envy. I was sure that medical care would make all the difference for David right up to his funeral. He was 25.

My effort to remember how flawed I am is a mechanical exercise, like doing yoga on a mat. Your spine doesn't want to stretch to the point where you can touch your toes, but you tell it to, so it does. There's no warmth involved, or spontaneity. I am a feral child. I do not possess the store of memories that, from what I hear, some others do, and can access in their love for the rest of humanity. Like a Linnaean botanist surveying varieties of plants, I mentally survey the species of intimacy I have not experienced. I discover them by overhearing other people talking about the kindly priest who said a memorable word at a funeral, the caring professor who offered just the right touch to a research paper before publication, the older brother who looks out for his kid sister. I just don't have those memories, and so they do not animate my muscles, and I cannot incorporate their absent warmth into my interactions with other humans. When it comes to "love," I am limited to mechanical exercise.

The verse to which you allude, Rand, is 1 John 4:20-21. "If anyone says, 'I love God,' but hates his brother, he is a liar; for whoever does not love a brother whom he has seen cannot love God whom he has not seen. This is the commandment we have from him: whoever loves God must also love his brother."

It would be extreme to use the word that John uses here, and say that I "hate" humanity. I do feel, as you put it, like a space alien, visiting this planet, among a biological life form that is not my own. Okay, I just found and am now rereading this e-mail from you, Rand, and it is not clear to me – were you using that space alien metaphor to ask about how I feel? Or to tell me how you feel? And if you feel that way, why do you? You're so successful, so well-connected. You can't feel alienated ... can you?

So, you ask, how do I reconcile my alienation from humanity with my Christianity? In other words, since scripture tells me that I am a liar if I say that I hate man but love God, how can I claim to love God, since I often hate man? This is how, Rand: I believe in these verses, from the first chapter of John: "In the beginning was the Word, and the Word was with God, and the Word was God ... And the Word became flesh, and made his dwelling among us."

The students in my folklore classes read myths from various cultures, and, especially if they're also reading authors like you, they dismiss all myths with a wave of the hand and a comment like, "It's all the same nonsense." It isn't all the same and it isn't all nonsense. These verses communicate the unique identity of the Judeo-Christian God. Our God is not Ba'al or Tiamat or Apollo or Allah. Our God is the Word – logos – truth and reason.

The village Hinduism I knew was typified by stories in which a not particularly good or even observant man accidentally engaged in an act that was similar to worship, and reaped rewards thereby. One example: the village drunk got lost in the forest and began to cry over his fate. His tears wet the exposed tip of a Shiva lingam, most of which was buried underground. The man didn't see it, had no intention of worshiping, and was not conscious of weeping on a lingam, but his tears were close enough to the libations a pious person would spill that Shiva rewarded the man anyway. A tale: a Brahmin leaves his wife for a prostitute, kills his parents, and eats taboo foods. One day he accidentally overhears a sermon about Shiva. When he dies, the god of death comes to carry him off to deserved punishment for all of his heinous crimes, but Shiva intervenes and takes the sinner to Mount Kailas, close to heaven. The moral is very blunt: all that matters to the gods is that they get what they want – worship – by hook or by crook.

In 2006, Pope Benedict gave a speech at Regensburg, highlighting the Christian God's nature as truth and reason. Benedict contrasted that with the notion of God held by many Muslims. Allah is not bound by reason, and is not bound even by his own word. You can please Allah by converting infidels to Islam by violence. It doesn't matter that the infidels are converting only out of fear. What matters is that they obey. Not so in Christianity. "Not to act in accordance with reason is contrary to God's nature," so said the Holy Father.

God isn't just reasonable, he is reason. God isn't just truthful, he is truth. What might sound like very dry concepts have been central to me. As you intuited, Rand, I am alienated from my fellow humans. I'll up the ante. I'm alienated from God.

"God, why do you hate me?" That prayer erupts from my lips spontaneously and sincerely several times a week. Why am I still a Christian? For the same reason I'm not yet an axe murderer. Yes, I have passing thoughts of pure hate for my fellow humans, and for God. But I pause, and give those thoughts some more thought, and I don't act on them.

After I spontaneously speak from my heart and ask God, "Why do you hate me?" I never end with that prayer. My next prayers are, "I do not know. I am not God. Deus meus et omnia." I may view a situation in which it appears clear to me that the only interpretation is that God hates me. My understanding is limited, because I am not God. I remind myself that my commitment is to God; my God is my all.

How do I deal with the verses from 1 John that you mentioned above, about how one must love one's brother in order to love God? Well, as I said, I don't know that I love God. At least not in the sense that "love" means "to have mushy-gushy, obsessive feelings about another."

This whole idea that feelings matter so much was pretty foreign to people like my parents. "You do what you have to do," was their motto. They worked lousy jobs, they went to church on Sunday, they voted the straight Democratic ticket, and they didn't act on their feelings. It's a relatively recent trend to think, "If I am feeling something, I have to act as if that feeling is the most important thing in the world." If I feel depressed because I gained seven pounds, I have to give that all my attention, because my feelings are the most important things in the world. If my best friend comes in and she says that her husband just died, that's not important, because I have to pay lots of attention to being depressed because I gained seven pounds. If a tsunami of world-record proportions hits Southeast Asia and millions are injured, dead, or homeless, I can't pay attention to that because I am depressed because I gained seven pounds. I have to get counseling because I gained seven pounds. If I start to feel better, I have to encourage myself to feel sad, because I don't want to be in denial over my grief for gaining seven pounds. Otherwise, for the rest of my life, I'll have a wound over my unexpressed, unhealed, undealt with grief over gaining seven pounds.

The Twelve Step approach is variously expressed as, "Fake it till you make it" and "Don't think yourself into a right way of acting; act yourself into a right way of thinking." You hate your life? You want to curl up and sob? You want to do your drug of choice till you are a Bowery bum? Who cares? Act as if you are strong. Act as if you are brave. Act as if you care about others, even if you are completely self-absorbed. "Bring the body and the mind will follow."

I do have mushy-gushy feelings, but mostly I have them about unattainable men I have crushes on, and dogs. Not about God, and not about the mass of humanity. So, if we define "love" as the mushy-gushy, obsessive feelings thing, then, no, I do not love God, and I do not love man, and I am going straight to hell. But I don't believe in a God who will damn me for a response that I can't help. That's because I believe in a God who so much personifies truth and reason that I can always be truthful with him, and he will still love me. What do I believe my reasonable God will attend to when he judges me? What Jesus talks about in Matthew 25:31-46, and what Twelve Step would call "act as if." I act as if I had mushy-gushy feelings for the mass of humanity. I donate to charities. I volunteer time. I am a supportive friend. To me "love" is a pretty empty word. I'm interested in actions. Don't tell me you love me; buy me a big car. You know what I mean?

save SEND delete

Wednesday 4:44 p.m.

Dear Rand,

Well, first, thank you for the compliment. But all credit for that goes to God.

I consciously feared, back when I was sick, and being betrayed at every turn, that I'd never be able to teach again. I was so afraid of how humanity's betrayals, stored in my body, mind, heart and soul, might manifest in the classroom. What actually did happen was a miracle. You atheists say, "show us a miracle." They happen everyday. As Rabbi Mendel of Kotzk might say, it's not resurrection of the dead that most awes; it's the resurrection of the living.

Rand, can I share something with you? Heck, I'm just going to splice it in here.

Professor:

I would like to thank you for being a great teacher and a beautiful human being. You put your heart in every class you taught, and you have been a source of information, inspiration and motivation to all of us, including my husband – he wished he could have gone to your classes!

I remember the second class we had, I started to cry and I couldn't explain why. I was happy, that's why. I knew I was in a class where I had to face my fears, my beliefs, my ignorance, my naiveness of things and I knew I had to work hard, not to get a good grade, but to face myself. I greatly appreciate you teaching us with sincerity, sensitivity, and understanding. For me this class has been an introduction of "thought" and "awareness" and you have inspired us to challenge ourselves.

Teachers are mothers (and fathers) to the students. As one of your students, I have felt your guidance just as a mother would be to her child. I thank you, Professor, I will never forget you.

Rand, this is why I believe in God. You know me, Rand. You read me very well. You see that I do not "love" my fellow man, in the sense of mushy-gushy, obsessive feelings.

I received the e-mail, above, from a student, my first semester teaching after I had the operation and was able to go back to work. I have no money. I live in a slum. I'm full of rage. I did what Jesus told me to do. I died to myself. I did not put my feelings first. I put Jesus' command to serve others first. And I got feedback like that from students. Not because of *me.* Because of the God I strive to serve.

And here's the thing. That striving opens the door for miracles. Before every class, I pray that I will die to myself, and put my students first, and that prayer opens the door for this miracle: I see curiosity in their eyes, and I know I can satisfy that curiosity, and I resurrect.

Gushy-mushy, obsessive feelings? If my students knew how much I love them, they would be embarrassed. I wish I could capture all the stars of the sky in a great, silken sheet and lay them down at my students' feet. I wish I could watch treasures tumble across the floor, as my students pick and choose their fortunes. Failing that, I do everything I can to be the best teacher I can be.

If I obeyed secular, selfish society, if I focused only on my feelings, I would not be able to experience that miracle that I do experience every time I teach.

save **SEND** delete

Wednesday 6:02 p.m.

Well, that's a change of subject.

Anyway, no, absolutely not. Never. Never even close. In fact, I saw right through it from when I was a little kid. Something I'm guessing that you and I have in common.

save **SEND** delete

Wednesday 6:17 p.m.
No. Never.

save SEND delete

Wednesday 6:27 p.m.
What part of "no, absolutely not, never," is not clear?

save SEND delete

Wednesday 6:40 p.m.
Dear Rand,
What have I said that is not clear? No, I have never believed in it. And I'm guessing you, skeptic and scoffer and pure materialist that you are, have not, either. So, we have that in common. What's not clear in what I'm saying?

save SEND delete

Wednesday 6:59 p.m.
Well, I don't know what to say. But, given your last e-mail, I guess I better say something.

I'm stunned. Knocked for a loop. I don't see how you reconcile that position with your materialism. I really thought that this would be something we'd have in common. And that's all I have to say, really. Do we need to discuss this?

save SEND delete

Wednesday 7:14 p.m.
Dear Rand,
Look, do you want me just to remind you that I know how smart and famous you are?

save send DELETE

Wednesday 7:20 p.m.

Dear Rand,

Okay. I hear you.

save **SEND** delete

Wednesday 7:39 p.m.

Dear Rand,

No, I am not humoring you.

save **SEND** delete

Wednesday 7:45 p.m.

Okay, I am humoring you.

What you're saying is ridiculous. Okay? There is NO support for it. And given that you are arguing for a position for which there is no support, you are utterly contradicting your status as a scientist.

save **SEND** delete

Wednesday 7:51 p.m.

It's bullshit. The entire thing is bullshit, from A to Z. It's a joke. It's a can of industrial strength baloney. And you BUY it?

Feh.

save **SEND** delete

Wednesday 8:01 p.m.

One piece of evidence, baby. Just one piece. Oh, what's that? You don't have any? Sorry. Next!

save **SEND** delete

Wednesday 8:03 p.m.

You better have yourself checked for early onset Alzheimer's.

save send **DELETE**

Wednesday 8:07 p.m.

Amanda! She who is worthy to be loved!

You will not believe this! Mr. World Class Scientist believes in *romantic love*!

save **SEND** delete

Wednesday 8:10 p.m.

Look, you're the one making extraordinary claims. You show the extraordinary proof. There's no onus on me to prove anything. Just because humans have believed in this crap for thousands of years – and is that really true? Social scientists argue that romantic love is a relatively recent invention, dating from the Middle Ages. How can you be so blind to your own inconsistencies! You know that people believe in God, and yet you insist that that belief counts for nothing.

I know you pal around with Edward O. Wilson, but have you actually read Edward O. Wilson? Wilson is one of my heroes. I teach him to my classes on feminism. His sociobiology is a better inoculation against belief in romantic love than graphic slides of advanced syphilis. High status males, that is, males with access to resources, select physically attractive, young, fertile, high status females. This happens among humans, mosquitoes, and bighorn sheep. If we don't call it "love" when naked mole rats do it, why call it "love" when humans do the exact same thing?

Humans pair for as long as they need to in order to raise their little clones, their little fingers in the face of their own mortality, their children. A drug cocktail makes it possible for them to overcome their natural aversion to long-term intimacy. These chemicals include testosterone, estrogen, adrenaline, dopamine, serotonin, oxytocin and vasopressin. Profiles of human brains on these chemicals are comparable to human brains on cocaine. Gimme a good lab and a syringe and I could get General George S. Patton to make a mixed tape for Field Marshall Erwin Rommel.

save **SEND** delete

234

Wednesday 8:30 p.m.

Do you hear that percussive sound way across the Atlantic? It's my fingers drumming my desktop. As I wait for ... hmmm ... what's it called again? Oh, I know. A word I learned in *science class.* Evidence!

Put up or shut up. Show me your hand or concede.

save **SEND** delete

Wednesday 10:03 p.m.

Ho, hum. I'm underwhelmed.

I just don't see it. I've never seen it. Have I ever actually met a "happy couple"? Sure, sure I have. The same night I met *SANTA CLAUS*!

The women I know feel ignored by their men. The men I know feel estranged from their women. I'll never forget a woman who summed up her marriage thus: "As long as I have a hot supper on the table when he comes home, and lay flat at night, he asks no questions, and I volunteer nothing." Or a husband who summed up his marriage to me thus, "I hope that my wife is not going crazy like her mother."

Men care only about appearance. Go ahead, hate me. Vault across your keyboard, clear the Atlantic Ocean, and go for my throat. I'll say it. Men care only about appearance. If this is an anti-male statement then Hugh Hefner, Bob Guccione and Larry Flynt are anti-male. You think that porn is one of the world's most profitable businesses because men care about any other feature of a woman besides the tautness of her breasts, the length of her legs, the roundness of her butt, and the shininess of her hair?

Women have porn, too – we get our intimacy needs met reading Jane Austen, or Harlequin Romances – do you really think that they sell so many books because there are so many *fulfilled* women out there?

Rand, why are we even talking about this?

Can we change the subject?

How about those Mets? Or … what's the name of your big soccer team … Manchester United?

save **SEND** delete

Wednesday 10:27 p.m.

Yeah, well, I'm an American, and we call it soccer. And the NFL is not exactly a cottage industry. Does it really contribute to world peace for me to call soccer "football"?

save **SEND** delete

Wednesday 10:43 p.m.

Manchester United Football Team.

Happy?

save **SEND** delete

Wednesday 11:00 p.m.

Manchester United Football Club.

I stand corrected.

It's got to be like four o'clock in the morning by you. Time to go to sleep?

save **SEND** delete

Wednesday 11:30 p.m.

Dear Rand,

Okay, you haven't written for a while, so I'm assuming that you are all peaceful and tucked in.

Good night. And …

… just … good night.

xxx ooo xxx

save **SEND** delete

INBOX

have penetrated to heart of issue … antigone is friend of bill!

re-doing entire production ... scrapping reverse chronological order innovation ... scene one ... antigone is seated around a table in a church basement ...

"hi my name is antigone and i'm an adult child of abusive parents ... my dad oedipus murdered his dad and married his mom, jocasta, who was my grandmom, and also my mom ... our home was very dysfunctional ... i grew up needing to parent my parents so i'm a bit of a control freak ... i'm getting very obsessive about my brother polyneices' funeral arrangements, and uncle creon is all bent out of shape ... i'm working to practice the twelve step principles in all my affairs ... to detach from polyneices' funeral with love" ...

only problem ... if we send antigone and creon to twelve step ... they both recover ... are at peace and happy ... no tragedy ... no immortal play ... how to solve ...

Thursday 4:32 p.m.
I love it. It's great. You're the best.
save SEND delete

INBOX
why the long face ... are you doing your basset hound imitation

Thursday 5:19 p.m.
You can intuit that from an eight-word e-mail message that never so much as alludes to chocolate chip cookie dough, sharp razors, or smooth jazz?
save SEND delete

INBOX
oh pumpkin ... we have known each other for many years ... banked all those years ... this is the interest

Thursday 5:45 p.m.

Tsover.

save **SEND** delete

INBOX

is there an echo in this room ... where have i heard that before

Thursday 6:07 p.m.

Yeah, but this time, tsreally over.

You know, for so long, he was so good, able to run with me, and think anything, or at least debate anything. And what trips him up and makes him go splat? Romantic Love. What a load of hooey. I should have just kept my big trap shut. But then talking to him would be just like talking to anyone else. Anyone else you have to lie to and keep secrets from and hide your exasperation and talk about behind his back just to relieve the pressure of taking all his BS.

And it's *soccer,* damn it. Not football. Soccer.

He's supposed to be this big QUESTIONER! This person who allows himself to think anything.

Men really need to be flattered. All the time. You can't say anything true to them.

And the thing is, this is HIS bailiwick! "Bailiwick"? Such a quaint word. It interrupts my rage-fueled rant. Where did I pick up that antique?

But this is exactly his area of expertise. Science! If science can tell us that there is no God, as he insists, why can't we use science to tell us that men are, as my high school sex education teacher, that proud dyke, declared, "plumbing"?

Too close to home. He doesn't care about God, and so it's no hardship for him to go around preaching that there is no God. But he cares about his sacred manhood all right.

I want to date Diogenes. That Greek guy who lived in a barrel, carried a lantern, and walked around saying, "I'm looking for an honest man." And you know what? He probably couldn't handle this, either.

Can any of 'em?

It's the last frontier of truth. When men finally acknowledge, publicly, "When it comes to fifty percent of the human race, all men are shallow and blind," we will know that we are close to the End Times.

save SEND delete

Thursday 6:58 p.m.

Dear Rand,

Hi.

Hi –

Nice to hear from you.

hi…

I'm listening?

save SEND delete

Thursday 7:31 p.m.

Dear Rand,

That's great! What a coup for you. Congratulations!

Me? Nothing much. Just sitting here reading and writing e-mails. It's a pleasant evening.

save SEND delete

Thursday 7:32 p.m.

Amanda!

He's gaslighting me. He just sent me a perky, friendly e-mail that acts as if nothing has happened. What to do?

save SEND delete

Thursday 7:37 p.m.

Wait. I get it. He wants something from me. He's not coming out and saying what it is. He's just sending me a nicey nice e-mail to get his toe in the door, and, then, when the moment is right, he'll ask.

Something was left unsaid in our most recent e-mails. I don't know what, but something. He's here to take care of unfinished business.

save **SEND** delete

INBOX

have complete faith in you ... must focus antigone ... later

Friday 4:42 p.m.

Dear Rand,

Hi. The vacation – the holiday – you describe sounds like so much fun. Send me postcards.

About that other thing. Yeah, you're right. I never did tell you. But why don't we just skip it? It's not important.

save **SEND** delete

Friday 5:30 p.m.

Dear Rand,

Hi.

Rand, I'm sorry. I should not have said what I said. Please forgive me. Can we let it go?

save **SEND** delete

Friday 5:59 p.m.

Rand, if this hurt you or bothered you, I'm sincerely sorry. I let you down and I

save send **DELETE**

Friday 6:02 p.m.

Rand, I'm really sorry. I should never have said that.

But for reasons that I can't explain, I hope that we can leave this topic.

I wasn't consciously lying to you. I just made a promise that I don't think it would be wise to keep.

It's nothing, really, I promise you. In a way my not wanting to answer is making it seem all dramatic and it's not dramatic. It's just

save send **DELETE**

Friday 6:34 p.m.

Yes. You are absolutely correct. It was stupid of me to say that. Can we just forget it?

save **SEND** delete

Friday 6:45 p.m.

Yeah, I could see where my hesitance might appear ominous. But, really, it's not. It's just something I don't think I should mention. I wasn't thinking when I said what I said the other day.

save **SEND** delete

Friday 7:03 p.m.

Dear Rand,

I am sorry I upset you. I am sorry I have not lived up to your expectations of me.

I am really, truly, genuinely sorry. When I spoke, I wasn't thinking. I'm trying to avoid making a further blunder by addressing the question further.

But, really, Rand, I don't think I should or could tell you why I asked you to convince me that there is no God. I know that I told you I would tell you but I don't think I should tell you.

I hope you can forgive me, and I certainly don't blame you for judging me.

save **SEND** delete

Sunday 10:04 a.m.

Dear Rand,

Hi. I just read the e-mail you sent me last night. I mean, I read it last night, thirty times, and then I read it again this morning, twenty times, and I thought about it countless times as I attempted to sleep.

How in God's name – how did you know? How did you know that that is why I asked you to convince me that there is no God?

save SEND delete

Sunday 10:16 a.m.

No, it's nothing like that. And, frankly, if you were to attempt to contact authorities in New Jersey, I would simply deny everything and never speak to you again.

It's not a pretty picture. I've never been through it but I've been involved in online discussion groups and people who've been through it talk about it and it sounds like punitive torture. They put you in a psych ward. I've read about people being strapped down, being forbidden to leave, being pumped full of drugs. Who knows if any of that is true, but that is what they talk about online. I hate cops anyway. I certainly wouldn't want a cop around me – a Paterson cop, no less – at a moment like that.

save SEND delete

Sunday 10:48 a.m.

Dear Rand,

I'm sorry, Rand. I'm very sorry if I've caused you any sadness at all. That's why I decided not to tell you why I asked you to convince me that there is no God. I should never have told you that I would. I wrote that without thinking. I was flippant.

save SEND delete

Sunday 3:02 p.m.

Please don't think that, Rand. Please don't think that. Please.

There may have been some of that in the beginning. Honest to God, Rand, I don't know what possessed me to author that lengthy e-mail I sent you that started this whole thing. I've never written such a manifesto to anyone, never mind a famous person. It's as if I were on auto-pilot. Automatic writing! No doubt another thing you don't believe in. Me neither.

But you have blossomed for me, Rand. You are so much more to me than ... than the guy who might convince me that there is no God. And thereby release me to do what I've been planning all along anyway.

I hope that that is obvious? That my affection and respect for you, my gratitude for every e-mail you send me, is obvious? The pleasure I get from your company. Please know that. Please.

Oh, everything is all icky and depressing now. Let's get into a rip-roaring fight.

Wanna debate the possible existence of Romantic Love?

Soccer?

There, I've said the taboo word. Soccer.

I've said it again.

I hope you are smiling.

I'm doing the best I can.

save SEND delete

Sunday 3:11 p.m.

How on earth did you know?

Do you really not believe in psychic abilities?

I've thought back over our e-mails and there is nothing in there that would make that the obvious conclusion.

save SEND delete

Sunday 3:57 p.m.

If you want. I can't see why you'd want that, but if you want, sure, I'll tell you. And we'll have a chance for a goodbye.

I can't imagine why you'd want that, though. I like slipping out when people are preoccupied with other things. I've never been one for goodbyes.

Are you ever going to tell me how you knew? Wild speculation? Lucky guess?

Or, is it, really, Rand, that there is some psychic bond?

save SEND delete

Sunday 4:11 p.m.

Yeah, you're right. It is a big no-no for Catholics. That anathema terrifies me. Suicides can't even be buried in consecrated ground. At least that's what I was told in church as a child. I'm not sure if it is still true. Not that burial concerns me. I've arranged for my cadaver to be donated to – hey, get this! – science. Do I get any points for that?

save SEND delete

Sunday 4:32 p.m.

I hope that you know ... I hope that this isn't a stupid thing to say, but I hope that you know ...

That you don't have to rescue me.

Good God, this is why I should never have said anything.

But I *didn't* say anything.

How *did* you know?

save SEND delete

Sunday 5:01 p.m.

Yes, you are exactly right. Geez, you are smart.

You've got it. I am terrified of going to Hell. That's the only thing that keeps me here. This terror of going to Hell.

Yes, that is why I asked you to convince me that there is no God. Because, no God, no Hell, maybe, and I can just leave. If only I could see things as you do.

It's not an abstraction for me. I've been to Hell.

I appreciate your curiosity. You know I adore curiosity. It's my favorite human trait. One of my favorites. Maybe my favorite. I've never been any good at choosing exclusive favorites. I even have trouble picking a favorite color. Of magenta and turquoise, who really can select the superior?

So, no, I don't at all mind your questions. But when it comes to Hell, I become terrified and paralyzed and depressed and afraid. Because I've been there.

See, my goal is not to get to Heaven or to Hell, my goal is just to disappear, and I want there to be nothing, absolutely nothing, left of me. In fact I wish that "me" had never come to be, at all.

You know, I've got to say, this is one way that you and your fellow atheists really drop the ball. You keep saying that religion is a Darwinian escape mechanism for a creature intelligent enough to understand that it will someday die. Religion, you claim, comforts us because it promises eternity.

Rand, I can't imagine any curse more terrifying. I can't imagine any oppression worse than waking up day after day after day after day after day to ill health and no doctors and poverty and ruined, broken dreams and loneliness and loathing and despair. Just typing the last sentence chokes me with tears. My throat constricts. I want to die, Rand, I want to die, just from contemplating the God-awful punishment of eternal life. I can't even stand the thought of there being enough left of my essence for anyone to remember. If I could do this the way I want, I would extricate every smudge of memory of me from anyone who has ever seen me and incinerate those memories, because otherwise, there would be enough of me left out there to hurt, to betray, to humiliate, to beat up, to rape, to destroy.

You say, Rand, that we humans, we Darwinian creatures, invented eternal life as a way to thwart our knowledge of death. Oh, Rand, that is so wrong. We yearn for death because we yearn for an end to our suffering. Have you never read Gerard Manley Hopkins?

Hopkins vibrated to the natural world; what moves a firefly

moved him. Have you ever read "God's Grandeur"? Of course, you have; every educated English speaker has. You think of the first line of "God's Grandeur" and the entire sonnet recites itself inside your head, it is so alive: "The world is charged with the grandeur of God. It will flame out, like shining from shook foil."

Hopkins captures God and nature and the force of life, and he places them on the page. Nobody illustrates that unbroken thread like Hopkins. Reading a Hopkins poem is like being alive twice.

But this man who so lived the beauty of life knew the allure of death. Of finally calling it a day. "Creep, Wretch, under a comfort serves in a whirlwind: all Life death does end and each day dies with sleep." He wanted to die, Rand. This man who, better than anyone else ever has, voiced the exuberance of merely being alive, wanted to die.

You're so wrong, Rand. You and your fellow atheists are wrong. We don't invent eternity to comfort ourselves. Eternity is the biggest damn punishment of all. Death is easy; death is child's play; death is the premium drug to which all other anodynes aspire. Death is escape, death is release, death is no consequences for the crime of raping a girl, or the big, fat chocolate cake you ate last night or for your twisted soul. Death means you get to spend all afternoon in the store and never have to confront the cashier on your way out. War criminals committing atrocities, mothers beating their kids, liars, con artists, cheats and frauds – do you really think that they plan on eternity? They bank on death. Rand, convince me that there is no God. Show me the cosmos you see: a psychopath's wet dream unencumbered by consequences, an amusement park blissfully free of meaning. Give me a shot at that blessed release, death.

save SEND delete

Sunday 5:14 p.m.

Yes, I can see why you'd say that and I appreciate your concern.

And, yes, Amanda *is* very special.

But there is something about Amanda, Rand, that if I told you, you would see that relationship very differently. But, I can't tell you

save send **DELETE**

Sunday 5:16 p.m.

Dear Rand,

Yes, Amanda is very special. But my relationship with Amanda is not what it once was, and we really aren't as close as it appears that you have concluded.

So, no, no one would care. And that's a good thing. Invisibility has its advantages. I go where I want, do what I want, and I owe nothing to anyone. If I had kids, I wouldn't even contemplate this. Heck, not even if I had a *dog.* My building doesn't allow dogs. In my planning, I've made sure that I don't do it during the semester. I've never missed a class, and I would not feel comfortable letting my students down.

I will be irrevocably forgotten in six months.

save **SEND** delete

Sunday 6:00 p.m.

You just made me smile.

I *love* how you put that.

Rand, I love your mind. Am so grateful for it. I completely lack the intellectual capacity to fathom the obviously grand contributions you have made to your field. I am an inadequate audience for you. But you are so smart in your e-mails to me that every time I read a message from you I get how special you are and how lucky I am.

I really admire your turning your questions into "an anthropological exploration." Your putting it that way takes so much of the burden off me.

One of the reasons I never talk about this with anyone is

because I don't want to have to add those I tell to the list of people I need to take care of.

I love the coolness of a highly intellectual mind. Thank you for never being overwhelmed by me. Thank you for being man enough, for being sturdy enough, to let me be who I am. Thank you for not rushing forward to declare yourself victimized by my existence. Thank you for not giving me one more thing I need to take care of.

save SEND delete

Sunday 6:01 p.m.

Dear Rand,

I love you. No, I'm not going to send you this. But I just had to type it out. Thank you so much. I love you.

save send DELETE

Sunday 6:16 p.m.

Okay, we'll talk again tomorrow.

G'night, sleep tight, and don't let the bedbugs bite.

save SEND delete

Monday 7:00 a.m.

Okay, I'm going to take these one at a time. I hope to be as clear and rational in replying as you have been in asking.

1.) Gun. Quickest, most certain. Haven't bought it yet. Am a bit horrified of guns. Must overcome that. Temporarily.

2.) Nnnno. I am not one of those people. They are not my tribe.

There was someone like that on the internet discussion list. When I first read her posts, I was very touched, and I liked her a lot. Becca grew up in a stable, comfortable household, she had a great job, she earned good money, she was physically healthy, and she was attractive, as she was sure to tell us, and she posted a photo that looked pretty good. Her posts were among the longest, they appeared with the greatest frequency, and she got

lots of feedback. People mostly responded to tell her how courageous she was, to offer sympathy to her in her plight, and to urge
her to carry on.

For most of the years that I was part of that discussion group,
I commiserated. The essence of my posts: "Oh, you poor dear."
After a few years, I realized that Becca's posts were always the
same: "I was raised in a good home. I have a good job. I am
pretty. I am healthy. I am unhappy." One day I finally broke
down and asked Becca things you are not supposed to ask. "You
say that you know that you are not depressed for material
reasons – the material realities of your life are quite good. Do you
ever address the immaterial stuff, by, say, consciously practicing
gratitude, or doing what researchers suggest to depressed
people, like aerobic exercise, walks in the sun, keeping regular
sleep-wake hours, eating light, healthy, regularly scheduled
meals, performing service work for others, following your
dreams, or taking calcium supplements?"

No, she said, she had never done any of those things. Hadn't
I understood? She was *depressed.* Depression is a *real* illness.
It prevented her from being able to do anything that I suggested.

Now, see, I don't understand how depression would enable
you to purchase a computer, set it up at home, and spend a few
hours every night typing messages, but prevent you from going
for a walk in the sunshine, or stacking shelves in a food bank –
I'm not casting the first stone. I'm saying, "Explain this to me in
terms I can understand, because there are facts here that don't
add up."

I'm not saying that I'm better than Becca. I'm saying that I'm
different than Becca, and that Becca has the microphone. I'm
saying that any conversation about suicide is so dominated by
middle-class, fully-employed, fully-insured, Americans like
Becca that people like me get drowned out, or are misunderstood
as being like her, when we are not, at all. I've never, not once in
my life, if I could walk, or even if I could crawl, spent a day in

bed. I exercise. I take calcium. I don't smoke. Don't drink. Don't purchase or consume foods containing hydrogenated fats. Although I respect her talent, I'm no fan of Sylvia Plath. I relish the life-affirming, heart-warming art of Norman Rockwell, and the vivacious tunes of Leroy Anderson. I have never worn black fingernail polish.

There was another member of that group. Posted only once. Did not give his name. Like me, he was from New Jersey, and, like me, he was suddenly stricken, as an adult, with a vestibular disorder. He had been a highly paid executive for a telecommunications company. His wife and kids were relying on him for a very comfortable lifestyle. And then, one day, his ability to provide that lifestyle was, without warning, snatched from him. He couldn't walk across a room. There were whispers at work about his termination. His one post was very concrete. There were no words about feelings. There were words naming objects and action verbs. He was going to go into the garage, close the door, start his Jaguar, and inhale the exhaust. Afterward, and "afterward" is always an interesting word choice when one is talking about one's own life, his wife and kids would be very comfortably taken care of. He had made sure of that.

"Hi, friend. I liked your post," I typed, immediately. "I can see why you feel the way you feel. It really does suck. How's it going? Can you give us an update?" I felt like a cop trying to talk someone down. Not make any false moves that might tip him from being perpendicular to the ledge.

The telecommunications executive never posted again. My best guess: he did what he said he was going to do. Anything a philosopher or a priest or an officer of the law might say that would be pertinent to Becca would not be pertinent to that guy. They are living two totally different stories.

I'm not Becca. I'm not the executive. I'm someone who can't get a job. I live in a slum. It's life unworthy of life.

In the years since getting the pro bono surgery that ended the chronic illness, and getting my PhD, I have spent every Saturday applying for jobs. I'm more scrupulous about this than church attendance. I don't go on vacations. I rarely go to the movies. I go through job listings. I've applied for teaching jobs. Hotel maid. Store clerk. Fund raiser. Grant writer. I've applied for five hundred jobs.

Most people would become depressed just passing through the city I live in full time. Piles of garbage in the streets. No "quiet time." Diesel engines and air breaks and honking horns and boom boxes pumping out aural garbage to match the garbage piling on the streets. There is no "walk after dinner." I strategize when and how I leave the apartment. A very good percentage of the citizens of this city are barking mad. Just walking from my apartment to the border of the town, I run a gauntlet of men who expose themselves, clinging beggars, stinking prostitutes, heroin addicts, drivers who shout, "I'm gonna kill that white bitch."

I am dying by pieces. My teeth go one at a time. One day I might fall. One day I might not hear the guy behind me. There was a flood in the city last April. Cops filled the streets. There were crowds and anger. Helicopters overhead. I don't want to die the way a lone woman might die when chaos breaks out in a city like this.

Is this all too raw for you, Rand? Is this all too weird? I am very careful to protect people I know from the life I lead. I don't mention it when I go outside the door of my apartment and see a man urinating in the hallway. But this is the world I've been sentenced to. Can you not see why I want to leave? I sometimes wonder if I have not killed myself already, but have forgotten that, and the life I lead now is my punishment, is my eternal hell.

3.) Yes, I have.

In fact, it's something that that the career coaches I've consulted told me to do: "Tell everyone you know that you are looking for work." I've got the contacts: a motivational speaker published an essay by me; a former Peace Corps buddy manages a multi-million dollar charity; one former boyfriend is now in charge of cultural programs in a major city.

They all find my story pretty interesting. "Oh, Mira, you are so dramatic. What a fascinating life you lead. You Bohemians. Well, thanks for sharing that. I've got to get back to work. The real world calls. Talk to you soon." You tell your story and I nod; I tell my story and you nod; we pay and we go. I can't tell you how many times I've mentioned to an acquaintance who has hiring power how desperate things are for me and they say, "Fascinating, fascinating. You were always such an interesting person, Mira," and then they ask me to donate to their favorite cause. "Maybe, Mira, you could throw in five hundred, as has our mutual pal?" Or else, they'll say, "We were in the Caribbean for the break. You?"

Can you see, Rand, why that Psalm 39 incident was such a mind blower? That someone was actually willing to hear me? As for these people, everyone, really, who doesn't hear me? I hate them. Wouldn't you? I don't hate them because they haven't offered me a job, or handed my resume to a potential employer. It's because they don't even see that that would be the decent thing to do. They really just do not understand that there are people who need work and can work and can't get work.

4.) You asked if there is anything I want to do before I go.

That is such a great question. I love your curiosity.

There is.

I had an art professor my freshman year of college, Prof. Lowe. As soon as we walked in, he flipped the light off, and went to the back of the room. He always stood in back of us, and never took questions. My guess is he had no idea who any of us were. It is possible that he couldn't bear to look at us, his working-class students at an undistinguished state school. To me, that did not matter. I loved him. He insisted, with a flamboyant consistency, on writing us into his slide show. "When *you* visit St. Peter's, as you jostle with the milling crowds, eagerly anticipating Michelangelo's Pieta for the first time ... When *you* dismount from your rickshaw in Agra, and as you brush the red road dust from your shoulders ... When in Chartres cathedral, she will entrance *you*, la Vierge Bleue, the stunning Blue Virgin." I love the color blue, and Prof. Lowe's mention of blue stained glass windows is why I went to Chartres nine years after he was my teacher. I wasn't expecting much when I pulled in to town, just: blue windows, a town in France that wasn't Paris or Marseilles or Nice, and a croque-madame sandwich.

Of all of the world's wonders past which I have respectfully trod, the velvet-roped, museum must-see masterpieces, battle monuments and grassy fields where religious leaders were born, died, or preached their first sermon, the place that I've never been able to shake, and would not want to shake, is Chartres.

I spent an entire day inside Chartres cathedral. I did not want to disconnect from whatever it was that Chartres was doing to me. Why Chartres? Language runs out. I don't believe in geomancy, but geomancers will tell you that it's the ley lines that make Chartres magic. They believe that Chartres is on a geologically sacred spot. I don't think that that is true, but that people resort to that theory to explain Chartres' power is telling. I offer no better explanation. Gothic cathedrals all offer splendor: the stained glass, the flying stone, the cool, quiet, sanctuary, the mathematics calculated to levitate a soul heavenward. I grew up with Sacred Heart in Newark, and St. Patrick's in New York. I'd been to Notre Dame de Paris several times. Washington's National Cathedral is very fetching, from its Darth Vader gargoyle to its stained glass window that contains a piece of real moon rock. But, for me, walking through the National, while a visual feast, was sterile.

Afterward, in London, I wrote a love poem about Chartres. The poem was terrible, and I don't know where I keep it. (This is what I do with embarrassing writing; I don't throw it away, so I can't escape it. I hide it, so I can't improve it.) The poem just kept apostrophizing, "You, Chartres," and then "telling" Chartres that, in all of my experiences, she made me believe. Not believe in God. I already believed in God. Believe in the thing we can't name. So, that's what Chartres is to me. I felt something in Chartres, that I could not deny, and could not empower myself by naming. My only choice was to surrender, wordlessly, to it, and I did: a humbling experience. I cede Chartres my awe.

Chartres – that's what I want to experience one more time. My curiosity would drive me in search of words. My soul would hope for, again, the experience beyond words' adequacy to name.

That is all of your questions. If I've missed anything, lemme know.

PS: Thank you.

save SEND delete

Monday 10:07 a.m.

I love you! That is the best thing anyone has said to me in a long time, if not ever. Holy cow, you are so great.

Okay, I promise. If I ever develop a secret, quiet hate for you, as I have for my acquaintances who ask me the last time I've been to the Caribbean, I will tell you.

You, too. Tell me if you ever get to the point where you hate me. It would be hard for me to hear, but I would want to know. The health of our relationship is more important to me than my ego.

And, sure, take a break, by all means. That sounds like a good idea. I look forward to talking to you again when we do talk, and I hope you enjoy the break while you are taking it.

And, sir, yes, sir, I will, sir. I promise I will. I will be here when you get back. You can put that in the bank.

save SEND delete

Monday 10:30 a.m.

Rand,

I just realized ... you did for me what I told you I do for my students when they come to me in pain. You asked me questions. Then you listened to my answers.

Thank you.

Bless you.

I love you.

Can't send this, but ... I love you so much right now.

Thank you.

save send DELETE

Tuesday 2:47 p.m.

Amanda,

I came perilously close to telling Rand the truth about you.

save SEND delete

INBOX

truth about *moi*??? *truth* about *moi*?!? there is no truth about moi except that i am a semi-undiscovered artistic genius, a great, but unconventional, beauty, and probably a bodhisattva ...

antigone very vexing ... we've got her and creon workshopping at area twelve step meetings ... i do get some stares with the ancient greek costume ... one *must* go braless ... women can be so envious of their better endowed sisters ... as for the men ... don't get me started ...

if we aren't careful, antigone and creon will both get recovery ... no conflict ... no suicide ... no play

Saturday 10:03 a.m.

Dear Rand,

It's nice to hear from you again. I was beginning to wonder.

Forgive me for stating the obvious, but the e-mail you just

sent contradicts everything you've ever said. And written. And broadcast. And preached to your followers. And been applauded for saying. And been quoted as saying on numerous, worshipful fan websites. And earned big bucks for writing, saying, publishing, and broadcasting. On the topic.

Given that you are trying to be kind to me, it would be in bad taste for me to debate with you, but … c'mon. You must see the inconsistencies. They're as big as a house.

save SEND delete

Saturday 3:56 p.m.

Well, I didn't think that you held my good taste in such low esteem.

In any case, you are being plainly inconsistent. In your every public statement you are a pure materialist. Material reality is all there is. There is no reality transcendent of the material. That is your position. I've told you my material reality. It sucks. Failing a miracle, and you don't believe in those, and I have no reason to expect that any are coming my way, my material reality will not change. Therefore, to be consistent, you should be gung ho behind my decision.

You don't get to champion material reality one day and the next insist, "Hey, don't kill yourself, even though everything you see, hear, smell, taste, and touch is utterly abysmal, beyond enduring, and futile. There is something out there that you cannot access through your senses that's really very important, and if you kill yourself, you'll ruin that." That's not a materialist's argument. That's the argument of someone who believes in a reality transcendent of the material. You, sir, are dropping the ball.

save SEND delete

Saturday 4:29 p.m.

Oh, come on. I may be suicidal but I haven't suddenly suffered a double digit drop in my IQ.

Your argument is pathetic.

Write me again when you can craft a position that would pass the standards I apply to my freshman comp classes.

save SEND delete

Saturday 4:36 p.m.

I am NOT being a bitch. And even if you put that captivating adjective in front of it, you still used a naughty word. Although I *am* impressed by your harnessing of both alliteration and internal rhyme.

Rand, now deploy your *logic* to impress me. If you are going to take an untenable position, well, tenablize it. Your position, I mean. Make some sense. You're a famous smart man. Or just cut to the chase, cave in, and admit that, yet once again, I've bested you in a debate.

save SEND delete

Saturday 4:48 p.m.

Very funny.

If nothing else, you've got a career in stand-up ahead of you.

Since you can't win a debate, I mean.

save SEND delete

Saturday 6:36 p.m.

So, you took an hour on a beautiful Saturday afternoon – or evening, by you – to compose this uplifting little religious pamphlet from the atheist's POV.

There are two responses below. The first was written by Bill Moyers, as channeled by me. I wrote the second. Choose your poison. Caveat lector.

BILL MOYERS: Our guest tonight is the magnificent Lord Randolph Court-Wright, world famous smart man. He is here to discuss his magisterial essay, tentatively entitled, "An Atheist's

Purely Materialist Arguments Against Suicide." Reading it, I became so excited I panted. I wet my pants. I then arose, washed my pants, and put them in the drier. I stood against the drier, enjoying its gyrations, warmth, and simple, good-hearted, polyrhythmic song. I recognized the seminal influence of Mississippi Delta bluesmen. I contemplated, "Why can I not be as smart as Lord Randolph Court-Wright?" I then sighed, heavily.

ME: You can use all the big words you want, Rand. I've got a thesaurus, same as you. But if you boil it down and put it in plain English, there is NOTHING materialist about your argument. You are chickening out and adopting the stance of a believer in a transcendent reality. "Precious," "sacred," "the dignity of the human person" – did you think I would not notice that you lifted that phrase straight from the Vatican? "a whole which transcends" – you even use the word!!! – "the sum of its parts." "Spirit" !!! Oh, Mister Man, you are in a world of trouble. The Vocabulary Police levy WEIGHTY fines when an atheist uses the word "spirit."

For the sake of your remaining dignity, milord, it is time to change the subject and start talking about Manchester United.

save SEND delete

Saturday 7:00 p.m.

You're kidding me. It's midnight your time. Witching hour. Rand, don't go to bed yet. Please answer this e-mail. Is this an elaborate joke? If it is, it's not funny. Really not funny. If you have any reason for saying this and it is not true, please just forget that reason and please just write me back ASAP and tell me. Rand, is what you just wrote true? Please write me.

save SEND delete

Saturday 7:07 p.m.

Omigod.

That is so weird.

I believe you. But I can't believe it. I'm getting chills.

Tell me this is just coincidence? Do your mathematical mumbo jumbo and convince me that this is just like somebody walking into a room with twenty-three people and meeting somebody else with the same birthday?

Right?

save SEND delete

Saturday 7:20 p.m.

Of course. I want you to be refreshed for your talk tomorrow. Go to bed.

It's just so incredible.

Thank you for telling me. I'm kind of stunned that you haven't told me till now. But thank you for telling me now.

I actually feel kind of nauseated.

It's probably just a coincidence.

I keep typing but I'm not saying anything. I'll just stop typing.

God bless you and God bless me and God bless this crazy world.

Amen.

save SEND delete

Saturday midnight

Amanda,

I know that you're busy with "Antigone." I know that that is more important than anything I have to say. And I know I've been taking a lot of your time. I'm here to take some more.

For the past five hours, I've been surfing the web, getting up, sweeping the apartment, scouring shiny surfaces, alphabetizing my clip files, watching the traffic, and then sitting down again, and just staring.

Rand said the most amazing thing. It's probably just a coincidence. I mean, Littlewood's Law of Miracles, and all. So many things happen in any given day that it is inevitable that something will occur that defies the odds.

All this time I've been wondering how it is that he and I are talking. Why would a celebrity who has lunch with the Queen of England so much as give the time of day to me?

The night that I wrote to him I felt like I was on a leash. I just kept writing and writing and this little voice inside my head kept nagging, "You haven't said it yet. You haven't said it yet." Eventually, I felt somehow like I was finished and I wrote a bit more and I just pressed "send."

Rand told me, today, and I don't think he's pulling my leg, because the tone of his post was way different, more urgent, more raw. He caved in and confessed that, yes, he doesn't know how to craft a purely materialist defense of the value of human life – we had been talking about that – and then he changed, jumped, from one tone to another. He said that the morning that I wrote to him, he was up early because his wife had to catch a flight. And they had fought, that early in the morning, and he interpreted that as a very bad sign. That they could fight with such venom before sunrise. This is the first time he has ever so much as alluded to his wife. It's the first time he's ever used the word "wife" in an e-mail.

He retreated to his office. He said that he was just sitting there, trying to regain his composure, and he had taken down a book, a book at random from his shelf, and opened it at random, it opened naturally to its most frequently read passage, and he was just trying to get to the point where he could actually internalize what he was reading, because he was so upset that he was just reading blah, blah, blah, and it was at that moment that he was looking at the book that my e-mail arrived – ping! – in his inbox, and he normally lets his secretary handle the hundreds of e-mails he gets from strangers in any given day, but something compelled him to look at that one. He began to read this e-mail and was amused by it and thought that this e-mail, better than the book he was reading, would help him to get over being upset by the fight with his wife, but then he kind of choked, because my e-mail just happened to include the very paragraph from Jung about synchronicity that he was reading from his book in his lap at that very moment.

People think, Amanda, that people like you and me who believe in something out there that is more than the material are comfortable with moments like this because these moments confirm our belief system. That is so not true. I believe in water but it's not any easier for me, as a believer, to be taken up by a wave. As much as anyone else, as much as any atheist, I also fear drowning.

save SEND delete

Sunday 7:36 a.m.

Yes!

YES! YES YES YES!

Ten thousand times yes!

In case I'm not being clear: Omigod, yes.

Oh, Rand, this is so wonderful!

Holy Cow! I am so happy! You are ... beyond my ability to say how wonderful.

Oh, I cannot wait! I cannot wait to meet you. And to be in Chartres again! Oh, this is going to be so fabulous. I don't know if I've ever been so excited about anything in all my life. I feel like a teenager!

To hear your voice speak your words, to see your mouth move and the words come out, to sit at a café table with you, to eat a croque-madame with you! (How are your cholesterol levels?)

To replace my ellipses with pauses and glances at your face to check if you are following me. To replace my asterisks with emphases that arise in my throat. To smell you. What do you smell like? What do I smell like? I will shower. Do you like Je Reviens? It's the perfume I wear.

Rand, we'll see – we'll witness – la Vierge Bleue ensemble. Together. Did you know that I speak French? C'est la plus belle langue du monde. We'll walk the labyrinth. I'll light a candle. You'll do what atheists do in Gothic cathedrals. Nothing illegal, I hope.

Holy cow.

I'm jumping around the room, Rand, I'm jumping around the room!

This will be so great!

Yes, Rand, yes, it is a wonderful idea. A fabulous idea. I am so thrilled. I am so excited. I am so happy.

save SEND delete

Monday 10:12 a.m.

Dear Rand,

It is September this morning in New Jersey, a phenomenon that makes belief in God plausible. The memory kicks up Keats – "season of mists and mellow fruitfulness; close bosom-friend of the maturing sun," segues into Gerard Manley Hopkins "golden grove unleaving" and, inevitably, culminates in Shakespeare, "when yellow leaves, or none, or few do hang."

God, I love the fall. I want to live forever in fall, on a hilltop, hiking, with a golden retriever, heading home, squinting against the setting sun, harvest moon over shoulder; I'm readying to bake apple strudel, with the apples from my backpack, which I picked in a wild orchard.

The mere air, the color of the sky, are so magical, so divine that I wonder if atheists believe in autumn …

save SEND delete

Monday 5:03 p.m.

Dear Rand

save send DELETE

Monday 6:33 p.m.
Dear Rand,

save send **DELETE**

Monday 7:10 p.m.

save send **DELETE**

Monday 8:32 p.m.
Dear Rand,
My, what a witty

save send **DELETE**

Monday 8:51 p.m.
Dear Rand,
Oh, you can be so funny sometimes

save send **DELETE**

Monday 9:10 p.m.

save send **DELETE**

Monday midnight
Dear Rand,

save send **DELETE**

Tuesday 4:16 a.m.
I'm sorry

save send **DELETE**

Tuesday 10:11 p.m.
D

save send **DELETE**

Tuesday midnight
Rand, we need to talk.

save send DELETE

Thursday 5:45 a.m.
Please

save send DELETE

Sunday 5:58 a.m.
Amanda,
I got up at 4:30, jumped rope 1,800 times, lifted my weights a hundred times, and took a cold shower. A Mason jar full of peppermint tea steams on the desk. Rumbling Mack trucks, transporting gravel from the quarry on the hill to road construction on route 80, make my desk tremble as they pass. I am naming what I can.

Treat this as a share at a Twelve Step meeting. "Take what you like and leave the rest." Don't "fourth step" me. Know that typing this out to you right now is the only thing I can do. I've got to do something. Rand has e-mailed about a thousand times.

He wants to meet me in France. I said yes.

When I read Rand's reply, everything went black. You hear about people seeing stars. I saw them. The street noise faded. I wish I could always blot it out so thoroughly. I went into the bathroom. Probably a memory from a Midwest tornado drill. If you don't have a basement, you are supposed to go into the bathroom. I leaned into the wall. Hyperventilated.

I came back out, and some part of me decided that I just needed to act as if I had never gotten that e-mail. In some other dimension, I had, and in that world, when I was ready, I would deal with it in a way that would make it all cool. But in my own world, I decided, I had never gotten it.

save SEND delete

INBOX
you know and i know that you never told me what his e-mail said ... you want twelve step? "just show up and tell the truth"

Sunday 2:42 p.m.
Dear Amanda,
Yes, that is a very good question. It is the obvious question. What did he say? Here's the thing. I've been very scrupulous about not showing his e-mails to anyone. He stipulated that, but even if he hadn't, I wouldn't. So how do I tell you what he said? Perhaps if I take a keyword approach, and just share with you his keywords.

He said nipples Amanda. He said nipples and he said tits and he said breasts. He said cock he said pussy he said touch he said pinch pull rub and bite he said yourself he said me he said slowly he said faster he said faster he said soft he said hard he said like a rock he said swollen lips wet hot like silk he said it burns he said I want it he said grip it and stroke it he said rub it and lick it he said taste it he said tease it he said agony he said sweet he said again he said again he said again he said you want it he said thrust he said harder he said burst he said cry he said please he said please again and he said please again and he said please again he said could not wait and he said love.

None of these are words I have not heard before. Indeed, I myself have spoken them, or others like them. I just have not heard them in this exact context.

save SEND delete

INBOX
topic: big deal ... question: what is the ... you've wanted this this whole time

Sunday 3:17 p.m.

He's a married man. I've never committed that particular sin.

save **SEND** delete

INBOX

repeating ... what is big deal ... i'm flattered ... thanks but no thanks ... you is a married man ... sheesh mira men say these things to me on a daily ... no ... hourly basis ... if i fell apart as you have every time i was propositioned ... the bay area's theater scene would come grinding to a sudden and undignified halt ...

Sunday 3:28 p.m.

Amanda, this is why I keep you around. You are so damn smart, and such a woman of a woman. And I offer this flattering preamble by way of saying, what I'm about to confess may sound really weird and I want to keep you on my side.

I suspect that Rand has been hurt by a woman. In his manhood. "Manhood:" such an old-fashioned word. But I bet there are cultures out there, somewhere, on this earth, where you could talk about "manhood" and not sound as if you are using a Ouija Board to invoke the spirit of that sweat-glistened, broad-chested, broad-lipped, 1950s gladiator film star, Victor Mature.

That e-mail he sent me was so masterful. He owned me. But it was also so vulnerable. I could auction it off on E-Bay. I have not responded and he's been sending me e-mails crammed with shame, rage and regret.

I *can't* say, "Oh, little man, put it back in your pants. You are married, after all, and we must remain chaste." If I play that card, I would just contribute to his wounded manhood. I don't want to sin with him, but I want to give him my risky, vulnerable lust. But if I say, "I can't have you, because you are married, but I just want you to know how truly sexy you are," I'm Lady Bountiful, and he is a beggar out in the snow, to whom I can explain charity, but to whom I can't give any.

I know that this is sick. My Christian desire to help another human being seems to be telling me that I have to break one of the Ten Commandments.

Otherwise, let's just leave God out of this. Being a spinster is the one thing in my life that's working out really well. In Twelve Step we refer to "The Priceless Gift of Serenity." I only had any idea what that was after I eliminated men from my life. I love not dealing with the heartache, the needing, not feeling cute enough, feeling too fat, all of that miserable crap. If someone told me, "You can have sex again, or we'll tinker with your lease so that you can get a puppy," I'd take the puppy.

save SEND delete

Sunday midnight
Amanda, you there?

save send DELETE

Friday 5:52 a.m.
Dear Rand,
Good morning. I'm sorry. Please let me explain. It is not what you think.

I am sorry I have not responded to your posts until this moment. Please know that this whole time I've been trying to figure out the best way to respond. Also, please know that what you've been speculating – that I'm disgusted by your offer, or that you misread my interest – please know that those speculations are not accurate.

I have imagined, over a hundred times, meeting you for the first time, and, immediately, before any words are exchanged, touching your face. I knew exactly how I would touch your face, what portion of my hands I would use, how long it would take. Our bodies aren't just flesh; they are also our mind's concept of that flesh. Some part of my conceptual body exists in anticipation of this act, like the athlete, in position, before executing a move. I promise my body that no matter how much you and I fight, or what obnoxious, atheist thing you say to me, no matter how wide and cold the Atlantic, or how wide and hot the flaming lava stream between fame and failure, that I will acquire for my anticipating body this satisfaction. I so desperately want this word to become flesh; I so want to touch your face.

Can't happen, Rand. Can't. You are married.

save **SEND** delete

Friday 6:57 a.m.

I am so sorry.

You know, I don't know what goes on in marriages, except by hearsay. But if what you describe is accurate, what you describe is abuse. That is the right word. I guess the best I can do at my end is pray for all concerned. For you, for your wife, for a happy outcome.

I really hope, and I do pray, that you two can find a way to work things out.

save **SEND** delete

Friday 7:15 a.m.

Yeah, I can see how those kinds of entanglements could make divorce difficult. Yikes. One would have thought that two people being forced to stay together in a loveless marriage would have gone out with "Jane Eyre."

save **SEND** delete

Friday 8:47 a.m.

I don't think that is a good idea. You know what Leviticus says, 19:14. Don't put a stumbling block in front of a blind man, nor curse the deaf.

You and I are the blind and deaf, Rand. We want each other. We can't have each other. We shouldn't meet. Let's not mess around.

save **SEND** delete

Friday 11:01 a.m.

Manda, I thought I had defenses for everything. I've got none for begging. What am I supposed to be doing? Can't you just tell me, and everything will be fixed?

save SEND delete

Friday noon

Dear Rand,

Those are some of the most beautiful words anyone has ever spoken to me.

Whatever happens, and, God bless you, and me, too, and your wife, I don't think we should meet, but, whatever happens, thank you for what you just said.

save SEND delete

Friday 12:17 p.m.

Amanda,

He still wants to meet. He promises that nothing "sinful" will occur. I won't go.

But then he said that he had a feeling about me. That maybe I was comfortable in my isolation. He said that maybe I would have been resistant to falling in love with him even if he were not married. He said that he understood perfectly why someone who'd been through what I'd been through would feel alienated. He said that it was okay if I, with him, performed "act as if" love. If I were just "indulgent" of him, while feeling some residual alienation. He said he would settle for that. And he said that, with time, he hoped to earn my genuine affection.

He's not a civilian, Amanda. You look at someone with money and success and you think, "Okay, this guy's got it all." He doesn't.

save SEND delete

Saturday 12:30 p.m.

Dear Rand,

Are you serious? That's incredible. I can't believe it. I mean, all this time, it never occurred to me. There are photos of me on the web, Rand. Not great and not obvious but if you Google my name you'll come to them eventually. I organized a protest against the bombing of Serbia, and our peace group posted photos on the web. I just assumed that when you Googled me that first time and read that essay that I wrote, the one you said you liked, that you continued in your search until you found photos.

This whole time, you've been writing to me without having any idea of what I look like.

You wrote that explicit sex e-mail … without any idea of what I look like.

Rand, you will discover what I look like. When we meet. In Chartres.

save SEND delete

Friday 7:20 p.m.

Dear Rand,

I can't believe that tomorrow I'm going to meet you in the flesh for the first time. I am so excited.

The flight over was uneventful. I'm in the Paris hostel now. Typing on their computers.

Rand, when we spoke on the phone before my flight you asked me why I had found it so difficult to type out sex words when we were typing about sex. You said that I had told you, after all, that I like to curse and that I had certainly used all those words before. I think I know the answer now.

I can fight, but love is scarier. If I use those words with you now that we've used the L word with each other, if I let you touch me the way you touch me, I am without defenses.

Rand, please know that that sex e-mail you sent me, the one I could not respond to, the one in whose absence of a response from me you apologized for and then raged against and then denounced and then trivialized and then repudiated. I loved that e-mail, Rand. I will keep it forever. I'm so glad that you sent me a crazy, raunchy, risky sex e-mail. "If I was on top of you": I reread that sentence fragment over and over and it thrilled me every time. Of course, it should be the subjunctive, "If I were on top of you." But, just the same.

I thought about this on the plane, Rand, and I decided. And, so, I am here to say I love you, Rand. I love you and cunt and cock and touch and come. Do you get what I'm saying? I understand the etymology of the word "ecstasy": "stand" "outside." Ever since your first sex e-mail, I have been standing outside of myself. I feel my essence flowing toward you. I am taking huge risks. I am taking them out of love for you. I'm not telling you this to demand your thanks. I'm reporting it to thank you.

Let's jump in with both feet, and leave our life preservers onshore. Let us stand outside of ourselves.

save SEND delete

Friday 4:57 p.m.

Dear Lord Randolph Court-Wright, Marquis of Alnwick,

Your e-mails have been unnecessary.

At the hotel, Madame Signoret was explicit. Friday night you were there, and then you left, at around ten p.m. That was all I needed to know.

I left within an hour of my arrival that morning. I did not go to the cathedral. I did not want that memory in my head.

I have not needed to receive e-mail after e-mail from you frenziedly explicating that you and your wife are working things out, that you were at a weak point, that you were very lonely, and that you made a mistake.

It wasn't all your other e-mails, your tortured logic and pathetic attempts to convince me that you and your wife now enjoy a marriage so blissful that Brad and Angelina could only look on in envy. It wasn't the "after all" e-mails. "After all" you are a man and men can't be held responsible for their horniness. Ha, ha, ha. "After all" I was a woman of the world, with quite a potty mouth. Wink, wink, nudge, nudge. "After all" I had Amanda to help me through any rough patches. How socially responsible you are. "After all" it was just a few naughty e-mails. Nothing "real" happened.

It wasn't these "after all" e-mails that finally prompt me to overcome my own good sense and respond to you now. It is, rather, this most recent e-mail, the one suggesting that it is because I am a person of faith that I have not yet written to offer you absolution and a shook hand. It is this e-mail, the one suggesting that it is something about my religious background that has warped me into an "unforgiving," "implacable," "punitive," "unrealistic" and "irrational" personality. It is this e-mail that prompts me to write to you this morning and to say, Lord Randolph Court-Wright, Marquis of Alnwick, you once asked me to promise to tell you when and if the moment ever came when I hated you. I hereby acquit that duty.

save SEND delete

Saturday 5:59 a.m.

Dear Amanda,

A brick wall self-erects when a love affair ends. It does not inhibit you spatially; you may go wherever you choose. Nobody cares. This brick wall demarcates time. You can never go back. Once you recover from the shock, you retire, to their various pensions, what had been the scaffolding of your reality. You retire the loved one, not just his presence; of course he's gone, you know he's gone. In this brick wall moment you confront your idea of him and realize that he will never live up to your dreams, or his own. In fact he has behaved toward you in far worse a manner than some common – truly, common – criminal. You retire your memory of a good man and never replace it with this common

272

man. This is different than death. There isn't anything to bury, because you now deny he ever existed. Your love had elevated not just the other, the loved one, whom you saw as good and high and shining; your love had elevated you. You retire the you who loved. She'll never speak such words ever again, never again be so generous, or hope, enthuse or enjoy with ever the same sparkle; in stopping the performance of these acts, she'll simply cease to exist. You retire the love itself. What had gotten you out of bed in the morning. What had gotten you through the day. At first, you place it on a difficult-to-reach shelf, somewhere, where you have some room, but it withers with time; it becomes unrecognizable, and it is discarded absentmindedly the next time you tidy up.

This is a death without flower arrangements or time off from work or condolences. It is a filthy swallow of grave dirt, so frigid you shudder and fear freezing. You, alone, experience this. Your continuity with your past self, with the you you were only yesterday, only an hour ago, has been severed, violently. The distant, recovered, carefree you is a stranger. You are completely alone, not just in space, but in time. Some new you you haven't met yet will emerge, some time in the future, who knows how far off, who knows who she will be, who knows how she will remember the you of this moment.

save SEND delete

INBOX

scrapping sophocles' script ... hopelessly dated ... entirely new concept ... a participatory theatrical event cum buffet dinner cum joyous family celebration cum twelve step meeting cum group hug ... antigone and creon serve moussaka, gyros and feta cheese with baklava for desert ... cash bar serves ouzo ... hello my name is amanda and i've gained ten pounds ... but amazing calf muscles with all the Greek line dancing ... Hopa!

Friday 12:14

Dear Amandarama, Amandelicious, Amandadream, Hail Go
Dess, She Who Is Worthy to be Loved,

You've single-handedly kept me sane through this whole
ordeal. Farewell now, pumpkin. We won't be writing again. I'm
going to "detach with love." Thank you. It's been real.

save SEND delete

Two days after Winter Solstice
Wednesday midnight

Dear Lord Randolph Court-Wright – strike that.

Dear Rand.

Dear Rand,

It's been a really dark day here. It's been a really dark week. I
was trying to read at three in the afternoon and the apartment
was so dark I had to switch on the lamp – and I've got two ten-
foot high windows facing south. Snow mixes with rain. I'm
listening to Paolo Conte. As soon as he's done, I'll slip in the
carols.

Three years, Rand. Can it really have been three years? Yes, it
can. My calendar tells me so.

You know, back in the day, when we were e-mailing, I
promised myself that I would never again Google you. It felt
stalker-like. I've been true to that promise. When I'm listening to
NPR and you come on, even if I'm in the bath, naked and
dripping wet, I run to the radio and tune to Led Zeppelin. I have
no idea how you are.

I don't even know why I'm writing you. Except that it is the
anniversary. It was three years ago that I first wrote. And you
blew my mind by responding.

I'm not dead by the way. Although this e-mail would be a lot
more thrilling to receive if I were. Suicide is just another onerous
chore I haven't been able to work into my schedule. I still assidu-
ously debate it on internet discussion boards. Nobody's given me

a good response so far. Actually, their responses are pretty intellectually flabby. Not everyone can think – like you. Like you, Rand.

I don't hate you any more. I just wanted you to know. That means, of course, that I don't love you any more. That is how that works.

If there is one thing that bugs me, and there is one thing that bugs me, and it's really just irritation, not anything I'd have to mount a terrorist assault against you for, it's this. I'll be teaching Jung's concept of synchronicity. One of my students, and it is always the same student, semester after semester, campus after campus. He's the angry young atheist man, the geeky kid, who sits by himself, and is humorless and intense, righteous and paranoid, and, in his papers, he damns the minds of fools who have any respect at all for religion or myth or magic – it's that kid – you know the one I mean. He asks for your autograph at conferences. He posts on his Facebook page, "When facing conundra in life, I ask myself, 'What would Randolph Court-Wright do?'"

Anyway, I'll be teaching Jung's concept of synchronicity and that boy will raise his hand and say, "Professor, you should familiarize yourself with Dr. Randolph Court-Wright. Using simple mathematics, he has completely debunked the concept of synchronicity."

You would think, given how often this happens, that I'd have worked out a reply. In fact, to say that I become like a "deer in headlights" would flatter me and insult deer. A deer frozen in the headlights of an oncoming car has a readier repertoire of snappy comeback lines than I do at that moment.

Don't worry, Rand. Nothing will ever make me talk. I'm never gonna tell that there is documentary evidence kept under tighter control than is exercised by the Vatican archives. The archives in question? The shoebox in which I keep the floppy discs on which I stored our every e-mail to each other. I'm Catholic, remember?

We Catholics know how to respect mystery. We're into secret societies and esoteric knowledge available only to a select few. So, even though there remains no other bond between you and me, Rand, there is this. We are members of a secret society of two, and we both know the world's most famous debunker of synchronicity once, investing in synchronicity, risked a great deal. How's this for our exclusive club's secret oath? "There are more things in Heaven and earth, and in e-mail, Horatio, than are dreamt of in your philosophy."

So, no, I don't hate you any more. In fact, I think that you were right, in all those nauseating e-mails you sent me after you cut and ran. I think it really was your loneliness talking, your, as you put it, penis. Opposites attract, but our bond is not stable. Truth to tell, I often found your coldness off-putting. I'm hot-blooded and I require some volcanism in my men. Not that you would care, at this point. I found it funny that you cared back then. But I'm not shopping. I'm back to being a spinster. "The priceless gift of serenity."

You? In that flurry of e-mails you sent me after I said that I wouldn't have sex with you because you were married, you said a lot about your wife. Your wife was a materialistic, manipulative, Neo-Pagan princess with a smokin'-hot bod she made you beg for the privilege to touch. She never forgave you your faults, had no faith in you, cheated on you, and tried to manage your every move. I'm sure you're very happy together.

Seriously. I think that my flood of love for you, a flood that would have intimidated the US Army Corps of engineers, I think that the intellectual delight I took in every word you sent me, my physical hunger for every inch of you, my total surrender to you, embarrassed you. I learned something about you when I couldn't respond to your sex e-mail. You were so quick to back-peddle, to abandon your own words, to reel in risk and scurry for shelter. I think that feeling and trusting frighten you. I think that being touched disturbs you. I think that that is because, for some reason

I can only guess at, you don't love yourself. That may be the most cliché analysis I've ever ventured. Sometimes clichés become clichés because they are true.

In any case, Mazel tov. I wish you and Cruella De Vil every happiness.

Rest assured, Rand. I have never shown anyone the e-mails you sent me. And that presents me with a quandary. No one ever saw you and me together. "You and me together" is utterly outlandish. Who would believe it? *Should* anyone? After you left France, you sent me all those e-mails insisting that nothing had happened between us. Maybe that's true.

Rand, there is something I never told you. I feared you'd write me off as utterly delusional. I made Amanda up. No, no, not out of whole cloth. I did once have a friend named Amanda. She stopped e-mailing me, though, a few years into the illness. She never told me why.

Here's my best guess. In addition to everything that you and I said about suffering, suffering is a story, one that demands attention. Friends want stories, and the attention that they demand, to be distributed equitably. I think it was hard for Amanda to be friends with a woman whose story just kept getting bigger and bigger. I think it would be hard for anyone. One of the reasons we have friends is to talk about our stuff. To receive commiseration, and praise, and to share laughter. How do you say to someone who has just gone deaf over night, or who is about to become homeless, "Hey, I had a date with a really cute guy!"

Amanda moved in that cloud of glittery allure that a beautiful actress can conjure, but it was much more than that that inspired me to cherish her. In her own smoky-bar, well-thumbed-poetry-paperback way, she was as smart as you. She understood, and never mocked, that I was in love with Gerard Manley Hopkins, a dead, gay, depressive poet priest who was, when alive, five inches shorter than I.

This is how special Amanda was. One night I watched a movie that ended badly. I'm not saying that it was an unhappy ending; some unhappy endings are perfect. This was narrato-cide – the murder by mangling of a narrative. I was crushed. I knew I'd never sleep. I phoned Amanda. As skillful as Scheherazade, she immediately launched into an extemporaneous production. She spent the next hour animating utterly integral characters she invented on the spot, vivifying sets and landscapes, and weaving a harmonious, satisfying conclusion.

When you responded to my first e-mail, I panicked. Writing brings me much of what peace I know. I can't do it just in my head. I need to feel letters surrender under my fingertips. I need to drown out extraneous noise with the percussion of keys unreeling a hundred words a minute onto the screen. Pressing the "send" button exorcises the energy. I wrote to Amanda, as if she were still there. I became an actress myself. To my own great surprise, as I was acting out Amanda, I found myself typing words that I might not have accessed without this performance.

Are you thinking what I'm thinking? I imagined a friend in Amanda. I imagined that you felt affection for me. Do we similarly imagine God? But doesn't it tell us something that we have to imagine someone who loves us, who is willing to read our long e-mails? Doesn't that inborn yearning tell us something about who we really are? Inhale as a believer, exhale as an atheist.

Rand, I told you once that I had a pet student in Nepal. He was around ten. He was a pet because he, as am I, was dyslexic, and a bit awkward, and alone. I told you that he died of dysentery. One day, he had given me a marble. I slipped it into my backpack, the very butterscotch-colored, internal frame, North Face backpack slouching on the chair next to me as I write to you now.

The backpack in question is a veteran of thousands of miles of low-to-no-budget travel. It has frozen and sweat, climbed and been man-handled along with me. It is something of an eyesore. The waist band, always a weak spot, has lost all of its sole means of fastening, Velcro. (As an outdoor gear enthusiast, I do curse the day that Velcro was invented.) I fasten the waistband, as best I can, with two shoelaces tied together.

Raveling selvage bleeds butterscotch-colored thread, and when the thread gets caught in the zippers, the zippers pop open. I thus lost a jar of roasted peppers. Thank God it was not my wallet that popped out. But, using multiple copies of the New York Times as insulation, on summer days of one hundred degree heat, I have safely carried home a half gallon of ice cream, even over a one-hour walk.

As a pedestrian, I am not confused about how the world – or humanity – will come to an end. Our garbage will suffocate us. Garbage clogs the roads I walk. In addition to endless discarded beverage containers, I step over useful things. A fine gauge crochet hook. Watches and gloves – I have never bought a watch, or a glove, and I lack for neither. Wallets, which I return, never accepting the reward, because my father was a pedestrian, and he never accepted the reward. Marbles. For years I have been finding the stray, isolated marble, blue, green, clear, yellow, and placing it in my backpack to nestle next to the marble that my Nepali student gave me before he died.

Marbles are smooth and round. Any jostle will send them careening, difficult to retrieve. I keep them in one of my backpack's pockets. The length of this pocket's side runs a zipper. I must zip and unzip it everyday. It would be very easy for the marbles to tumble out. I keep these tiny globes in this insecure environment for a reason.

If I've just come in from walking miles with groceries in my backpack, if the mail contains nothing but rejection letters, if I'm unpacking in an unheated apartment far from any place I'd want to call home, I have to stop. I cannot allow my movements to reflect impatience or hostility or despair. I must breathe, and I must take a bit more care, and be a bit more present, to unzip this pocket, and remove its parcel of the week's haul of groceries.

There is something precious in that pouch. The marble my pet student gave me, that little earth, and its atmosphere of memory and honor due him, and every other poor kid who died before he got a chance. I no longer remember which marble was his. If I lost any, I'd not know if I'd lost his. I have not lost any.

Rand, a week ago I had a moment when I was close to being ready. It's the end of the semester. I haven't yet been assigned any classes for spring. I could get my grades in, and then just do it. I was walking to campus. It was just before winter solstice. I stood atop the hill. The setting sun was to my right; the waning moon would not be up for hours. I prayed. "I am so tired. Please let me. I don't need to go to Heaven. Just don't send me to Hell. And, if this is really not what I'm supposed to do, give me a sign." I stood and waited. Down below, I saw my student, Sheila Gambino, a Type A personality and early as usual, pulling into the parking lot. It was time for me to go to work. I walked in to teach the final session of my night class: "Folklore for Elementary School Educators."

Sheila is a delightful returning student. She lost her long-term, well-paid position at an investment house that went south with the mortgage crisis. Sheila is now, in middle age, studying to be a primary school teacher. In spite of her husband's last name, Sheila is Irish. Her thick hair is snowy white.

Displaying a bit more mischievousness than is normally allotted to adjunct professors, I had suggested that Sheila might devote her final research paper to the Irish folklore motif of the Sheela-na-gig. I have to admit that I got a kick out of the look of horror on Sheila's face when she saw a photo of a Sheela-na-gig.

I wasn't playing around. I want the students to understand that folklore isn't all Johnny Appleseed and black cat superstitions and "I've been working on the railroad, all the live long day." Folklore is the repository of our people's efforts to wrestle with the big questions. We secular moderns forget it, or ignore it, or think it's enough merely to debunk it, at our own risk.

Sheila wasn't interested in working on the big questions her first semester back in school. She wrote her final research paper on the folk significance of colors. She would be presenting her research this night to her fellow students. She would be presenting it in the form of a simulation of a lesson plan for primary school kids. Sheila is one of the best students I've ever had. She has never been late, never been unprepared. She's the kind of student who, if I have to leave the room for an emergency, I'd just hand the chalk to, and say, "Vamp for me for a little bit," and feel secure that the class was in good hands. I was looking forward to being her simulated primary school student.

Sheila dug into her bag for her carefully prepared ingredients: Styrofoam trays, a children's book on color, tubes of blue, red, and yellow paint, and, "Oh, no," Sheila's voice, usually so in control, sounded suddenly vulnerable.

"What is it?" we asked.

"I forgot them in the car," she said. Sheila slumped, displaying that despair that hyper-competent people display on those rare occasions when they screw up.

"What did you forget in the car?" we all asked, anticipating a boring wait as Sheila traipsed out into the ten-degree cold to fetch whatever she had forgotten.

"The marbles," she said.

"How many do you need?" I asked, getting up and going to my backpack.

Everyone laughed. "You're kidding, right?"

"Is that why your backpack is so heavy?"

"Have you got a microwave in there, too?"

Inevitably: "Prof, have you lost your marbles?"

"Two for each person," Sheila said dubiously, plainly not believing that I had that many marbles in my backpack.

I counted them out. I had plenty and to spare.

My students couldn't stop talking about it. "And then Sheila said, 'I forgot them in the car!' And then Professor Hudak said, 'How many do you need?' And whipped them out of that backpack she's always carrying!"

In the eyes of those who determine who is worthy of full-time employment, publishing contracts, healthcare, and love, I am about to enter my sixth decade of complete and utter worthlessness. But maybe what we do here, that is any good at all, is something we don't know enough to assign value to. I don't know. Inhale as a believer, exhale as an atheist.

Rand, I am here to say that you were right. As you so clearly stated in the e-mails you sent me after we did not meet in France, the verifiable facts clearly indicate that we were wrong for each other. That nothing *real* happened between us. We would have caused each other nothing but pain. And it was really painful, Rand. I won't even go into how much I cried – okay, the correct word is "sobbed" – how many months it was before your name stopped repetitively announcing itself in my head. Okay, that hasn't actually stopped yet. But the thing is, now that I'm not in love with you any more, I can see that all those facts that you adduced were unimpeachable.

And … just one more thing. I don't know if I ever told you this. You made me so happy. Happier than I've ever been. You redefined life for me. I saw it as I never had. You made me want to live.

SAVE send delete

References

Scripture texts in this work are taken from the "New American Bible with Revised New Testament and Revised Psalms" © 1991, 1986, 1970 Confraternity of Christian Doctrine, Washington, D.C. and are used by permission of the copyright owner. All Rights Reserved. No part of the New American Bible may be reproduced in any form without permission in writing from the copyright owner.

Carl Jung's story of the scarab beetle is found in:
Campbell, Joseph. "The Portable Jung." New York: Viking Press, 1971.

Quote from Tadeusz Rozewicz's poem "Saved" / "Ocalony" is from:
Strzetelski, Jerzy, PhD, editor. "An Introduction to Polish Literature" Krakow: Jagiellonian University, 1977.

Quotes from St. Jerome are from:
Pence, Mary Elizabeth. "Satire in St. Jerome." The Classical Journal 36.6 (1941): 322-336.

Quote from the Nasadiya is taken from:
Kramer, Kenneth. "World Scriptures: An Introduction to Comparative Religions." Mahwah, NJ: Paulist Press, 1986.

Quote from the Upanishads is taken from:
McKenzie, John. "Hindu Ethics: A Historical and Critical Essay." Oxford: Oxford University Press, 1922.

Quote from the Garuda Purana is from:
Naunidhirama, Ernest Wood and S. V. Subrahmanyam. "The

Garuda Purana." New York: The AMS Press, 1974.

The quote from Nostra Aetate is taken from the full text:
"Nostra Aetate: Declaration on the Relation of the Church to Non-Christian Religions, Proclaimed by His Holiness Pope Paul VI on October 28, 1965" http://www.vatican.va/archive /hist_councils/ii_vatican_council/documents/vat-ii_decl_19651028_nostra-aetate_en.html (Accessed June 7, 2011.)

Quotes from Jim Zwerg are taken from the PBS website devoted to their television series, "The People's Century," "Interview with Jim Zwerg Civil Rights Activist, United States." PBS http://www.pbs.org/wgbh/peoplescentury/episodes/skindeep /zwergtranscript.html (Accessed June 7, 2011.)

Jim Zwerg discusses reading Psalm 27 in
Blake, John. May 16, 2011. "Shocking Photo Created a Hero, But Not to His Family": CNN. http://articles.cnn.com/2011-05-16/us/Zwerg.freedom.rides_1_greyhound-bus-bus-station-bus-trip?_s=PM:US (Accessed June 7, 2011.)

Stefania Podgorska's story is found in:
Block, Gay, and Malka Drucker. "Rescuers; Portraits of Moral Courage in the Holocaust." New York: Holmes and Meier, 1992.

Sor Juana's quote, translated by Michael Smith, is from the website of Shearsman Books:
"Sor Juana: Eleven Poems. Translated from the Spanish by Michael Smith." "You Foolish Men."
http://www.shearsman.com/pages/gallery/smith/11sorjuana.html (Accessed June 7, 2011.)

The Twelve Steps of Alcoholic's Anonymous are visible on their webpage:
http://www.aa.org/1212/ (Accessed June 7, 2011.)

Quotes from Sigmund Freud's letters to Carl Jung are from:
McGuire, William, editor. "The Freud-Jung Letters: the Correspondence between Sigmund Freud and C.G. Jung." Princeton, NJ: Princeton University Press, 1974.

Carl Jung's "spiritus contra spiritum" letter to Alcoholic's Anonymous founder Bill Wilson is found in:
Sullivan, Lawrence. "The Parabola Book of Healing." New York: Continuum, 1994.

Carl Sagan's essay on marijuana is found in:
Grinspoon, Lester. "Marihuana Reconsidered." Cambridge, MA: Harvard University Press, 1971.

Quotes from Gerard Manley Hopkins and T. S. Eliot's poetry are from:
Eastman, Arthur M., coordinating editor. "Norton Anthology of Poetry." New York: W. W. Norton & Company, 1970.

The text of the e-mail from the former Peace Corps Volunteer who calls himself "Lamjung" is used by permission:
D.B., a.k.a. "Lamjung." (Author prefers that his full name not be used.) May 28, 2008. Memorate. E-mail to Danusha V. Goska.

Quote from Avrom Sutskever's poem is from:
Kremer, S. Lillian. "Holocaust Literature: An Encyclopedia of Writers and Their Work." New York: Routledge, 2003. Translator: C. K. Williams.

Quotes from Viktor Frankl are from:

Frankl, Viktor. "Man's Search for Meaning." New York: Simon and Schuster, 1962.

Joseph Campbell's quote from Igjugarjuk is in:

Campbell, Joseph and Bill Moyers. "The Power of Myth." New York: Doubleday, 1988.

The quote from a student e-mail is used by permission:

Martinez, Anna. May 15, 2005. E-mail to teacher. E-mail to Danusha V. Goska.

Roundfire Books put simply, publish great stories. Whether it's literary or popular, a gentle tale or a pulsating thriller, the connecting theme in all Roundfire fiction titles is that once you pick them up you won't want to put them down.